D0206027

Berlin in Focus

BERLIN IN FOCUS

Cultural Transformations in Germany

Edited by
Barbara Becker-Cantarino

Westport, Connecticut
London

Library of Congress Cataloging-in-Publication Data

Berlin in focus : cultural transformations in Germany / edited by
   Barbara Becker-Cantarino.
       p.   cm.
   Includes bibliographical references and index.
   ISBN 0–275–95507–9 (alk. paper)
   1. Berlin (Germany)—Intellectual life—20th century.   2. Berlin
(Germany)—Cultural policy.   I. Becker-Cantarino, Barbara.
DD866.8.B53   1996
306′.09431′55—dc20   95–50531

British Library Cataloguing in Publication Data is available.

Library of Congress Catalog Card Number: 95–50531
ISBN: 0–275–95507–9

First published in 1996

Praeger Publishers, 88 Post Road West, Westport, CT 06881
An imprint of Greenwood Publishing Group, Inc.

Printed in the United States of America

The paper used in this book complies with the
Permanent Paper Standard issued by the National
Information Standards Organization (Z39.48–1984).

10 9 8 7 6 5 4 3 2 1

Contents

Photos follow page 34

Preface

This volume will, I hope, shed some light as to why the city of Berlin has held such a fascination and crucial position in recent German developments. The articles assembled here focus on important cultural developments and changes in Germany as they occurred, particularly in Berlin during the last decade. The introductory chapter provides a brief factual survey of recent major events and reflects on areas of conflict in the cultural and social sphere of the newly reunited city. Subsequent chapters address problems of coming to terms with life in Germany and in the formerly divided Berlin, and with the changes brought about by unification. They examine women's participation in the restructuring of higher education in Berlin, the impact of State Security at Humboldt University, problems relating to Berlin's (and Germany's) growing immigrant population, and the innovative counterculture ventures in the Prenzlauer Berg district of Berlin. Two chapters, on renowned filmmakers Wim Wenders and Helke Sander, address major cinematic responses to the metropolis. Two final chapters discuss literary reactions to, and representations of, the divided and now united city: perceptions of the "wall"—its physical disappearance and new presence in "people's heads"—and reflections of prominent women authors on the past, as well as coming to terms with present-day Berlin as a locus of terror. A new understanding of the fascinating and feared Berlin, once again the capital of Germany, evolves from these essays, and a variety of views on German culture and society emerges.

While the various chapters bring out some of the complex issues of Berlin and Germany—problems of recent unification and the heritage of the postwar period, particularly as respects the German Democratic Republic—they explore history and developments over time. Some provide substantive factual information on social transformations, while others reflect on cultural visions and expressions of the metropolis, including the refiguring of a united city and country and the merging of asymmetrical halves. It is not the goal of the authors to identify solutions to the multifaceted cultural and social problems of Berlin, nor to find some universally shared, homogenized view of a city where fractures, disparities, and paradoxes abound. There is no commonly accepted, unified image of Berlin, nor does this metropolis have a homogeneous identity—to apply a term in constant use in German Studies. On the contrary, it is the diversity of its people and cultures, its capability for change and transformation, and the multiple perspectives it presents that make Berlin's ongoing cultural process such as fascinating project.

It is with great pleasure that I express my gratitude to those individuals who contributed to this project. Apart from the contributors, I would like to thank my many friends in Berlin who inspired and advised me in matters pertaining to the city, especially the late Gerhard Spellerberg (Free University) and Christiane Spellerberg (Senatsverwaltung für Kulturelle Angelegenheiten), and Hannelore Scholz (Humboldt University). I owe many insights on the changing nature and problems of Berlin to the students in my seminars at the Free University during several guest semesters in the 1980s and 1990s; they taught me more about the city and its people than I could ever have learned from visits or research. I am especially grateful for generous support for my research from the Alexander von Humboldt Foundation. My thanks go to Dr. Heidrun Suhr and the DAAD for assistance with the earlier conference "Berlin—A City of Change" at the Ohio State University, and to the Goethe Institute, C incinnati and Ohio State University for valuable support for the conference and this project. I wish to thank Sibylle Arnegger, Elèna Chandler, and Sven Merkel for assistance with some translations.

Barbara Becker-Cantarino

Berlin in Focus

1

Reflections on a Changing Berlin

Barbara Becker-Cantarino

Berlin has been the primary site of political, social, and cultural transformation in modern Germany. Unlike any other German city, Berlin, known as the "Athens on the Spree and City of Crisis,"[1] has witnessed, influenced, and mirrored the political metamorphosis of Germany during the entire twentieth century. The years 1918, 1933, 1939, 1945, 1961, 1989, and 1990 represent special markers in political and social upheaval; in each the city of Berlin figured prominently as a locale and as a symbol: World War I and the 1918 November Revolution led to the establishment of the Weimar Republic; Hitler's rise to power, with the burning of the *Reichstag* on February 27 and 28, 1933, was a visible sign and sinister omen; the invasion of Poland on September 1, 1939, signaled the beginning of World War II, with the war eventually ending with the Red Army's conquest of Berlin in April 1945 and the *Wehrmacht*'s unconditional surrender signed in Reims and in Berlin on May 7 and 8 of that year; the division of Berlin and Germany was most painfully enacted and visibly demonstrated by the initiation of construction of the Berlin Wall on August 13, 1961, and unexpectedly breached on November 7, 1989; and German unification, marking the end of the postwar era, took place on October 3, 1990.

The abruptness of political and social transformation during this century has meant that the relationship between Berlin as a cultural site, its varying groups of inhabitants, and Germany at large had to be renegotiated repeatedly. During the past decades, Berlin has also been the trendsetter for German avant-garde and counterculture groups, albeit often to the chagrin of more conservative forces in the rest of Germany—East and West.

Because the essays in this volume explore aspects of transformation in German society and culture in recent years and employ the city of Berlin as a seismograph for Germany and symbol for that nation, a sociocultural introduction to the city's historical and topographical reality during the twentieth century becomes a necessity.[2]

CAPITAL AND METROPOLIS (1871–1920):
"ATHENS ON THE SPREE AND CHICAGO"

At the turn of the century a young and decidedly upper-class Walther Rathenau, who as Foreign Minister became a victim of political assassination in 1922, observed about his native city: "Athens on the Spree is dead and Chicago on the Spree is emerging."[3] Such a dichotomy, a clash between tradition and modernity, between a nostalgia for "high culture" and an avant-garde, urban civilization in transition, has pervaded perceptions of twentieth-century Berlin. Unlike Paris, London, or Rome, Berlin did not so much evolve as Germany's capital over many centuries, but was able to assume that role as a result of the Franco-Prussian War and politics—Bismarck's diplomacy—as well as economics and, of course, people. When the city became the capital, not only of Prussia but of the new German Reich, in 1871, Berlin was a relatively provincial city, the center of Prussian militarism and the heart of Prussian hegemony over Germany. The city's rapid growth during industrialization began to accelerate even more during the expansive, optimistic Wilhelmine era and the prosperous decades leading up to World War I. Berlin's economic opportunities attracted not only businessmen, bankers, industrialists, intellectuals, writers, and artists, but streams of impoverished people from rural areas as well as many immigrants, especially from Eastern Europe. They would work in the factories and as domestic servants, join the many small businesses, shops, and trades, or find jobs in newly forming enterprises such as construction, transportation, gastronomy, and entertainment. By 1910 there were 3.7 million people living in the metropolitan area, compared to about 100,000 a hundred years earlier.

In 1920, an urban reorganization created Greater Berlin (*Groß-Berlin*),[4] then the second-largest city in Europe with approximately 4 million inhabitants. But by the end of World War II, the city had lost more than one third of its population. During the postwar division, West Berlin, until the construction of the Wall a favorite destination for refugees from the Eastern territories of the former German Reich, from the German Democratic Republic (GDR), and from Eastern Europe, grew to a population of approximately 2 million.[5] East Berlin, as capital of the GDR, attracted residents from throughout the Republic and had about 1.17 million inhabitants. These numbers, however, conceal an unusually high fluctuation in the city's population; moving to, through, or away from Berlin has affected many lives during the twentieth century.

In 1920, *Groß-Berlin* had a territory of almost 878 square kilometers (some 340 square miles); it was an urban conglomerate of diverse parts with a territorial expanse unusually large for a German city. Its size, variety, and open spaces helped the city to survive the post–World War II partition and to make the island of West Berlin a liveable, functional place with sprawling suburbs like Wilmersdorf, Steglitz, Charlottenburg, Dahlem, and Zehlendorf; its large forest preserves like Grunewald; and parks and recreational areas. Open spaces allowed limited construction and building activities, most notably in the American sector in Zehlendorf where a large American community of troops and dependents was accommodated until their official departure in the summer of 1994.

It was the urban development of the nineteenth century that shaped much of Berlin's topography and infrastructure and thus has had a profound influence on society and culture. With the economic growth and population explosion during industrialization, the city's many new and mostly poor inhabitants moved into the dismal, overcrowded public housing projects (the so-called *Mietskasernen*, or rental barracks—multistory blocks constructed around a maze of small, paved courtyards, the *Hinterhöfe*), which were built in such suburbs as Wedding, Moabit, Gesundbrunnen, and in the Prenzlauer Berg district (then called Königsviertel).[6] Not until the 1920s, with backing from the trade unions, were large and functionally designed housing projects, such as Siemensstadt designed in 1929 by the Bauhaus architect Walter Gropius, built to accommodate working-class families more adequately. To this day, these boroughs, often now antiquated, house blue collar workers and new immigrants. In the case of those located in East Berlin, there has been an almost total lack of maintenance during the past fifty years. They are now, once again, the locale for social conflicts.

Because of exploitative working and living conditions in the German Reich, these boroughs were fertile ground for the rapidly growing Berlin socialist movement. Although the first Workers' Alliance had been outlawed from 1878 to 1890 by Bismarck's Anti-Socialist Laws, it reorganized into the Social Democratic Party (SPD). By 1912, the Socialists received 75.3 percent of the Berlin vote (34.8 percent nationally) during the elections for the German *Reichstag*. "Berlin belongs to us" was the Socialists' slogan, and they proudly dubbed their city "Red Berlin," capital of the German worker's movement. The Socialists strove for parliamentary, democratic, and social reforms in the authoritarian, though constitutional, monarchy;[7] they were especially successful with cultural, recreational, and social programs and services that were organized for their Berlin constituents, as well as with the newly established trade unions. With this tradition, the socialist movement, though fractured into several groups, has remained a large and decisive force in Berlin politics and social affairs.

Profiting greatly from working-class Berlin, the city developed into an elegant metropolis and cultural center during the Wilhelmine era. Lavish villas and wide boulevards began to grace fashionable parts of the city like the West-End. Between 1880 and 1886, the Kurfürstendamm, later to become a trendsetting commercial center during the 1920s and the heart of the "Western showcase" of West Berlin in the post–World War II era, was transformed into a wide, tree-lined boulevard leading to the Grunewald from the newly built, neo-Romanesque Kaiser-Wilhelm-Gedächtnis-Kirche. This structure, built from 1891 to 1895, was to become the landmark ruin of West Berlin a century later. To Berlin's historical center district (*Mitte*), which extends from the Alexanderplatz to the Brandenburg Gate and is connected by Unter den Linden and the area north and south of it, more monumental buildings representative of an ambitious national culture were added: the Museum Island complex; the *Reichstag* (in 1884–94); the symbolic Victory Column (*Siegessäule*), which was dedicated in 1873; and in 1901 the Victory Boulevard (*Siegesallee*), which Wilhelm II had lined with statues of his Hohenzollern ancestors. The city's building boom created libraries, theaters, churches, concert halls, banks, grand hotels, railroad stations, post offices, often in the fashionable neo-Romanesque or neo-Gothic style, and palatial residences. The official, imperial Berlin had become the center of German industry, business, and commerce, as well as public administration and high culture.

Of these buildings, hardly anything remains today with the exception of the massive Brandenburg Gate, the *Reichstag*, and a few equally massive or reconstructed buildings. Most of Berlin *Mitte* was destroyed by the bombings during World War II and the siege and capture of Berlin in 1945, especially the buildings appropriated or built by Hitler, as was his vision of Berlin's grandiose urban renewal as "Germania," a city for ten million, to be completed in 1950. A number of historic buildings were later removed by the Communists to erase the symbols of a Prussian feudal state: In 1950 the only partially damaged City Palace (*Stadtschloß*) had to make way for Marx-Engels-Platz as a parade ground, the East German State Council building, and the Palace of the Republic. Only the ornate balcony from which Karl Liebknecht had proclaimed the socialist republic in 1918 was preserved, becoming the centerpiece of the State Council building. Farther to the east of Alexanderplatz, much of the heavily bombed historical center gave way to the socialist showcase: large residential blocks lining the Stalinallee (the former Frankfurter Allee, renamed in honor of Stalin's seventieth birthday in 1949, and then renamed Karl-Marx-Allee in 1961 after the demise of Stalinism).[8] With the heritage of the imperial age gone and most visual traces of the divided city removed, today's Berlin *Mitte* still contains huge empty spaces at the very center of the metropolis—the wasteland around the Potsdamer Platz where Sony, Daimler-Benz, Hertie, and Asa Brown Boveri are now constructing commercial centers. Much of the city is again the site of transformation, over which social, cultural, political, and commercial interests are clashing.

FROM THE WEIMAR REPUBLIC TO THE END OF WORLD WAR II (1920–45): CULTURAL MECCA AND POLITICAL INFERNO

During the November Revolution in 1918, the socialist Philipp Scheidemann announced from a *Reichstag* balcony: "The rotten old monarchy has collapsed. . . . Long live the German Republic!" A few hours later the competing Spartacist Karl Liebknecht, an ardent admirer of the Russian revolution, proclaimed a "socialist republic of workers and soldiers," a German Bolshevik Republic, from the *Stadtschloß* balcony (Ribbe 1988, 799). Following the military defeat of Germany in the First World War and William II's abdication, Berlin became the site of political power struggles, bloody street clashes, and assassinations, notably the 1919 killings of Rosa Luxemburg and Karl Liebknecht, founding members of the newly constituted German Communist Party and guerrilla fighters. But Berlin remained the capital of the newly created Republic whose constitution was established in Weimar in 1920. The subsequent years were marked by social unrest, street demonstrations because of unemployment, dire poverty, supply and food shortages, real hunger, and high inflation. The situation began to slowly stabilize when in late 1923 Gustav Stresemann, the son of a Berlin brewer and by then the young Republic's eighth chancellor, introduced a controversial new currency, the *Rentenmark*. A short boom, the "Golden Twenties," followed. But by 1929 the great depression hit Berlin; hundreds of thousands of unemployed took to the streets and shouted "Hunger" and "We want work." By November 1932, there were 650,000 unemployed in

Berlin. The young democracy survived only until 1933 when Hitler came to power.

As the capital of the Weimar Republic, Berlin, with its new freedom and cultural diversity, became a magnet for the young avant-garde. It quickly gained fame for its innovative cultural scene, for its theaters, musical events, art studios and galleries, for its nightlife and entertainment of all sorts and for all tastes, and for its liberal and diverse sexual scene. The Berlin of Max Reinhardt and Heinrich George, of Bertolt Brecht and Carl Zuckmayer, of George Grosz and Otto Dix, of Christopher Isherwood and W. H. Auden, of Josephine Baker and Marlene Dietrich has been enshrined in numerous books, plays, musicals, and films such as *Cabaret* (1972)[9] and *Mephisto* (1981).[10] Nearby Potsdam, with its then ultra-modern UFA studios and popular early German film productions, contributed to the nostalgic dream of an uninhibited, free-spirited creativity and a truly modern city.

The glamour of Berlin's Golden Twenties contrasted garishly with the violence, poverty, social conflicts, and poor living conditions for the masses of working people, small shopkeepers, impoverished pensioners, the unemployed, the homeless (many women among them), and the immigrants, mostly from the Eastern provinces, Poland, and Russia. This was the Berlin that came alive in Döblin's *Berlin Alexanderplatz* (1929) set in the old part of the *Mitte* district (*Scheunenviertel*), where most Eastern Jews settled, often displaced by new technical and commercial developments. Fassbinder recreated this milieu meticulously in his film adaptation of the novel.

Berlin's Golden Twenties were admired for being anti-bourgeois, anti-imperialistic, and anti-aristocratic, a break with stolid, authoritarian, conservative German tradition. This was reflected, for instance, in the rejection of "old" Fontane, who had died in 1898, by the young and brash Roth, Benn, and Döblin. And nostalgia for this Berlin looms in autobiographical text passages and memoirs, based on childhood memories of the now prominent generation of authors born in the 1910s and 1920s. A generation of survivors, emigrants, and visitors who witnessed that decade as children or young intellectuals has written or reminisced about it in earlier or recent memoirs: Berlin authors such as Günter de Bruyn, Hans Knobloch, and Christa Wolf; and visitors and emigrants like Elias Canetti in *Die Fackel im Ohr. Eine Lebensgeschichte 1921–1931* (1980). But there was also the negative view of Berlin as the "Babylon-on the Spree" as expressed by Oswald Spengler,[11] who saw a decadent civilization and destructive modernity at work in the city; such popular cultural pessimism was later embraced by the Nazis.

With Hitler's appointment as chancellor on January 30, 1933, the Nazi's dictatorship fundamentally transformed the city in its relatively short rule of twelve years. The burning of the *Reichstag* a few weeks later has become a symbol of Nazi subversion, propaganda, and destructive power. Octogenarian Stefan Heym, the senior member of the Bundestag and representative of the PDS, the SED successor party, from former East Berlin, witnessed the event as a youth, and still vividly recalls the burning. With the dissolution of parliament and the prosecution of opposing parties, especially the communists and socialists, the Nazis quickly controlled the city and tightened their grip on the population,[12] when the Enabling Bill of 22 March gave Hitler and his party uncontrolled power. Joseph Goebbels, with his propagandistic and organizational talents and ruthlessness, was almost single-handedly responsible for the rise of the Nazi Party in Berlin, and Adolf Hitler made no secret about his dislike of the modern metropolis and of hating "Red Berlin." Every institution and association in the city was either transformed according to Nazi ideology or eliminated.

In May 1933, the first spectacular book-burning, with students and Storm Troopers bringing over 20,000 books seized from area libraries and bookstores, took place on the Opernplatz next to the university and the State Library. It signaled Berlin's demise as a great European cultural center. Intellectuals and artists who refused to buckle under the tight censorship of press, radio, film, and all cultural events began leaving Berlin and the country. Political prosecution, terror raids, and murders further silenced any effective opposition from within. The Nazis' racist, antisemitic propaganda, *Juden raus*! (Jews out!), became government policy after April 1933, with store boycotts and vandalism against Jewish merchants, harassment and imprisonment of dissident civilians, and removal of Jews from public office.[13] By November 1933, 117 Jewish professors had been dismissed from Berlin universities and the State Library, and universities had been closed to Jews. While the well-known Berlin Rabbi Leo Baeck, president of all Jewish organizations in Germany (*Reichsvertretung*), initiated self-help measures such as establishing schools for expelled Jewish pupils, and while the Jewish Cultural Alliance (*Kulturbund*) provided some temporary refuge and relief in Berlin, the organization of their own emigration became the only hope of the Jews against the increasingly brutal repressions that escalated after the Nuremberg Laws were enacted in 1935.

After the international visitors for the 1936 Olympic Games had left, economic pressures to eliminate "nonaryan" ownership and workers were stepped up again. In October 1938 as many as 15,000 Polish Jews living in Berlin were forcibly returned to Poland. After the infamous *Reichskristall-*

nacht pogrom of November 9, 1938, when nine of the twelve synagogues in the city, most Jewish schools, and a number of shops and offices were destroyed, the mass exodus of Berlin Jews began. In September 1939, Hitler's declaration of war on Poland made an escape impossible. Mass deportations to concentration camps followed from October 1941 to 1943 when the Wannsee Conference's "final solution" policy was carried out. At war's end, only about 1,400 of the 160,000 Jews in Berlin in 1933 had survived in the city, many of them living in mixed marriages and saved by their wives' mass demonstration against deportation.[14]

Thousands of Jews resurfaced from hiding places, some from the camps, many from Eastern Europe as Displaced Persons (Ribbe 1988, 1007). After the split of the city in 1953,[15] a group of survivors reestablished a Jewish community of about 5,000 in West Berlin, is now serving again as a center and host for Jewish immigrants from the East. But almost none of the emigrants of the 1930s returned for more than a visit. About 40 percent of Germany's Jews lived in Berlin during the 1920s, but this culturally important, wealthy, and powerful Jewish community of Berlin has vanished. A younger generation of writers and intellectuals who returned to their Jewish roots, like Jurek Becker, Ansgar Hilsenrath, Andreas Sinakowski, and Irene Dische, has been writing and living in Berlin in recent years. In *New York Times*'s Paul Goldberger's view, the Jewish community in Berlin appears "highly visible, in part because of an effort on behalf of the city government" (51), which sponsors restoration, the construction of a new Jewish Museum, cultural activities, and security.[16]

On May 2, 1945, soldiers of the Red Army hoisted the Red flag on Schadow's Quadriga atop the Brandenburg Gate while the Reichstag burned again, signalling the end of the Third Reich and destruction of its capital Berlin.[17] During the preceding months, some 100,000 civilians, among them forced laborers from Poland and many refugees from the Eastern provinces, died in the battle for Berlin launched by the Red Army. Allied aerial bombing during the war had killed an estimated 52,000. Many of Berlin's factories, public buildings, military installations, cultural facilities, streets, transportation systems, hospitals, and large sections of its residential areas had been reduced to rubble. Starvation and disease threatened the survivors, mostly women, children, and old people. Most men, tens of thousands of soldiers, were rounded up and marched away to captivity in the Soviet Union. After almost two weeks of unchecked looting, violence, and rape,[18] the Red Army took control and organized food and water supplies by the end of May.[19] Life was reduced to the barest essentials for survival. Women were called in to start clearing the main arteries of rubble. During the ensuing years, the

Trümmerfrauen (rubble women) were crucial in recovering construction materials such as bricks from the rubble, restoring minimal living quarters, and putting the people of Berlin back on their feet.

BERLIN RECONSTRUCTED (1945–61): "IT'S GOT TO LOOK DEMOCRATIC BUT WE MUST HAVE EVERYTHING IN OUR CONTROL"

By the time the Western Allies were allowed into Berlin in July, the Soviets had tightened their grip on the city that, according to the London Agreement of 1944, was to be divided into sectors to be occupied and administered by the individual powers.[20] The Soviet Sector was the largest, with 45 percent of the land area, including the historical and administrative central district (*Mitte*) and 36 percent of the population. The Americans controlled six, mostly affluent residential districts in the south and west including Zehlendorf and Dahlem, the British four including Charlottenburg with the Kurfürstendamm, and the French, who had not been included in the agreement, received two from the British in the northwest. The city was to be run by the four-power Kommandantura with veto powers for each member; likewise, a four-power Allied Control Commission seated in Berlin was set up to govern Germany, now carved into four zones of occupation. The control of Germany, with Berlin a strategically and symbolically central site, was to become a focal point of conflict. While the Western Allies wanted to establish their sphere of influence by stressing democratization (besides denazification, dismantling of industry, and disarmament), the Soviets wanted to establish a Communist regime as a satellite of Moscow.[21] This had been carefully planned by the Soviets together with German Communists living in exile in Moscow during the Nazi period, among them Walter Ulbricht, one-time Spartacist and leader of the 1920s Berlin Communist Party, who had returned with the Red Army and a Communist Action Group. "It's got to look democratic but we must have everything in our control," was Ulbricht's mission and formula for success as the founding father of the GDR (Leonhardt 1955). He was to become the leader of East Germany until he was forced out by his protégé Erich Honecker in 1971.

Following the capture of Berlin and before the Western Allies were allowed into the city, the Soviets immediately appointed Communists as wardens (*Obleute*) for each city block and party members to all key administrative posts, often as a deputy to a well-known personality who would serve as figurehead and have no choice but to obey Soviet orders. In

April 1946, the Socialist Unity Party (SED), a fusion of communists and left-wing socialists from the Weimar era, and its official press organ *Neues Deutschland* was formed under the leadership of Otto Grotewohl and Wilhelm Pieck. Eighty percent of the rank-and-file members of the Social Democrats in the Western sector dissented. When the SED sought to extend its authority over all of Berlin, it received only 19.8 percent of the votes in the first citywide City Council elections (October 1946); 48.7 percent of the vote went to the Social Democrats, and the rest to the Christian Democrats (22.2%) and the Liberals (9.3%). This was a clear victory for Berlin's democratic socialist tradition and against SED rule and the communist takeover of the city. The ideological and personal rift, if not animosity, between socialists favoring the western democracy and communists oriented toward a Soviet-style Marxism and Stalinist dictatorship dated back to the Weimar Republic and exists to this day in the form of Social Democrats and the SED-successor PDS, albeit with changing subgroupings and fluctuating alliances. In order to absorb Berlin's socialist tradition and to inherit the Social Democrats' voters, the SED embraced the vocabulary of a socialist (not communist) democracy in establishing its "real existing socialism" (*real existierende Sozialismus*) while adopting a Stalinist-type, one-party-ruled political organization controlled by a small, elite, all-powerful committee (*Politbüro*).[22]

The Cold War sealed the division of Berlin and Germany. In response to Stalin's increasingly aggressive and expansionist foreign policy, to extend Communist rule over Eastern and Central Europe, Churchill spoke of the "iron curtain" that had descended and divided Europe. In 1947, the so-called Truman Doctrine was formulated to defend against Communism, while the Marshall Plan brought economic aid. The 1948 Currency Reform introduced by the Allies eliminated major shortages, ended the black market bartering, and united the three Western zones and Western sectors of Berlin into an economic union (see Wolff 1991). It paved the way to recovery, to West Germany's "economic miracle." West Berlin was soon to become a living showcase in the midst of an austere, if not starving, tightly controlled East Germany. The Soviets protested against these economic measures and in retaliation cut off access to Berlin from the West. It was the Social Democrat Ernst Reuter, a former Spartacist-turned-anti-Stalinist and the elected mayor of Berlin, although vetoed by the Soviets, who was instrumental in convincing the U.S. Commandant in Berlin, General Lucius D. Clay, to resist the blockade and to fly in all vital supplies for the Western sectors. Reuter's speeches to the Berliners, which were widely circulated, helped maintain their spirits: "We shall fight those who want to turn us into slaves and helots of a party. We have lived under such a slavery in the days of Adolf Hitler. We want no return to those days" (Craig 1982, 38). The Berliners' determination impressed the West; these events cemented a positive relationship with the Western Allies, especially the United States, and embittered the people even more against the Soviets, who abandoned the year-old blockade in May 1949. The American airlift saved West Berlin as a democratically governed entity. In the minds of Berliners, of most Germans, as well as in the Western press, it transformed Berlin, the "island city" and "bulwark of the West," into a symbol of liberty.

In the political history of Berlin, the immediate postwar period was one of rapid change, and the blockade was only the first of many Berlin crises to come during the 1950s and 1960s. It signaled the vulnerability of West Berlin and its anomaly as a political organism. By October 1949, the Federal Republic of Germany, newly established in a merger of the three Western Zones, followed its first chancellor Konrad Adenauer's bidding and chose Bonn as its capital (although the Social Democrats had proposed Frankfurt). Situated deep within the Soviet Zone, West Berlin insisted on its ties to the West and became a quasi-federal state when the FRG joined NATO and rearmed in 1954. Its representatives had no votes and its inhabitants were not subject to the draft. East Berlin became the capital of the German Democratic Republic, the *Hauptstadt der DDR,* as it was always referred to in East German parlance, when the GDR was established in October 1949.

The two Berlins soon rivaled each other in building activity, cultural and sports events, and political propaganda and ideology. A priority for the GDR was to "construct Berlin as a socialist capital" (Keiderling 1987) featuring, among other monumental buildings, the Walter-Ulbricht-Stadium (in 1950)—the massive Olympic Stadium of 1936 was located in West Berlin—the Palace of the Republic on the site of the war-damaged Hohenzollern City Palace that had been blasted in 1950–51, as well as the "first socialist street" in Berlin, the Stalinallee (renamed Karl-Marx-Allee in 1961). After the blockade, West Berlin began to rebuild and modernize at an amazing pace using investment money from the United States and West Germany. There was much commercial development along the Kurfürstendamm; the shopping complex Europa Center, topped with the gleaming Mercedes star, and several luxury hotels were built; the then ultra-modern Congress Hall was a gift from the United States. In 1952, the international building exhibition *InterBau* began and created a strikingly modern suburb, the Hansaviertel, in response to the Stalin-Allee project in the East; by 1957, some 100,000 municipally funded apartments had been constructed. Major new industrial plants were erected by, among others, Siemens, Osram,

Borsig, and AEG. Cultural institutions were reestablished: The *Deutsche Oper* received a new building; the Free University of Berlin with its center in the Henry Ford Building in the American sector Dahlem opened its doors in 1948; the annual Film Festival *Berlinale* was established in 1953; and the 1960s saw the realization of the *Kulturforum* complex, designed by Bauhaus architect Hans Scharoun, with its Philharmonic Hall, State Library, and National Gallery. Like West Germany, West Berlin began to adopt a thoroughly Western, that is, American, life-style including valorizing consumer goods, economic growth and increasing affluence, political freedom in a multiparty democratic system, a free press, social mobility, and economic opportunity for its citizens.

Concurrently, East Germany and East Berlin were converted by the SED, under Ulbricht's leadership, into a state-controlled, planned economy and socialist society modelled after Stalinist Russia. Despite receiving preferential treatment and supplies, East Berlin continued to suffer from acute shortages of consumer goods and at times even of food supplies well into the 1960s. The 1953 worker's protest—perhaps the first popular revolt[23] against Stalinism in Eastern Europe—started with construction workers on the Stalinallee. They protested high work quotas, calling for a general strike in support of their demand for free elections, the reunification of Germany, the return of German prisoners of war held in Russia, and the removal of Ulbricht. Russian tanks rolled into Berlin's center and crushed the demonstrations, as was later to be the case with similar protests in Hungary in 1956 and in Czechoslovakia in 1968.

The display of military force, the many restrictions on its citizens, the intense pressure for socialist reforms, and the austere living conditions in the East caused people to seek out Berlin, where they could cross over into the Western part of the city with relative ease. The "iron curtain" had by this time become a reality, a heavily guarded and fortified border sealing off the GDR and the entire Soviet bloc from the West. The first major stream of refugees into Berlin had come from the Eastern provinces during the final months of the war. Although access to Berlin and settling there were officially restricted, refugees continued to come by the thousands, especially after the implementation in 1946–1947 of the Potsdam Agreement concerning the German-Polish border of the Oder-Neisse Line. Around five million people were expelled from the formerly German territories taken over by Polish settlers, who had in turn been removed from Polish provinces in the East that were annexed by the Soviet Union.[24] Many of these expellees (*Vertriebene*) came to the Western Sectors of Berlin in spite of being refused residence permits there; many also tried to move there from the GDR when economic conditions did not improve and the West German "economic miracle" and its consequent opportunities began to beckon. Many were deeply dissatisfied with the process of socialization, the planned state economy, the land and property confiscations, the collectivization, the intense political propaganda, and repeated party purges. Many belonged to the so-called bourgeois who were denied professional training or jobs in the GDR where "workers and peasants" were given preference; many were dissenters and afraid for their personal well-being and safety, distrusting the SED's ideological pressures and controls and resenting the process of social transformation. The more enterprising, more mobile, and younger people often fled the collectivized farms, factories, businesses, and professional jobs leaving all belongings and relatives behind, causing serious gaps in the GDR economy. Despite ever more strict controls on East Germans traveling to Berlin, where barriers were set up around the outskirts and sector borders within the city were controlled and fenced off by East German police, refugees by the thousands managed to slip into West Berlin each month by taking the subway and city-rail, which still ran mostly unhindered. From the establishment of the GDR until 1961, over 2.5 million of its citizens had passed through West German refugee reception centers, some 80 percent of these through West Berlin.

THE WALL AND THE TWO BERLINS (1961–1989): "DIVIDED HEAVEN"

On August 13, 1961, the Berlin crisis came to a head with the building of the Wall.[25] Planned with military precision, supervised by Erich Honecker, and backed by East German troops and Soviet tanks, the enterprise of tightly sealing off West Berlin started with barbed wire and quickly grew into a wall of concrete slabs 13 feet high; it contained over 300 watch towers equipped with powerful search lights and machine-gun ports. When the project was completed many months later, buildings had been razed to create a "death strip" alongside the concrete wall. It consisted of a bare track, an antivehicle ditch, a patrol track, a run for guard dogs, and a high wire fence with built-in alarm systems. The Wall completely encircled West Berlin; twenty-seven miles of it cut across the city separating East and West; seventy miles cordoned off West Berlin from East Germany in its hinterland. By 1952 telephone links between the two Berlins had been severed (to be restored only after the 1989 opening of the Wall), and in 1953 buses and trams had been discontinued. The Wall closed all public transportation into West Berlin from the East.[26] One subway and one city-rail line from

West Berlin was allowed to enter East Berlin; they ended at the Friedrich-strasse station in a heavily guarded, fortress-like border post. One "international" crossing was established for diplomats, the Allied military, and foreigners in cars—the famous "Checkpoint Charlie."[27]

The day construction of the Wall began, about 60,000 commuters (*Grenz-gänger*) who lived in the East and worked in West Berlin earning D-Marks were immediately shut off from their jobs. Indeed, the intended function of the "anti-fascist protective wall," as it was referred to in GDR parlance, was to keep East Berliners and East Germans from moving, from being "lured or kidnapped," it was said, to the West and thus to stabilize the GDR economy and the socialist state. Moreover, the Wall was to have an immediate impact not only on people's personal lives but also production in West Berlin. It also was meant to impede West Berlin's ties to the West, to isolate it, and to freeze out its existence. "The Wall will be there until the reasons for its existence have been eliminated," Erich Honecker remarked as late as January 1989 in a public appearance, "it will still be there in 50 and even 100 years" (McAdams 1993, 3).

The construction of the Wall heightened most Berliners' distrust and dislike of the SED regime, for its immediate and lasting effect was a painful severing of ties between families and friends. The Wall was to keep East Berliners and East Germans from visiting the West for almost thirty years except for special "travel cadres," a privileged elite of loyal party members who were also important scientists, scholars, intellectuals, artists, and some sports personalities. Also, senior citizens (men above the age of 65, women above 62) were later allowed to travel to the West for as much as one month per year. Yet West Berlin remained, much more so than West Germany, the forbidden city, especially for East Berliners and for the citizens of the GDR. As to West Berliners, for the first two and a half years after the Wall went up, none were allowed to visit East Berlin. They pressured publicly in the press and with the politicians for access to their families so that at Christmas 1963, limited day passes (*Passierscheine*) were negotiated with the GDR in return for a fee.[28] These passes allowed them to visit only close blood relatives and only at major family events in East Berlin, but not in the GDR. Thereafter restrictions and conditions for passes changed over the years, as the GDR used these (as well as the official transit routes to West Berlin) for political leverage by unpredictably creating and modifying impediments, a practice that was finally largely forestalled by the Four-Power-Agreement in 1971. When Honecker became First Secretary of the SED (1971–1989), the GDR exploited access to East Berlin as a source of hard currency income by requiring all visitors to exchange Western currency into East German marks at exorbitant rates. In 1981, for example, the GDR set the minimum required exchange[29] at 25 D-Marks (for almost worthless 25 East German Marks) per day for West Berliners, including retirees and children. This made it financially very difficult for low-income groups, although a maximum of 30 days for visits in East Berlin and the GDR were permitted. Thus the Wall disrupted family relations, personal ties, and professional, as well as business, associations of long standing; it divided the people of Berlin into two distinct populations almost as much as the different ideological allegiances had done. It created two cultures in Berlin, a "divided heaven" that Christa Wolf's 1963 Berlin novel envisioned, although she never mentioned the forbidden word "wall."

The Wall proved to be effective and deadly; by December 1961, the numbers of refugees arriving in West Berlin was a mere 2,000 (many among them border guards, policemen, and soldiers stationed at the Wall), down from 25,000 in August. By early 1962, the stream of refugees had stopped completely, except for daredevil or ingenious attempts to cross at which the guards were ordered to open fire. During the almost thirty years of the Wall's existence, more than 5,000 would-be escapees were caught; the guards are known to have fired in some 1,600 escape attempts; at least 80 people died, some left by the guards to bleed to death while in full view of, but out of reach of, West Berliners who had to watch helplessly. Family members of some of those killed, silenced and threatened by the authorities at the time, have come forward recently during trials of several border guards now convicted of murder, a muddled legal issue but a sign of the human suffering the Wall caused for all involved. Recalling the physical effects of the Wall helps to understand its singular unpopularity with Berliners whose personal lives were deeply affected.[30]

The Wall also became a major attraction for politicians and tourists visiting the city. Kennedy's spectacular visit in June 1963 was preceded by retired General Lucius Clay and Vice President Lyndon Johnson denouncing "communist tricks and threats." In his famous speech to 450,000 Berliners, Kennedy emphasized West Berlin's right to exist: "I know of no town, no city, which has been besieged for eighteen years that still lives with the vitality and force, and the hope and determination of the city of West Berlin. While the Wall is the most obvious and vivid demonstration of the failures of the communist system, for all the world to see, we take no pride in it. . . . All free men, wherever they may live, are citizens of Berlin, and therefore as a free man, I take pride in the words 'Ich bin ein Berliner'" (Simmons 1988, 214). Kennedy's defense of freedom also meant a defense of the status quo, of American rights, and especially of the military presence

in West Berlin (McAdams 1993, 58–60). It came just a few months before
the Cuban missile crisis, the last serious saber-rattling of the Cold War.
Willy Brandt, closely associated with West Berlin's Social Democrats and
city politics as its mayor from 1957 to 1966, was an equally eloquent
spokesman for West Berlin. Brandt's *Ostpolitik*, begun as Foreign Minister
and continued as Chancellor (1969–1974), replaced Cold War confrontation
with an easing of tension through dialogue with, and official recognition of,
the GDR as well as East-West negotiations and treaties during the 1970s.
The 1971 Four Power Agreement, concerning Berlin, brought relative
stability and relatively smooth, though uneasy, coexistence for the two
Berlins. Acceptance of the status quo, nonrelations, and simply ignoring the
other side, punctured at times by noisy gestures of solidarity, friendship, or
animosity, became the order of the day during the 1980s. The Wall was then
largely ignored and overlooked by those who could afford to do so. The
flood of Berlin literature surrounding the city's 750th anniversary in 1987
rarely even mentioned the Wall, nor did West Berlin's intellectuals or those
who could move freely across it refer to it.

During the three decades of the Wall's existence, West Berlin and East
Berlin underwent social and cultural transformations, growing apart from
each other. As a federal state of the FRG, West Berlin saw major changes
in its population. It was losing middle-class, career-oriented residents
because its shrinking and highly subsidized industry did not provide enough
economic opportunity. Moreover, the political situation was unstable; West
Berlin's survival appeared perhaps doomed. The Wall also severely restricted mobility by limiting its inhabitants to West Berlin's territory. If they
wished to leave West Berlin, they had no choice but to make the long and
bothersome trip through GDR territory along one of the three prescribed
transit routes into West Germany. This trip was hampered by thorough
border controls and petty regulations on the part of the GDR. Expensive air
travel was the alternative for the well-to-do. This lowered the quality of life
for many residents. Older people did not leave, and West Berlin's population
was aging rapidly. By 1963, West Berlin began to recruit foreign workers
from Spain, Italy, Greece, and Yugoslavia, and after 1968 mainly from
Turkey to compensate for labor shortages; most of these workers remained
with their families as permanent residents in Berlin and established their
own neighborhoods, most notably the Turkish community in Kreuzberg.
They are now experiencing ambivalence, hostility, and violence over housing, job competition, and cultural, social, and political differences with
other groups in unified Berlin.[31]

At the same time, since the 1960s, a new generation born during and after the war had been making West Berlin a center of politicized social movements: from the radical, militant terrorists to the feminists, ecologists, and pacifists. Most visible was the student protest movement, the "sixty-eighters," who clashed with police in West Berlin in mass demonstrations. They protested against the Vietnam War, against conservative FRG politics, against encrusted university and social structures, and against the conservative German press.[32] Benno Ohnesorg, a student, was killed by a police bullet in 1967 during demonstrations against the Shah's visit; the student leader Rudi Dutschke barely survived an assassination attempt in 1968, which led to a rampage against prominent West Berlin stores, banks, and the traditional Springer publishing house. With its dailies *Bild*, *Die Welt*, and *Berliner Morgenpost*, the Springer Press publications were vocal advocates of conservatism, Cold War politics, and a strong anti-communist stance in Berlin. Springer's high-rise press building overlooked the Wall, a shining symbol of Western presence in Berlin; it became the target of many demonstrations. As the students in Berlin debated a wide range of marxist, anticapitalist, and anti-Western positions and activism, the movement soon splintered into a number of politicized factions: anarchists (*Spontis*), Marxist-Leninists and Maoists (*K-Gruppen*), violent *Autonome*, and the notorious RAF (*Rote Armee Fraktion*). The RAF was born in 1970 when Andreas Baader, a member of the Berlin counterculture scene who was in Tegel prison for setting fire to a Frankfurt department store, shot his way to freedom with the help of Ulrike Meinhof, then a part-time instructor at the Free University. In 1974, a Berlin judge, Günter von Drenkmann, was assassinated in his chambers; in 1975, a leading CDU politician, Peter Lorenz, was kidnapped. To combat the underground terrorist activities in West Berlin and in the FRG, and the violent tactics of the city guerillas, including murder, arson, kidnapping, and hijacking, in 1972 the *Radikalenerlaß* (extremist directive) was enacted under the leadership of Social Democratic Chancellor Brandt. Ironically, Brandt was forced to resign when his closest personal adviser turned out to be an East German spy.

By the late 1970s, a squatters movement began to attract attention because of its successful efforts to occupy older city blocks owned by speculators, who could use Berlin subsidies and tax write-offs, evict tenants, and let the buildings decay for a profit. This led to fights with the police to rampages and window smashings by demonstrators on the Kurfürstendamm and in prominent establishments elsewhere. Enabling squatters to renovate flats and buildings diffused the movement after the mid 1980s. The reunification of Berlin put an end to this by totally eliminating subsidies, creating a run on real estate, and thus, once again, exacerbating the housing shortage for middle and low income groups.

The enclave of West Berlin became a magnet for unconventional young people. The development of the alternative lifestyles of the counterculture—the *Szene*—with its collectives and shared living quarters (*WG: Wohngemeinschaften*) and its experimental forms of living arrangements, education, and art forms attracted young West Germans. They flocked to Berlin, to visit friends for a while and take in the many outstanding offerings of "high" culture and the popular "counterculture," to study at the comparatively progressive, liberal Free University, the Technical University, the prestigious art institute (*Hochschule der Künste*), or the numerous specialized colleges for the social, administrative, or medical professions. Some came to dodge the draft, since residents of West Berlin were exempt from military service, some to do drugs more freely, and some to escape restrictive families or boring small towns while enjoying the anonymity and freedom of the big city.

A decade after the Wall was built, East Berlin began to prosper as *Hauptstadt der DDR*, the political, administrative, and economic center of the GDR. An elite of young professionals, skilled and trained workers, and political functionaries moved in from other parts of the GDR. As the GDR's capital, East Berlin received preferred treatment and supplies of consumer goods. It was the undisputed cultural and economic center of the country with much new construction, notably in the districts of Marzahn and Lichtenberg, and the renovation of historical buildings after the mid-1970s.[33] While East Berlin did not experience overt radical groups and changes until 1989, individual dissidents received much publicity in the Western press—Humboldt University physics professor Robert Havemann, who was removed from office after a critical lecture and interview in 1976, or Wolf Biermann, who was stripped of his citizenship and not readmitted into the GDR after giving a concert in Cologne in 1976 at the invitation of the Metal Workers Union (IG Metall).[34] Prominent East Berlin writers, among them Christa Wolf, Volker Braun, Franz Fühmann, Stephan Hermlin, and Heiner Müller, protested in an open letter; some left and went no farther than West Berlin, as did Thomas Brasch and Sarah Kirsch in 1977; some resettled in the FRG, as did Günter Kunert did in 1979 after being removed from the SED membership list; Monika Maron[35] followed a decade later. Artists and intellectuals who went against the party line were silenced or expelled because trials and prison terms proved embarrassing for the regime; this was the case in the Rudolf Bahro affair. Bahro had criticized SED policy in his *Die Alternative* and in 1978 was sentenced by an East Berlin court to eight years' imprisonment; an amnesty in 1979, however, allowed him to move to the West. During the early 1980s, the FRG negotiated the emigration into the West of some 35,000 GDR citizens in return for hard currency; among them were pacifists, dissident professionals and intellectuals, those separated family members, and political prisoners including *Fluchthelfer* (people who had helped with escape attempts) and spies.

The new wave of GDR citizens who desperately sought to leave was by no means limited to East Berlin; by the mid 1980s tensions rose between the Honecker government and its population over access to the outside world and travel to the West. By the end of the 1980s, when Gorbachev's reforms seemed to elude an increasingly stubborn Honecker and his ineffective and aging SED leadership, and when the Soviet Union's economic difficulties escalated, the pressure to leave mounted. Consequently over 30,000 persons were allowed to emigrate from the GDR in 1988. By August 1989, some 1.5 million GDR citizens were impatiently waiting for exit visas and some 5 million out of a total population of 16.5 million wanted to leave (Naimark 1992, 85). Entire families forced their way out by seeking refuge in the FRG's permanent mission in East Berlin and in West German embassies in Eastern European countries, hoping to gain free passage to the West. Many young working people fled via Czechoslovakia through Hungary, taking advantage of the first hole in the Iron Curtain since the building of the Berlin Wall. The surprise opening of the Wall on November 9, 1989 resulted from the people's unprecedented pressure for free movement and travel, but more concretely from the young East Berliners' desire for access to the forbidden half of their city.[36]

REUNIFICATION AND CAPITAL OF THE FRG:
"IN THE WAITING ROOM OF HISTORY"

Few events were of greater significance for the city of Berlin than the opening of the Wall, which led more rapidly than anyone had anticipated to the reunification of the divided city and country. It was the most visible sign and starting point of what is referred to as *die Wende* (the turning point), a process whose events are much contested in their interpretation.[37] East Germany's "peaceful revolution"[38] forced Honecker, his successors Krenz and Modrow, and the SED party elite out by dismantling the much-hated *Stasi* and occupying its offices all over the GDR; and even its Normannenstraße headquarters in Berlin were stormed on January 15, 1990.[39] Plans for a socialist renewal, a reformed GDR, or a "third way" between capitalism and communism, advocated by some within the civil rights groups and supported by prominent intellectuals and writers, failed to rally popular support. The continuing flow of people into the West, the mass demonstrations against the regime, the vocal criticism by opposition groups, and the bankrupt East German economy hastened the GDR's collapse and the unification process (Glaessner 1992, 93–102). After the first general, free elections in the GDR in March 1990, its *Volkskammer* voted to join the FRG, and its last government under Lothar de Maizière negotiated a monetary, economic, and social union with the FRG. The unification treaty was signed on August 31 in the old Crown Prince's Palace at Unter den Linden. The "Two Plus Four Treaty," consisting of the two Germanies and four Allied powers, which abolished the rights of the victors of 1945 over Germany and in particular over Berlin,[40] was signed in Moscow twelve days later. The GDR was legally incorporated into the FRG on October 3, 1990.

At the time of German unification, the entire city of Berlin, with its 23 boroughs, became a *Land* of the FRG like the five new federal states of the former GDR. A "marriage" with the surrounding Brandenburg to create an economically and administratively more viable state has been put on hold. East Berlin's city administration (*Magistrat*) joined West Berlin's *Senatsverwaltung* and for the first time since 1946, citywide elections selected an all-Berlin city council in December 1990.[41] The Bundestag's June 1991 choice of Berlin as capital of the Federal Republic was a narrow victory, rekindling old fears and bitter memories for some, for others sending a signal of hope and commitment to a new Germany including its East German constituency. The acrimonious dissent from residents of Bonn and western areas of Germany has since given way to procrastination in what is to be a complicated and costly move set for 1998 to 2000. Whether it is but a "capital lie" (*Hauptstadtlüge*) as *Der Spiegel*, weary of the everlasting Kohl government, put it remains to be seen.

Within less than a year of its opening, the Wall had almost completely disappeared, except for a stretch along the Spree serving as an open-air museum, with many pieces having been chiseled off and sold as souvenirs. Most of it was crushed to rubble to be used as a foundation for a high-speed rail track and new construction. With amazing speed, minutely detailed planning, and sophisticated engineering, Berlin's severed and deteriorating infrastructure—those cut-off streets, highways, waterways, telephone and postal service, utilities, transportation (metro, city rail, and bus lines), water, and power supplies—was reconnected and modernization begun.[42] "Reunification" was indeed an appropriate term for rejoining the divided metropolis into one smoothly functioning urban structure. But it would be a different story with people and their institutions. All of a sudden Berliners were again part of a country that had a voluminous recent past to grapple with and in which forty years of division had produced social and cultural separation.

Willy Brandt's words: "Now must grow together again what belongs together" echoed the longing for political unity of many postwar generation Berliners as whose most articulate spokesman Brandt had first gained world prominence. Like many of his generation, Brandt, who died in 1992, did not anticipate how difficult the process of reestablishing social, cultural, and human ties would be; forty years of separation into two opposing political systems had created two different cultures. After euphoric celebrations of new freedom and a rush to consumer goods, differences surfaced between the people in the West and the East, quickly dubbed *Wessis* and *Ossis*. Longing for the former bliss of West Berlin as a protected island, West Berliners began to resent the influx of visitors and new residents from the East eager for Western goods and amenities, the traffic jams, construction noise, and inconvenience, the escalating real estate prices, the run on affordable apartments, and the strain on public and social services. But in general, *Wessis* could continue in their way of life.

The *Ossis*, on the other hand, experienced drastic changes as "their" system was taken over and replaced by another, the Western system. The immediate effect of the currency union (July 1, 1990) and the GDR's subsequent accession to the FRG meant that the legal, political, and economic structure of the FRG was accepted by East Germany. That brought the dissolution and privatization (*Abwicklung*)[43] of all socialized enterprises and state-owned property, completed by the end of 1994 by the *Treuhand* (trust agency), which had been established by the Modrow government in March 1990. For East Berlin, this meant the downsizing or closing of all major factories and businesses and endless law suits over the return of, or compensation for, real estate property expropriated since 1950. It also brought fundamental changes in education, public administration, the legal system, police and army, and the economy, which were rebuilt and supervised by often arrogant and insensitive Westerners, quickly dubbed *Besserwessis*. "We preach, punish, ignore, and exclude," Richard von Weizsäcker, former mayor of West Berlin before his two terms as Federal President, remarked to explain why disillusioned East Germans increasingly turn to the PDS, the SED's successor party, which enjoys strong support in former SED territory in East Berlin. The PDS won direct mandates with prominent personalities, like writer Stefan Heym, and 20 percent of the vote in Berlin, compared to 4.4 percent nationally, during the second all-German *Bundestag* elections in October 1994. These victories were all clustered in East

Berlin districts, especially Marzahn, Lichtenberg, and Prenzlauer Berg. Five years after the *Wende*, the PDS is even embracing a neo-Stalinist wing among its members.[44]

Heated controversies raged about prominent politicians and intellectuals and their political past and involvement with the SED and State Security, as was the case with Manfred Stolpe, Protestant Bishop and popular Minister President of Brandenburg, with Heinrich Fink, the first elected, then discredited and fired President of Humboldt University, and with prominent authors like Heiner Müller and Christa Wolf. These much publicized debates in intellectual circles overshadowed many victims' stories such as that of Vera Wollenberger. Now a *Bundestag* representative for the newly formed party *Bündnis 90/Die Grünen* (Alliance 90/The Greens), Wollenberger discovered from reading her *Stasi* files that her husband of ten years had served as State Security's paid informant about her most private life, as well as her political activities, her friends, and family.

But one need not be a prominent person to feel displaced and disinherited in the new Berlin. Many East Berliners, who were forced into early retirement, lost their jobs, or work below their qualifications in the new system, and, especially many women,[45] long for values and recognition, often nostalgically recalling their former "niche," their role in, and protection by, a socialist enterprise. In East Berlin that often meant a relatively privileged position in the socialist state among the country's elite workers and intellectuals. Coming to terms with the past and facing the present is an ongoing, unresolved, and unsettling process. The long-time premier East Berlin cabaret, *Die Distel*, seems to echo many Berliners' frustration with politicians and their utter pessimism about any future in the Western system with its recent program *Völker hört das Finale!* (Nations Listen to the Finale, a clever play on the socialist hymn's rousing call to action *Völker hört die Signale!*).[46]

While the cultural and political divide, the "Wall in people's heads," has taken center stage in recent discussions, the city's new populations have received much less attention except for xenophobic violence. Berlin is again growing rapidly with immigrants and asylum-seekers (many undocumented) from Eastern Europe, especially Poland, Romania, the former Yugoslavia, from areas of the former Soviet Republic, as well as from troubled areas of Asia and Africa. Berlin has become, once again, a favorite place for various streams of immigrants.[47] Added to the sizable Turkish population in West Berlin, to foreign workers from southern Europe and the former Yugoslavia, the new migrants from Eastern Europe and refugees from Bosnia and Africa are taxing the city's resources, services, its job market, and public housing. The *Wende* has heightened, though certainly not initiated, social and ethnic frictions. Clashes with, and violent attacks by, right-wing youth groups, gang members, and latent and overt hostility from residents and newer arrivals to the city have revived the specter of racism, anti-semitism, and neo-Nazi activities. The open borders—unthinkable for Berliners before the *Wende*—have made Berlin a major attraction and are changing Berlin's population once again.

Even what at first seemed an unpolitical reshaping of Berlin's cultural institutions brought endless headaches. To name only the most visible places of metropolitan "high" culture: What was to be done with Berlin's 29 museums, among them two national galleries and two Egyptian museums? What with two official state libraries? (All museums, public libraries, and public art collections have been reorganized.) How can three flourishing, well-equipped opera houses, dozens of publicly funded fine theaters, numerous experimental stages, lay groups, and cabarets be supported? (All continue to exist so far, except for the closing of West Berlin's *Schillertheater*; some have been privatized partially like Brecht's former theater *Berliner Ensemble*.) What was to happen with three major symphony orchestras and two symphonic choirs dating back to the traditional Singakademie? With two Academies of Art? (They entered a controversial merger under Walter Jens's leadership.) The abundance of cultural institutions of very high quality (festivals, theaters, orchestras, museums, art galleries, libraries, special schools, and colleges) originated from the postwar division and eventual duplication of all of Berlin's numerous traditional institutions, a sign of the cultural rivalry of the two Berlins. In 1989 West Berlin's annual culture budget alone amounted to well over 550 million marks. [48] Since half of West Berlin's entire budget came from special subsidies from the FRG, which have now been discontinued, the large number of cultural institutions poses a financial strain on a city that also faces a multitude of demands for social services for a rapidly growing, diverse population with many new immigrants from the impoverished East European countries. Berlin's ongoing restructuring and economic downsizing adds to the problems of unemployment,[49] housing, and social tensions brought on by the *Wende* and conveys a sense of loss of valuable cultural traditions to Berliners. Reunification has meant a rethinking of cultural identity and the difficulty in starting afresh has translated into a hotly debated *Kulturpolitik* for all areas of culture, from the *Szene* and counterculture to the showy, internationally acclaimed and contested "high culture."[50]

"Berlin is a city reborn" was the optimistic prognosis of British TV broadcaster and businessman Alan Watson[51] in 1992. This may well have been more an expression of hope than a view based in reality. The city's refusal or inability to reform its political organs; its corruption, scandals, and party cliques (*Filz*) in local government, like the one surrounding the ill-fated bid for the Olympic Games for 2000; its lack of first-rate leadership, all these important issues have hampered the political, social, and economic "rebirth." On the positive side, time and the necessity to live together in one big city seems to diminish the bitter clash of *Wessi* and *Ossi* in Berlin. Not that Berlin as a city is providing a newly established identity for its inhabitants, but a process of "reimagining Berlin," as the *New York Times*'s Paul Goldberger has called it, is underway. With much of the major technical changes behind them or at least clearly outlined, Berliners simply have to go on living and to come to terms with their new roles and changing city. Since 1990 major competitions to redesign the city were held. For some time to come Berlin will be a huge building site for new commercial development and to prepare for the federal government's move to the city. The public debate about Berlin's historical center district, *Mitte*, with its intensive architectural planning and redesigning, is but sign of the ongoing transformation (see Schumann 1995).

"The entire city is sitting in the waiting room of history. People here are waiting for new construction at the Potsdamer Platz, for the move of the government, for immigrants and for investors," an observant Cees Noote-boom, the Dutch author and journalist, who had reported on the GDR since 1963 and who spent 1990–1991 in Berlin publishing his impressions, remarked during a recent interview (Nooteboom 1993, 54). When he refers to present-day Berlin as "a slow drama," Nooteboom echoes the mood and expectations of new and old Berliners and those who have visited the city frequently during the past decades with an open mind toward its tumultuous history and its present transformation. On a recent visit, the *New York Times* correspondent was first struck by "the startling discovery that [Berlin's] center is 17 acres of weeds and debris" where once the city's commercial heart stood. Now it is "empty, damaged by Allied bombs and finished off by the East Germans, who rammed the Berlin wall right through its center and tore down what remained of the surrounding blocks" (Goldberger 1995, 45). The city struggles to reinvent itself and to define itself as the cultural and political capital of a united Germany. Berlin has, I think, rightly been called "the ultimate postmodern space" (Borneman 1992, 1); it is the metamorphosis of the city, especially during the past decade that has earned it this challenging, but by no means unequivocal, reputation. With all the controversy over reunification and its aftermath, we might better remember, as Berlin-based journalist Klaus Hartung has put it, "that it was not a catastrophe that stood at the beginning of Berlin's reunification, but self-liberation and the end of the Wall."

NOTES

1. With this heading, Gordon Craig's chapter on Berlin (*The Germans*, pp. 261–86), published in 1982, reflects the dichotomous view of the post–World War II city in American and English historical narratives. Others operate with the rise-and-fall scenario, see Anthony Read and David Fisher, *The Fall of Berlin* (1992) and *Berlin Rising* (1994). For a review of historical Berlin narratives, see Brunn and Reulicke (*Berlin. Blicke auf die deutsche Metropole*); for literary images and perceptions of the city, see Glass, Rösler and White's *Berlin. Literary Images of a City* (with its extensive bibliography); for a more critical reflection on cultural and literary images, see Haxthausen and Suhr (*Berlin. Culture and Metropolis*).

2. That a description of "historical, cultural reality" reflects only an author's perspective, construct, and fiction is now considered commonplace. However, in order to place the following essays into the broader context of Berlin's history, culture, and society, I wish to provide some factual, historical information, which in so many recent accounts involving Berlin and Germany seems to be eroded in the rush for interpretation.

3. See Walther Rathenau, "Die schönste Stadt der Welt" (1902); see Haxthausen and Suhr, *Berlin*. p. 40. All translations from the German are mine, unless otherwise noted. The image of Berlin as an "American" metropolis clashing with tradition became a standard one for twentieth-century observers.

4. After about a decade of annexation attempts and rigorous city planning by the authorities, the Prussian Diet passed the reorganization legislation, with the votes of the SPD and USPD (Socialist parties). Effective on October 1, 1920, the creation of *Groß-Berlin* brought eight separate municipalities (Berlin, Charlottenburg, Köpenick, Lichtenberg, Neukölln, Schöneberg, Spandau, Wilmersdorf), 59 villages and 27 rural districts (*Gutsbezirke*) under one administrative umbrella.

5. West Berlin's population peaked in 1957; after 1961, the stream of refugees from the East was totally cut off. Although businesses, investors, and West Germans transferring to West Berlin were offered tax incentives, housing subsidies, and special monthly payments, these measures by the Federal German government did not reverse the trend of slowly decreasing population.

6. See Friederike Eigler's essay in this volume and the section "Wir machen Epoche" in Boberg, Fichter, and Gillen, *Die Metropole. Industriekultur in Berlin im 20. Jahrhundert*, pp. 16–102.

7. See the colorful contemporary accounts in Eduard Bernstein, ed. *Die Geschichte der Berliner Arbeiterbewegung*; Annemarie Lange, *Berlin zur Zeit Bebels und Bismarcks. Zwischen Reichsgründung und Jahrhundertwende*; and "Das rote Berlin" in Boberg, Fichter, and Gillen.

8. See "Die sozialistische Metropole" in Boberg, Fichter, and Gillen.

9. John Bruten's popular Broadway dramatization, *I am a Camera* (1952), of Christopher Isherwood's story of Sally Bowles (from *Goodbye to Berlin*, 1945) was adapted for the musical stage in 1966 as *Cabaret*. This musical was popular-

ized in Robert Fosses's movie version with the singing and dancing of Liza Minelli and Joel Grey. This complex and contradictory image of Berlin of the twenties is as much a fantasy of British and American pre- and postwar visitors to the city as it is a creation of Broadway and Hollywood culture. While musical and movie were great box-office successes, Christopher Isherwood said in 1968 about the transformation of his Berlin tale: "It's an ill bird that fouls its nest where the golden eggs are laid. Especially when the nest is anyhow made entirely of sawdust and shit" (Glass, Rösler, and White, p. 134). Most West Berliners saw and loved the movie as a film reminiscent of *The Blue Angel*, but they felt it was an essentially American view of the "Golden Twenties."

10. For a more authentic social portrait of Berlin's varied population and living conditions, see "Metropolenkultur" in Boberg, Fichter, and Gillen and "Berlin in der Weimarer Republik (1918–1932)" in Ribbe (*Geschichte Berlins*).

11. Oswald Spengler's influential *Untergang des Abendlandes* (1922) included a negative view of Berlin in his chapter on the "soul of the city"; the colossal stone monument of the city stands at the end of man's human development, will swallow its own creator and make him its victim (see Brunn and Reulicke p. 65ff).

12. With most of the opposition suppressed, thousands of voters imprisoned, and terror squads in the streets, the Nazis received 31 percent of the Berlin votes during the last national elections—even fewer votes than the outlawed Communists and harassed Socialists in local elections—winning only 86 out of 225 seats in the Prussian parliament. Hitler then dissolved the Prussian state government, appointed a Reich commissioner, and filled all key positions (mayor, police chief, etc.) in Berlin with loyal Nazis.

13. For a detailed, up-to-date account of the fate of Jews and Jewish communities under the Nazis in Berlin, see Monika Richarz, "Jüdisches Berlin und seine Vernichtung," in Boberg, Fichter, and Gillen pp. 216–25 and 389; for accounts of survival in Berlin, see Gross (*Versteckt. Wie Juden in Berlin die Nazi-Zeit überlebten*); for a study of prosecution and resistance in the central, upper-middle-class district of Tiergarten, see Roskamp (*Verfolgung und Widerstand*).

14. See the documentation in Jochheim, *Frauenprotest in der Rosenstraße*.

15. From 1953 on, the Rykestraße synagogue in the Prenzlauerberg district served as the only Jewish center in East Berlin; built in 1903, it is also the only intact old synagogue in the city. Not far away, the New Synagogue, a huge Moorish structure with a gilded dome built in 1866 and heavily damaged during the war, has recently been restored.

16. In November 1992 ground was broken for the Jewish Museum, adjoining the Berlin Museum in Kreuzberg and designed by the renowned architect Daniel Libeskind, and for the Hans-Galinski School. Commemorating the longtime leader of the postwar Jewish community in Berlin, the school opened in 1995 with a Jewish Studies curriculum and instruction in Hebrew (*Der Tagesspiegel*,

November 9, 1992). See also Susan Neiman, *Slow Fire: Jewish Notes from Berlin* (New York: Schocken, 1992).

17. See the memoirs and accounts in the Höcker, Kardoff, and Schäfer works.

18. Helke Sander's (thoroughly researched) film *BeFreier und Befreite* (Liberators and Liberated) (1992) examines mass rapes of women by allied soldiers, especially by Red Army troops, at the end of World War II, a tabu subject until now. Its controversial reception has set off an inquiry into the role of women in the immediate postwar period.

19. Numerous witnesses' accounts and personal memoirs (e.g., the works of Conradt, Höcker, Schäfer) published in recent years agree in their descriptions about the Red Army's looting and violence, a topic totally ignored in GDR history (see, for example, Keiderling, *Berlin 1945–1986*).

20. The Soviets had also dismantled almost all still functioning industrial installations in the Western sectors before the Americans were allowed into the city; they also carted off private and public property of value, from art works to telephone equipment and railroad tracks; see Hillenbrand, *The Future of Berlin*, pp. 3–6, Grosser, *German Unification*, pp. 29–30, and Ribbe, *Geschichte Berlins*, pp. 1028–34.

21. See Hillenbrand's discussion of Soviet intentions, the role of Berlin in the immediate postwar period, and revisionist and anti-revisionist views of the Cold War (especially pp. 3–39) for a detailed, dispassionate discussion of the period. The accessibility of East German and some Russian archives has brought to light definitive evidence of aggressive plans for a Communist Europe during the Stalinist era. The city of Berlin was a key object in that policy. The postwar political history of Berlin is presently undergoing substantive revisions on the basis of newly accessible documents. See Erler and Lauder, eds., *"Nach Hitler kommen wir." Die Planung der KPD-Führung in Moskau 1944/45*, and the interesting (and influential) eyewitness accounts by prominent journalists Wolfgang Leonhardt and Carola Stern.

22. See Glaessner, *The Unification Process in Germany*, pp. 103–15; Borneman's "process of mirror-imaging," his model of the two states "fabricating themselves as moieties in a dual organization," and his assumption that "the proposal for a socialist GDR was a response to the actually existing capitalism in West Germany" (17) disregard chronology and the Soviets' Stalinist master plan for the postwar period. The Moscow-trained SED leadership was to carry out this plan. By contrast, the Allies considered several differing plans and did not present a united front. Borneman's competition-driven, dual-system model does not account for fundamental differences between the two systems, with the Western democratic system being an open one allowing for dissent, unprecedented spontaneous changes and developments, and unplanned-for, irrational individual action. Much of Borneman's theoretical constructs and discussion appear heavily influenced by GDR cultural politics of legitimization and demarcation vis-à-vis the "imperialist West" during the 1970s and early 1980s.

23. Recent access to archival material in East Germany revealed a much larger dissatisfaction and wider participation than had been admitted before; see Hagen (*DDR—Juni '53*). After this revolt, the party elite moved to the exclusive, gated community of Wandlitz.

24. GDR leaders had accepted the Oder-Neisse Line as Germany's Eastern border by March 1948; it was called officially the "frontier of peace" in the East German-Polish declaration and treaty of June/July 1950 (Grosser, p. 260). Brandt's *Ostpolitik* included renunciation-of-force agreements with Moscow (August 1970) and Warsaw (December 1970), which contained a clause recognizing state boundaries in Europe as "inviolable." This included West Berlin and the Oder-Neisse border (McAdams, p. 82). In 1991, the FRG signed a treaty of friendship and cooperation with Poland, recognizing the Oder-Neisse border and pledging to support Poland's admission to the European Community (McAdams, p. 225).

25. See McAdams (especially pp. 3–55) for a detailed discussion of the political events leading up to the building of the Wall, including still ongoing discussions about Khrushchev's ultimatum, an offer of a peace treaty for Germany, and plans for a demilitarized free city of Berlin, as well as Kennedy's reactions and role at the Vienna summit in June 1961.

26. The border crossings of the three official transit routes from West Berlin into West Germany were also reinforced with elaborate security measures. There were continuous squabbles and chicanery with regard to free land and air access to West Berlin.

27. It was only during the 1980s that seven border crossings with differing regulations were opened.

28. For three decades after the Wall went up, much tension, discussion, and negotiation revolved around visiting rights in East Berlin. Small concessions on the part of GDR authorities were coupled with often ludicrous restrictions, tight controls, and hefty entrance fees by requiring a minimum exchange (*Mindestumtausch*). This restricted the flow of visitors and incensed West Berliners.

29. The money had to be exchanged at the GDR's highly inflated official exchange rate of one West to one East German mark when the actual value (black market exchange) fluctuated between one to five to one to ten; the GDR in fact acknowledged the black market rates by changing East German money into Western currency only at these rates. Also, East German retirees visiting the West were not allowed to take any money with them to the West, a measure that made them dependent on Western relatives. Thus West German communities provided "welcome money" (*Begrüßungsgeld*) of some 100 marks and more to each East German visitor, a practice that was criticized by the East as a capitalist bribe. Yet Western currency was much coveted in the GDR as a means to purchase many consumer goods available only in special government-run "Intershops," which accepted only Western currency and Rubles. It was in the city of Berlin where

people experienced most acutely the GDR's paranoid restrictions on travel, money, and its lack of many consumer goods.

30. For a sensitive discussion of the Wall's effect, see Siegfried Mews' essay in this volume.

31. See the article by Carol Aisha Blackshire-Belay in this volume.

32. A history sponsored by the Free University addresses the tumultuous 1960s: Tent, *Freie Universität Berlin 1948–1988. Eine deutsche Hochschule im Zeitgeschehen*, pp. 296–486. For a more critical view of the protest movement see Dutschke-Klotz, Gollwitzer, and Miermeister, eds. *Rudi Dutschke. Mein langer Marsch*, and Levitt, *Children of Privilege. Student Revolt in the 1960s*.

33. On the perception of East Berlin, mostly by East German writers, see the articles by Tate and Bullock in Glass, Rösner, and White, and by Rosenberg and Suhr in Haxthausen and Suhr.

34. For an insider's treatment of the Berlin situation, see Hartung, "Lyric Poetry in Berlin since 1961," in Haxthausen and Suhr, especially pp. 199–205. The literary and intellectual scene and individuals in the GDR have been the subject of much discussion before and after unification; see related articles by Siegfried Mews and Anna Kuhn in this volume.

35. See Maron, "Warum bin ich selbst gegangen?"

36. For a detailed account of the events leading to the Wall opening, see McAdams pp. 175–206.

37. See Kuhn's essay in this volume for major aspects of the literary discussion surrounding *die Wende*.

38. For a detailed discussion of the events and the use of the term "revolution," see "Collapse from Internal Weakness—the GDR 1989–90" and "The GDR on Its Way to Democracy" in Dieter Grosser pp. 55–87. The discussion is, of course, an ongoing one.

39. See Walter Süß, "Entmachtung und Verfall der Staatssicherheit," and the journalistic report, with the hindsight of five years, by Hans Halter, "Keiner wird verschont."

40. During the summer of 1994, the last of the allied troops, including all of the Red Army stationed in East Germany, left Berlin after spending almost fifty years as "occupying," then as "protective," forces in the city.

41. East Berlin city employees, including the police force and educators without incriminating *Stasi* connections, continued in their jobs. The December 2, 1990 elections for an all-Berlin city council showed many political differences: the Christian Democrats (CDU) received 47.8 percent of the vote in (the much more populous) West Berlin, 24.3 in the East, and a citywide figure of 40.4 percent; the PDS (SED successor party) received 1.3 percent in West Berlin, 24.8 in the East, and a citywide margin of 9.2 percent. The CDU's Eberhard Diepgen (West Berlin mayor during the 1980s) replaced SPD's Walter Momper as mayor in the Socialists' first loss of city hall in the postwar era.

42. While West Berlin had built a self-sufficient, but limited, utility system after the blockade, East Berlin's had not been modernized since the 1920s (the telephone network, except for State Security's own system, dated back to the Olympic Games of 1936), had been poorly maintained, and still had some war damage. The economic and ecological costs (e.g., raw sewage seeping into the city's shallow water table, 25 percent of households lacking indoor plumbing) were enormous and represented a financial liability for the city long after federal Berlin subsidies were discontinued.

43. The official term *abwickeln* was resented even more when it was pointed out that it had also been used by the Nazis for forced sales of Jewish property.

44. "Das Strafen muß ein Ende finden." *Der Spiegel* 4/1995, p. 23. The same issue carries a report on the comeback of Stalinism and old SED hardliners within the PDS, "Stalins Geist in der PDS," pp. 27–29.

45. See the article by Hannelore Scholz in this volume.

46. The Distel's recent program titles reflect East Berliners' changing moods: "Mit dem Kopf durch die Wende" [With the Head through the *Wende*–a play on *Wände*—wall] (January 1990), Über-Lebenszeit" [Survival] (March 1990), "Uns gab's nur einmal" [Only Once It Was Us] (Sept. 1990), "Wir sind das letzte . . . " [We Are the Last . . .] (May 1991), "Wir haben uns übernommen" [We've Overworked Ourselves] (Aug. 1992), "Reichtum verpflichtet" [Wealth Obliges] (Feb. 1993), and "Glaubt mir kein Wort" [Don't Believe a Word from Me] (June 1993).

47. Since the Bundestag's controversial changes on asylum went into effect in July 1993, migration from the former East Bloc states to Berlin has not declined, but the number of asylum-seekers for all of Germany dropped by some 70 percent in the first quarter of 1994 versus 1993. With a comparatively high foreign population of 7.8 percent, Germany has taken in as many immigrants proportionately as the United States did during its peak years of immigration in the early decades of this century. "This makes Germany the nearest thing Europe has to a melting pot—and a place where neo-Nazi groups and violent young people make foreigners the targets of their rage" (*The Economist*, May 24, 1994).

48. By comparison, West Berlin's culture budget amounted to more than half the federal outlays for culture in the entire United States (Haxthausen and Suhr, p. xiv).

49. In 1994 there were 450,000 Berliners without a regular job; Berlin's economic recovery is severely hampered by the loss of economic ties with its surrounding territory, loss of industry during the past forty years, and the enormous costs of renovating East Berlin and reunification of city services and infrastructure (Neubauer, p. 9).

50. See the essay by Friederike Eigler in this volume; the culture and identity debate continues in major journalistic articles on Berlin by, among others, Schwartz (her pieces first appeared in the *Washington Post*), Kipphoff and Sack

(*Die Zeit*), Nooteboom and Schneider (*Der Spiegel*), and Goldberger (*New York Times*).

51. The influential British journalist, businessman, and politician was writing shortly after unification (Watson, *The Germans*, p. 96).

REFERENCES

Bernstein, Eduard, ed. *Die Geschichte der Berliner Arbeiterbewegung.* 3 vols. Berlin, 1907–1910.

Boberg, Jochen, Tielman Fichter, and Eckart Gillen, eds. *Die Metropole. Industriekultur in Berlin im 20. Jahrhundert.* Munich: Beck, 1986.

Borneman, John. *Belonging in the Two Berlins. Kin, State, Nation.* Cambridge: Cambridge University Press, 1992.

Brunn, Gerhard, and Jürgen Reulicke, eds. *Berlin. Blicke auf die deutsche Metropole.* Bonn: Bouvier, 1989.

Conradt, Sylvia, and Kirsten Heckmann-Janz. *Reichstrümmerhauptstadt: Leben in Berlin 1945–1961.* Darmstadt: Luchterhand, 1987.

Craig, Gordon A. *The Germans.* New York: G. P. Putnam's Sons, 1982.

Darnton, Robert. *Berlin Journal, 1989–1990.* New York: Norton, 1991.

Dutschke-Klotz, Gretchen, Helmut Gollwitzer, and Jürgen Miermeister, eds. *Rudi Dutschke. Mein langer Marsch.* Hamburg: Hoffmann und Campe, 1980.

Eckhardt, Wolf von, and Sander Gilman. *Bertolt Brecht's Berlin. A Scrapbook of the Twenties.* Lincoln, Neb./London: University of Nebraska Press, 1993.

Erler, Peter, and Horst Lauder, eds. *"Nach Hitler kommen wir." Die Planung der KPD-Führung in Moskau 1944/45.* Berlin: Akademie Verlag, 1994.

Friedrich, Heinz, ed. *Mein Kopfgeld: die Währungsreform—Rückblicke nach vier Jahrzehnten.* Munich: C. H. Beck, 1988.

Friedrich, Wolfgang-Uwe. *Totalitäre Herrschaft. Totalitäres Erbe.* German Studies Review (Fall 1994).

Glaessner, Gert-Joachim. *The Unification Process in Germany. From Dictatorship to Democracy.* Translated by Colin B. Grant. New York: St. Martin's Press, 1992.

Glass, Derek, Dietmar Rösler, and John J. White, eds. *Berlin. Literary Images of a City. Eine Großstadt im Spiegel der Literatur.* Berlin: Erich Schmidt, 1989.

Goldberger, Paul. "Reimagining Berlin." *New York Times Magazine,* February 5, 1995, 45–53.

Gross, Leonard. *Versteckt. Wie Juden in Berlin die Nazi-Zeit überlebten.* Hamburg: Rowohlt, 1983.

Grosser, Dieter, ed. *German Unification. The Unexpected Challenge.* Oxford: Berg, 1992.

Hagen, Manfred. *DDR—Juni '53. Die erste Volkserhebung im Stalinismus.* Stuttgart: Franz Steiner Verlag, 1992.

Halter, Hans. "Keiner wird verschont." *Der Spiegel* 3 (1995): 44–55; and 4 (1995): 108–15.

Hartung, Klaus. "Bühne des Übergangs." *Die Zeit* (Overseas Edition), November 11, 1994, 5.

Haxthausen, Charles W. and Heidrun Suhr, eds. *Berlin. Culture and Metropolis.* Minneapolis/Oxford: University of Minnesota Press, 1991.

Hillenbrandt, Martin J. *The Future of Berlin.* Montclair, NJ: Allanheld, Osmun Publishers, 1980.

Höcker, Karla, ed. *Beschreibung eines Jahres. Berliner Notizen 1945.* Berlin: Arani Verlag, 1984.

Jochheim, Gernot. *Frauenprotest in der Rosenstraße: "Gebt uns unsere Männer wieder."* Berlin: Edition Hentrich, 1993.

Kardoff, Ursula von. *Berliner Aufzeichnungen 1942–1945.* Edited by Peter Hartl. Munich: Beck, 1992.

Keiderling, Gerhard. *Berlin 1945–1986. Geschichte der Hauptstadt der DDR.* Berlin: Dietz Verlag, 1987.

Kipphoff, Petra. "Violette Schweine, geplantes Chaos." *Die Zeit* (Overseas Edition), March 4, 1994, 13–14.

Kramer, Jane. *Eine Amerikanerin in Berlin.* Berlin: Edition Tiamat, 1995.

Lange, Annemarie. *Berlin zur Zeit Bebels und Bismarcks. Zwischen Reichsgründung und Jahrhundertwende.* Berlin: Akademie Verlag, 1972.

Leonhardt, Wolfgang. *Die Revolution entläßt ihre Kinder.* Cologne/Berlin: Kiepenheuer & Witsch, 1955.

Levitt, Cyrill. *Children of Privilege: Student Revolt in the 1960s.* Toronto: University of Toronto Press, 1984.

Maron, Monika. "Warum bin ich selbst gegangen?" *Der Spiegel* 28 (1989): 22–23.

McAdams, A. James. *Germany Divided: From the Wall to Reunification.* Princeton: Princeton University Press, 1993.

Micksch, Jürgen. *Deutschland—Einheit in kultureller Vielfalt.* Reinbek: Rowohlt, 1991.

Naimark, Norman M. " 'Ich will hier raus:' Emigration and the Collapse of the German Democratic Republic." In *Eastern Europe in Revolution*, edited by Ivo Banac, 72–95. Ithaca/London: Cornell University Press, 1992.

Neiman, Susan. *Slow Fire: Jewish Notes from Berlin.* New York: Schocken, 1992.

Neubauer, Ralf. "Warten auf den Urknall." *Die Zeit* (Overseas Edition), April 1, 1994, 9.

Nooteboom, Cees. "Berlin—ein langsames Drama." *Der Spiegel* 25 (1993): 51–58.

————. *Berliner Notizen. Berichte aus der Wendezeit.* Frankfurt: Suhrkamp, 1991.

Rathenau, Walter. *Impressionen.* 2d ed. Leipzig: S. Hirzel, 1902.

Read, Anthony, and David Fisher. *Berlin Rising: Biography of a City.* New York/London: Norton, 1994.

Read, Anthony, and David Fisher. *The Fall of Berlin*. New York/London: Norton, 1992.

Ribbe, Wolfgang, ed. *Geschichte Berlins. Zweiter Band: Von der Märzrevolution bis zur Gegenwart*. 2d ed. Munich: Beck, 1988.

Roskamp, Heiko, ed. *Verfolgung und Widerstand: Tiergarten, ein Bezirk im Spannungsfeld der Geschichte 1933–1945*. Berlin: Edition Hentrich, Frölich & Kaufmann, 1984.

Sack, Manfred. "Berlin für alle." *Die Zeit* (Overseas Edition) December 16, 1994, 13–14.

Schäfer, Hans-Dieter. *Berlin im Zweiten Weltkrieg. Der Untergang der Reichshauptstadt in Augenzeugenberichten*. Munich: Piper, 1986.

Schumann, Harald, et al. "Metropolis Berlin. Die unheimliche Hauptstadt." *Der Spiegel* 8 (1995): 42–78.

Schwartz, Amy E. "Berlin, Reunification, *Kulturpolitik*, Cultural Identity and the Difficulty in Starting Afresh." In: *From Two to One. U.S. Scholars Witness the First Year of German Unification*, 9–32. Bonn/Bad Godesberg: Alexander von Humboldt Foundation, 1992.

Simmons, Michael. *Berlin: The Dispossessed City*. London: Hamisch Hamilton, 1988.

Stern, Carola. *Walter Ulbricht. Eine politische Biographie*. Cologne: Kiepenheuer & Witsch, 1964.

Süß, Walter. "Entmachtung und Verfall der Staatssicherheit. Ein Kapitel aus dem Spätherbst 1989." *Deutschland Archiv* 28 (1995): 122–51.

Tent, James F. *Freie Universität Berlin 1948–1988. Eine deutsche Hochschule im Zeitgeschehen*. Berlin: Colloquium Verlag, 1988.

Watson, Alan. *The Germans. Who Are They Now?* London: Thames Methuen, 1992.

Wolff, Michael W. *Die Währungsreform in Berlin 1948/49*. Berlin: de Gruyter, 1991.

Zohlen, Gerwin. "Was wird aus dem Pariser Platz?" *Die Zeit* (Overseas Edition) March 4, 1994, 16.

1910: Imperial Berlin. The then new cathedral (to the right of the Spree river) is the only building to have survived in this central area of *Berlin-Mitte*. Today the *Berliner Dom* houses the theology department of Humboldt University and other civic offices.

1925: *Hausvogteiplatz* by Rudolf Schlichter depicts vamps during Berlin's "Golden Twenties" as harbingers of a doomed metropolis.

1945: Women, later dubbed *Trümmerfrauen*, cleared city streets of debris and worked for several years to restore bricks for rebuilding.

1951: West Berlin before reconstruction (Tiergarten district, Corneliusbrücke).

1960: The centerpiece of the socialist metropolis, Stalinallee (today Karl-Marx-Allee), looking eastward.

1980: The Wall as it cuts through an inner city residential area.

1990: Unter den Linden, street party in celebration of reunification on 3 October. The massive building complex in center back is the main building of Humboldt University.

1995: Berlin counterculture near Prenzlauer Berg district, "Tacheles" sculpture park.

2

"A Free University—Free of Women?" Women and Higher Education in Berlin since 1989

Hannelore Scholz

A massive loss of the scholarly potential of women has occurred in the new states of the Federal Republic of Germany due to reunification and its aftermath. Further, there is great concern that the number of women faculty and the percentage of women students will continue to decrease. It seems that, in the transition from the socialist welfare state of the German Democratic Republic to a social market economy, women bore a large proportion of the costs. Are women the losers in reunification?[1] The October 1990 joining of the GDR with the FRG canceled a number of entitlements for women "rarely found in Western market economies—guaranties of employment and affordable housing, free medical care and education, paid parental leave and day care, and a variety of other benefits, transfer payments, and subsidized services" (Rosenberg 1991, 129). Education and university reform are important and sensitive areas that I am familiar with because of my long association as a student and faculty member at Humboldt University in Berlin. In the following, I will explore developments affecting women in higher education in Berlin during the years since German national unity.[2]

Political and economic considerations were driving forces in the restructuring of East German universities. During the so-called renewal (*Erneuerung*) of a large number of ideologically tainted institutions, there was considerable concern about the problematic nature of dealing with people who were the academic elite of the former GDR and with the "dismissal" (*Abwicklung*)[3] of about two thirds of all faculty and staff for political and economic reasons. In contrast and despite earlier pronouncements and intentions, university reforms failed to materialize in the old federal states, and they were dropped from the agenda. At the same time, controversy arose with regard to the difficulties of an East German adaptation to West German norms and patterns. From the West German point of view, these problems were mainly questions of investment. Because the new Germany must remain competitive in the world markets, a highly trained, creative, and innovative academic work force is a necessity; there is great stress on, and support for, industrial research,[4] engineering, medicine, economics and business, and legal studies. This is evident in the political-economic agenda "Boom in the East" (*Aufschwung Ost*) as well as in the academic funding initiative "University Renewal Program" (*Hochschulerneuerungsprogramm*) for the new federal states. In my opinion, these two programs articulate inadequately and fail to address the important issue of cultural difference between the former GDR and FRG.

Generally speaking, the renewal of East German universities was not a reform program that sought to effectively include as responsible participants those who actually worked in the former East German universities. Instead, the reform program was a historically unique process of the "systemic evaluation" of one academic landscape by another (Brocke and Förtsch 1991). Its main feature was the evaluation, carried out by predominantly West German academics, of all former GDR faculty and academic institutions according to FRG standards: this meant the imposition of the structures of the evaluating academic system upon the other system. It was "an exchange of power elites that is associated with radical social transformation everywhere" (Dölling 1994, 739). Of course, these reforms affected the role of, and opportunities for, women as well, most notably the introduction of a representative for equal opportunity for women.[5] It is evident that during the transformation of East German higher education to West German university standards, the deficits in women's policies were likewise taken over from the West. Furthermore, with their different socialization, East German academic women could not participate as equals; in particular, they could not embrace the new identity offered in a "United Fatherland."

ON THE CURRENT SITUATION OF WOMEN IN
BERLIN UNIVERSITIES

Concerned about the declining number of women faculty in universities in the new federal states, the Chair of the Conference of University Presidents, Hans Uwe Erichsen, appointed women to the University Restructuring Commission and the University Foundation Committees responsible for reorganizing the universities in the new federal states. A brief look at student enrollment and faculty development figures by gender will document an ongoing process of erosion of women faculty.[6] Of all students entering the university in the old federal states in 1992/93, about 107,000 were women, while 148,000 were men. In the new federal states, 17,000 were women and 18,000 were men. This meant a 3 percent decrease of female students entering the university in the old federal states compared to the previous year with, however, a concurrent 8 percent drop in the number of entering male students; thus it accounted for an increase in the proportion of women from 40.8 percent to 42.0 percent. In the new federal states, the rate of entering female students increased by 3 percent in 1992/3, while the rate of entering male students dropped 14 percent; thus the rate of women climbed from 43.4 percent to 47 percent of the entering class.

To support highly gifted students, a total of 2,225 National Merit Scholarships were awarded in the old federal states in 1991, of which 1,433 were given to male and 792 (35.6 percent) to female applicants. In addition, the federal states awarded nearly 3,000 dissertation fellowships; the federal government does not record gender-differentiated statistics on these stipends. In the spring of 1992, the German Research Foundation (*DFG, Deutsche Forschungsgemeinschaft*) awarded 1,137 stipends in its *Graduiertenkolleg* program (for predoctoral and postdoctoral studies); 345 (30.3 percent) went to women. Statistics about the women's share in doctoral stipends are not available as yet for the new federal states. The German Research Foundation recently introduced a quota for stipends for women, but only for those working on their *Habilitation* (qualification for a professorial position). These data indirectly reflect the program's lack of support for female advanced degree candidates with small children. Their situation is particularly problematic in universities in East Berlin and East Germany because the GDR had introduced several measures to assist women during their childbearing years.

SUPPORT FOR ACADEMIC WOMEN
IN THE FORMER GDR

We know, of course, that true gender equality did not exist in the former GDR either. The government's policies for women emphasized a compatibility of family and social measures as part of the structure of socialist patriarchy. Nonetheless, the net effect for women was a higher rate of employment and a higher level of income and professional qualifications. That also explains the higher percentage of female university graduates in the new federal states. The GDR's support for women is reflected in the following gendered university statistics: The GDR's rate of 51.2 percent female university students in 1989 was among the highest in the world. The proportion of women was also relatively high in comparison with the old FRG in the engineering and technical fields; approximately 30 percent were females. Women as a whole amounted to 35.3 percent of all scholars in 1989, a figure that was twice as high as in the old FRG. The proportion of women, however, decreased with increasing status on the academic ladder. Of the full professors, only 4.9 percent were women—on par with the old FRG.

The crucial career obstacle for women came between the levels of lecturer/assistant professor as the lower rank and tenured associate or full professor as the most prestigious faculty position.[7] In 1989, 37.8 percent of temporary lecturers and 40.0 percent of tenured lecturers/assistant professors were female. This makes the women's proportion in the lower academic level twice as high as that in the old FRG (in 1988 it was 20.2 percent) in this category. Yet the rate of women's *Habilitationen*, qualifications for the top level, amounted to only 16.0 percent (still twice the rate of those in the old FRG and three times the rate of women professors actually appointed in either Germany). This phenomenon of "blocked resource of qualified women" could now serve as a solid pool of qualified female applicants in affirmative action hirings. But the very opposite is taking place. In the recent and ongoing hiring and rehiring of university faculty in the Berlin area, affirmative action policies are disregarded and East German women are very rarely among the candidates selected for appointment.

Take, as an example, the situation at the Humboldt University. Because of their previous position in the divided city of Berlin, the members of this university were confronted directly and harshly with the East-West conflict. Every single university employee who had not resigned voluntarily was evaluated for political clearance and professional qualifications. In May 1993, *Humboldt. Zeitung der Alma Mater Berolinensis* reported on the following new appointments: 200 professors had accepted an offer from Humboldt University; 97 of these new appointees came from the old federal states, 103 from (former) Humboldt University faculty and the new federal states; 28 of the newly appointed professors were women. We note that despite measures in effect to promote women, only a relatively small number of women regained faculty positions.

It is important to look at the former GDR's support for women within every institution of higher education; these measures were introduced in addition to general sociopolitical support for women. In order, these measures were:

- since 1952: plans to support women in every structural unit; setting up of women's committees
- since 1959: founding of a Women's Commission in the Free German Federation of Trade Unions
- since 1966: special training courses for women in the technical colleges and since 1970 in universities
- since 1967: qualifying and candidacy positions created specifically for women (since 1970 stipulated by law)
- since 1972: support and financial aid for female students with children
- since 1977: doctoral and postdoctoral positions or fellowships for female scholars
- since 1988: Council for the Advancement of Women at the Ministry for Higher Education

These measures sought to make the rearing of children compatible with a university education; an academic career for women would no longer mean a renunciation of having children. However, after 1989 the plans to aid and support women and the women's commissions were abolished. Since then, the proportion of women in academic positions at Humboldt University has been in continuous decline as the following data illustrate. As of the summer of 1993, the percentage of women at the Humboldt University (excluding the Charité hospital) were: full/associate professors, 7.1 percent; assistant professors, 20.1; tenured lecturers, 41.5 percent; untenured teaching/research assistants, 44.4 percent; staff, 61.7 percent; women students, 52.0 percent.[8] Due to the drastic reduction in positions, the largest university in East Germany now has the smallest percentage of women professors. Restructuring at the lecturer level also hit women hard: One third of the women who lost their jobs are presently unemployed; compared to their male colleagues, twice as many women are unemployed. For almost all of these women, their academic careers have abruptly ended. This dilemma leads to the Humboldt University being dominated by men, and the process is continuing. A large number of assistant professors/lecturers are slated for dismissal through 1996, meaning that the burden of the restructuring process will fall upon women academics. This remains true despite some legal initiatives supporting academic women.

RECENT EQUAL OPPORTUNITY INITIATIVES FOR
ACADEMIC WOMEN IN BERLIN

The Berlin University Law of October 12, 1990, expressly addresses the question of support for women: "The Academic Senate enacts, in agreement with the Board of Trustees, guidelines for the advancement of women in research, teaching, and study as well as for the support of female staff members. Guidelines for the Support of Women also regulate the assistance for women through budgetary means," and: "Women are to be adequately represented in all bodies."[9] Application of the Berlin University Law and the Federal Anti-Discrimination Law of Berlin[10] is still in its infancy. Take, for example, the specific passage regarding women's committee participation: It is very ambiguous. What is "adequately"? Adequately might mean in proportion to their status group, but at least one woman in every committee. Although the "adequate" representation of women in university structures remains a troubling issue, one step in the right direction is the institution at Berlin universities of "women's equality offices," which have proliferated rapidly at the state and local level in the West since about 1985.[11] In recent years, full-time Equal Opportunity Officers have been appointed at most Berlin universities, among them the Technical University, Free University, Humboldt University, Hochschule der Künste, Fachhochschule für Wirtschaft, and Fachhochschule für Sozialarbeit und Sozialpädagogik.[12]

Still another open question is the effectiveness of new special programs in providing adequate opportunities for women, such as the University Renewal Program (*HEP*) for the restructuring of East German universities; within *HEP*, the Academic Integration Program (*WIP*), which supports scholarly projects by individuals and groups of the former East German Academy of Sciences; and the Young Scholar Qualification Program.[13] Preliminary figures from the *HEP* program concerning East Berlin scholars (university professors and members of the discontinued Academy of Sciences) indicate much less activity on the part of women and a slight preference for supporting male scholars: Of the 975 research projects submitted, 207 came from women (21.23 percent); the approval rate for women was 19.94 percent (139 proposals); a total number of 3,668 (principal and associate) investigators applied, 17.09 percent of whom were women; 1,924 received funds, of whom 292, or 15.18 percent, were women. Thus the success rate in receiving support was about 2 percent lower for women than it was for male academics.

The Young Scholar Qualification Program launched by the West Berlin Senate in 1989 meant a definite initiative for women—that is to say for young women postdoctoral scholars at West Berlin universities. Five million German marks were set aside for improving the underrepresentation of women in the sciences, particularly at the professorial level. These funds support lower-level academic positions[14] for women in which they can do research and teach in order to obtain the academic degree of *Habilitation* essential for an appointment as professor. Altogether 40 positions were created for female scholars who came exclusively from the western part of Berlin. While a breakdown of support figures is not yet available, anecdotal evidence strongly suggests that the vast majority of *HEP* funding (2.43 billion DM) is supporting new appointments from the West at East Berlin universities and colleges.

INSTITUTIONS FOR THE ADVANCEMENT OF WOMEN'S STUDIES IN BERLIN

In contrast to the rather bleak picture for women in academia in general, especially in prestigious, tenured positions, considerable institutional resources exist for women's studies in the two major Berlin universities: There are the Central Institute for the Promotion of Women's Studies and Research on Women at the Free University and the Center for Interdisciplinary Feminist Research at Humboldt. There is now also an important citywide effort, the Program for Research on Women of the Berlin Senate, as well as a number of private initiatives.[15]

On July 2, 1980, the Academic Senate of the Free University of Berlin resolved to actively support female scholars. In the fall of 1981, the *ZE* (*Zentraleinrichtung zur Förderung von Frauenstudien und Frauenforschung*[16] [Central Institute for the Advancement of Women's Studies and Feminist Research]) was established at the Free University of Berlin. Its tasks have ranged from the integration of women's studies and research to the establishment of equal employment opportunities for women in the university. The *ZE* is not an independent academic department but operates in conjunction with the teaching staff and research projects in other interested sectors of the university. It organizes lectures, symposia, lecture series, and colloquia; compiles and interprets statistical data on the situation of women at the Free University and comparable data of other universities; documents research projects related to women carried out at the Free University; maintains a research library systematically collecting bibliographic information, journal articles, monographs, conference proceedings, etc., for all fields of women's studies, research on women, and on women in universities and academia in general; stimulates and supports activities in university departments and institutes relating to women; drafts recommendations for committees and resolutions dealing with women; and compiles an index[17] of all female scholars with *Habilitation* in the FRG. It presently has five permanent staff members, who do not have faculty status and do not teach, and several student assistants. The *ZE* publishes an informative newsletter, *Frauen-Informations-Blatt*, twice a year and was instrumental in setting up the scholarly series *Ergebnisse der Frauenforschung* in which some forty volumes of research on women have appeared to date (now published by Metzler Verlag, Stuttgart). In its twelve years or so of operation, the *ZE* has clearly had an impact on making the topics of women's studies and women faculty an important issue at the Free University. It has served as a focus for research on women and as a support for academic women. Its support for women faculty and students is invaluable but is not sufficiently recognized, because the *ZE* does not have faculty lines, let alone (famous) professorships. Much of the *ZE's* innovative work and vitality derive from the enormous potential of academic women, mostly students, at the Free University and from the incredibly lively and unorthodox women's movement in the metropolis of Berlin.

The Center for Interdisciplinary Women's Research (*ZiF* for *Zentrum für interdisziplinäre Frauenforschung*) at Humboldt University was established in December 1989 by a group of women academics from different disciplines who were able to take advantage of the period of radical change during the final months of the GDR. In the preceding years, a few academic women at Humboldt had attempted individually and collectively in a semiofficial work group to conceptualize feminist scholarship and to lay the groundwork for feminist research independent of the prevailing SED party line. The *ZiF* was the first successful example of the institutionalization of women's research in the new federal states.

The *ZiF* serves female professors, students, and independent women scholars and seeks to advance feminist research with an interdisciplinary approach within Humboldt University.[18] For the purpose of academic exchange and cooperation, the *ZiF* functions as a network to bring together female scholars interested in feminist research from inside and outside the University. A network is needed because many scholars still work largely isolated in their departments. Thus the *ZiF* seeks to support research on women in various university departments and to create a wide academic audience for the results of such research. An important aspect is the integration of feminist research into teaching through regular course offerings as part of the curriculum and for continuing education. The *ZiF* plans to develop programs of women's studies in the individual disciplines and to form an interdisciplinary study program with emphasis on gender research as a minor and a specialization. The *ZiF* also serves as an information and documentation center for research plans and publications at Humboldt University and in the new federal states. Its organizational structure fosters interdisciplinary networking and support for academic women and feminist research. The full assembly of all associates and employees of the *ZiF* elects the academic advisory committee (nine women from different academic disciplines) and its faculty director for a two-year term. The business office is staffed by a full-time managing director, a secretary, and an associate in charge of reference work. The *ZiF* has its own budget but is affiliated with the Department of Culture and Arts through its business office. Because of its institutional anchoring and independent budgeting, it has been both effective and relatively autonomous. It is hoped that, because of its distinct structure and clear mission, the *ZiF* will survive the present budgetary crisis of Humboldt University relatively intact (Dürkop 1993).

Such survival is less assured for the broad-based and well-funded Program for the Advancement of Women's Research of the Senate of Berlin (*FPFF* for *Förderprogramm Frauenforschung*), which was implemented in 1988 after years of planning and lobbying by women professors and women artists from West Berlin. Funded by the City of Berlin and directed by the Senate Administration for Labor and Women, the program has also included scholars from East Berlin since reunification of the city administrations in 1991. The innovative scope and financial support (3.7 million DM annually) of this program are as yet unmatched elsewhere in Germany, where many academic institutions render little more than lip service to women's studies.

A closer look at this rather unique public funding for women by a city (not a foundation or federal agency) is in order. The *Förderprogramm Frauenforschung* intends to promote research on women and gender (feminist or otherwise); to support existing structures, networking, and cooperation between women in the city of Berlin who are engaged in such research; and to assist university educated women with their integration into the labor force (*Förderprogramm* 1994, 13–18). Thus for the past five years, the program has supported research projects in women's studies for up to two years, including conferences, lecture series, and similar events. In particular, it assisted independent female scholars with monthly stipends in order to complete degree work and to qualify for university positions or for jobs in the educational and cultural sector. For female residents of West Berlin, stipends range presently from a modest DM 1,200 to DM 2,000 according to age, not rank or qualifications. Residents of East Berlin receive lower stipends according to the wage scales set for persons living in East Berlin and the new federal states during the transitional period following unification. Women with dependent children receive additional funds (*Kinderzuschlag*). Stipends may also include support for equipment and research-related travel. While making some allowances for the social obligations of individual women, these stipends are comparable to the support of regular university students (*BAFÖG*) and dissertation fellowships. Thus the program has been very successful in its assistance to untenured and often unemployed women scholars striving to gain qualifications for university appointments and the job market in the cultural sector. It has also undoubtedly given these women valuable research skills, pride and self-esteem in their work and accomplishments, opened new insights, and provided important networking; and it has produced important research and cultural materials including films, exhibits, radio scripts, as well as videos on women and gender questions.

Nevertheless, such short-term success for individual women raises several questions for their future. Where will these women find employment when restructuring in the cultural and educational sector in Berlin has already meant a severe reduction of jobs? What are the prospects for the many older women, those beyond the age of forty or fifty, when ever more institutions push early retirement (*Vorruhestand*) and when universities, as a rule, do not hire persons beyond the age of 45 for a regular, permanent academic appointment unless the individual is an already well-known and well-established scholar at another school? Only lectureships (*Lehraufträge*), which are outside the qualifying ladder for young academics (*Jungakademiker*), are available on a one-semester basis and pay very little (sometimes as little as DM 500–800 per course).

We must also ask how much employment opportunity is available for those qualified in feminist research and women's studies. In German higher education circles, such qualifications generally appear too narrow and specialized and may even close doors rather than opening them, especially since token women's studies appointments in relatively few areas (sociology, literature, political science, psychology) have been made in German universities. In 1994, there were a total of 13 at Berlin universities (7 at the Free University, 3 at Humboldt and 2 at the Technical University). And while Berlin in general has a very lively and innovative cultural scene open to women and areas related to women's studies (museums, bookstores, theaters, TV and radio stations, social services, independent cultural ventures, adult education, and cultural centers and projects), adequate and permanent employment in the city even in "typical" women's jobs is becoming increasingly difficult, if not impossible, to find.

COPING WITH UNEMPLOYMENT AND UNDERREPRESENTATION

Unemployment is a threat and a reality for many academic women in Berlin, especially from East Berlin and Humboldt University. Changing economic conditions in the city are only partly to blame. In 1992, recession set in for Berlin; federal subsidy payments for West Berlin, which served as an economic stimulus for the creation of jobs during the years of division, have been eliminated, and industry has reduced its labor force thus especially affecting semiskilled women and the social, educational, and cultural sector. East Berlin has lost its preeminence as the capital of the GDR, and with it the concentration of high-level administrative and academic jobs, many of which ceased to exist or were abolished, as was the case during the restructuring of Humboldt University and the dissolution of the Academy of Sciences. By 1991, one year after reunification, the unemployment rate for women in East Berlin had climbed from zero to 14.7 percent (some 52,000 women registered as having lost their jobs); in West Berlin, 38,531 were registered as unemployed in 1991, an unemployment rate of 10.4 percent.[19] The latest available, official figures (September 1993) show 44,444 (15.1%) women unemployed in East Berlin; 50,556 (11.2%) women unemployed in West Berlin; and 9,919 female alien residents who had lost their jobs. These are utterly depressing figures, even if academic women comprise only a relatively small number for whom exact statistics are not available. We can only point to 5,735 academic women in the so-called Temporary Job Creation Measures (*ABM*)[20] for East Berlin in August 1992. They are 5,735 highly qualified individuals, most of whom have earned a doctorate, not in women's studies—such a field did not exist in the GDR— but in any one of the traditional academic fields. However, these *ABM* term contracts only seem to defer unemployment, and the end of an academic career, for a few years.

Since roughly one third of all women employed in 1989 at Humboldt University had been dismissed by 1992 (only a few left voluntarily) and since the dismissal of academics—and a significantly larger percentage of women than men—is still continuing, the downsizing process has hit women especially hard. An ongoing empirical study is investigating the gender factor in this process in interviews with a representative sample of the group. Women react to the abrupt and destructive change in their professional and personal lives with anger, strong feelings of rejection, and a certain resourcefulness. By and large more than men, older women reported that they felt pressured and pushed into early retirement and resented it. All women felt that the dismissal from their university position meant the end of their academic careers, a dequalification of their professional skills, and a serious blow to their self-image. "I like to work," 94 percent of all dismissed women answered; "I need my profession for my self-esteem," some 61 percent of the women interviewed said. It is interesting to note that in this group only 2 percent had received a negative evaluation of their qualifications and performance. The women also indicated a willingness to move to a new job, if offered; 17 percent had taken training courses in the old federal states and 12 percent in a Western foreign country. These figures can only hint at the human and professional loss reflected in the "renewal" process of an institution.

Though much more progressive than in the old federal states, the various legal and administrative efforts in Berlin to promote and support women in academic careers have had only very moderate success. Women remain underrepresented in both the HEP Program and in the Job-Creating Measures (*ABM*) for academia and in higher education in general. The under-representation of women in the teaching body has become more and more striking since unification. With the selection criteria and qualification mechanisms (the so-called Structure and Appointment Commissions, *SBK*) presently in place, the ongoing wave of appointments is piling up a "third mountain of men" on top of the existing male professoriate and administration ("Gleichstellung 2000?" 1991, 7). Likewise, in the new federal states, the process of reordering and restructuring the universities has included far too few women.

Against this backdrop, pronouncements for the advancement and equal standing of women appear to be empty words. The Senator for Research and Higher Education of Berlin, Manfred Ehrhardt, was unable to come up with new concepts in his 143-page university reform plan. In this strategic plan, the subject of women's studies is given only a mere half page. In this way, men and women in elected office render lip service and make promises instead of pressing for the observance of the equal opportunity provisions in the Berlin University Law of 1990 and for sanctions against violations. As a consequence universities will probably remain a man's domain—in Berlin as well as elsewhere in Germany.

Translated by Barbara Becker-Cantarino

NOTES

1. In my "East-West Women's Culture in Transition," I address questions concerning the unemployment of women and their absence from important functions of the East European and German transformation process.

2. A comprehensive analysis of the role of women in the universities of the former GDR is not available. In this study, I will restrict myself to recent statistics and commentary based on specific events in Berlin, especially at Humboldt University.

3. Translator's note: The term *Abwicklung* (wrapping up, winding down) is officially used for the ongoing process of dissolution of industrial and business establishments and of social, cultural, and scientific institutions in East Germany since unification on October 3, 1990. See Dölling, "On the Development," p. 739.

4. Industrial research suffered the heaviest losses. In May 1992, Research Minister Riesenhuber mentioned a figure of approximately 35,000 to 40,000 employees in industry-related research in the new federal states (see *Frankfurter Allgemeine Zeitung*, May 2, 1992); this means that more than 75 percent of former GDR employees lost their jobs in this research sector.

5. *Frauen- und Gleichstellungsbeauftragte* (Representatives for Women and Affirmative Action) have been appointed at most West German universities during the past decade; they have the task of furthering equal rights and opportunities for women in a totally male-dominated and male-controlled academic system. The evidence of their effectiveness or success is inconclusive, but it is a visible innovation in a university system structured for and by men. East German universities have adopted this form of representation and advocacy for women.

6. Data from "Antwort des Parlamentarischen Staatssekretärs Torsten Wolfgramm vom 8. Januar 1993," p. 22.

7. Data from "Gleichstellung 2000?," p. 7, which represents a statement by the Federation of Democratic Scholars on the final report: "Zukünftige Bildungspolitik—Bildung 2000" concerning university policy recommendations of the Committee for Education and Science of the German Bundestag on December 5/6, 1991. Translator's note: The distinction of *Mittelbau* and *Hochschullehrer* refers to term and tenured lecturers (*Mittelbau*) who cannot direct dissertations, sit in on exams for advanced degrees, and are restricted to lower level graduate courses, and tenured associate or full professors (*Hochschullehrer*) who represent the top researchers and academic teachers in the German university system.

8. Data taken from "Die freie Wissenschaft ist auch frauenfrei."

9. *Berliner Hochschulgesetz* of Oct. 12, 1992, para. 45a, 46.

10. *Landesantidiskriminierungsgesetz (ADG)* was enacted in Berlin on December 31, 1990. It has yet to be aligned with the Berlin University Regulations.

11. See Ferree (1992, 63) for an interesting comparative analysis of these "equality offices" in East and West Germany: "Now that there are women's affairs officers/gender equality officers spread thickly throughout both halves of the

country, they have a considerable potential to be an organizing and mobilizing force for feminist politics."

12. College of Arts, College of Business, the College for Economics, Technical College for Social Work and Pedagogy. There is a part-time Equal Opportunity Officer at the *Kunsthochschule Weißensee* (art academy), *Hochschule für Musik* (conservatory), and *Hochschule für Schauspielkunst* (drama school). See also Dölling, 1994, 742–43.

13. *Hochschulerneuerungsprogramm (HEP),Wissenschaftler-Integrations-programm (WIP), Nachwuchsqualifizierungsprogramm.*

14. The actual titles are: *Assistentin* and *Oberassistentin*—something like untenured assistant professor—paid according to the category C1 and C2 (German professors are paid according to the scale of C3 and C4, the latter being the most coveted and increasingly the most powerful academic position).

15. Best known is the Center for Research, Education, and Information on and for Women Inc. e.V. (*FFBIZ* for *Frauen-, Forschungs-, Bildungs- und Informationszentrum*), an autonomous institution which grew out of the women's movement and was established in 1978. It supports women's education and interdisciplinary research on women, as well as the exchange of literature and information. The *FFBIZ* maintains an archive, a library, and a gallery. It organizes seminars, courses, discussion groups and conferences, and it publishes diaries, documentary accounts, and research findings. It also supports many worldwide activities for the advancement of women's interests. The *FFBIZ* cooperates with other women's archives and women's initiatives in Berlin, the Federal Republic of Germany, Europe, and other areas.

16. Translator's note: The German term *Frauenforschung* literally translates as "research on Women"; in the German context, it denotes women's and feminist studies at the university level. Regrettably, the word *Feminismus* is usually avoided in German academic circles because it seems to carry with it the negative connotation of aggressive partisanship instead of scholarly objectivity.

17. This is a continuation of Elisabeth Boedecker's and Maria Meyer Platz's *50 Jahre Habilitation von Frauen in Deutschland 1920–1970* (1975). The registration of all female scholars with *Habilitation* will facilitate the search for qualified candidates for university professorships and for identifying women for special committees and academic commissions.

18. The Preamble of the Statutes of the *ZiF* stipulates: "Women's research includes an understanding of science that (a) defines gender as a structural category, (b) negates an objective science free from women's interests, (c) regards the cause and manifestation of the structural discrimination of the female gender as a central issue, and (d) wants to use the scientific results to further the development of women to self-determined, autonomous subjects."

19. Data from *Situation der Frauen in Berlin*. In 1993 there was a total of 25,291 unemployed alien residents (formerly called *Gastarbeiter*) in Berlin. Fig-

ures represent persons collecting unemployment compensation to which every member in the labor force in Germany is entitled after the loss of his or her job.

20. *ABM* stands for *Arbeitsbeschaffungsmaßnahmen*, a program for public work—much of it in the social and educational sector—and some retraining opportunities that has been in operation in the FRG since the 1970s. It is funded by the Federal Bureau of Labor (*Bundesanstalt für Arbeit*) and is intended to lower the jobless rate and facilitate reintegration into the job market.

REFERENCES

"Antwort des Parlamentarischen Staatssekretärs Torsten Wolfgram vom 8. Januar 1993." *Deutscher Bundestag. 12. Wahlperiode*, 1993. Drucksache 12/4133.

Arndt, Marlies, et al., eds. *Ausgegrenzt und mittendrin—Frauen in der Wissenschaft: Dokumentation einer Tagung an der Humboldt Universität am 23./24. Oktober 1992*. Berlin: Edition Sigma Bohn, 1993.

Das Bildungswesen in der DDR. Berlin: Volk und Wissen, 1983.

Brocke, R. H., and E. Förtsch. *Forschung und Entwicklung in den Neuen Bundesländern 1989–1991*. Stuttgart: Raabe, 1991.

Dölling, Irene. "*On the Development of Women's Studies in Eastern Germany.*" *SIGNS. Journal of Women in Culture and Society* 19, 3 (Spring 1994): 739–51.

Dürkop, Marlis, Präsidentin der Humboldt-Universität. "Zur Haushaltssituation der Humboldt-Universität zu Berlin." *Humboldt. Zeitung der Alma mater berolinensis* 9 (1993/4): 3.

Ferree, Myra Marx. "Institutionalizing Gender Equality: Feminist Politics and Equality Offices." *German Politics and Society* 24–25 (1992): 53–66.

Förderprogramm Frauenforschung des Senats von Berlin. Bericht 1993. Berlin: Senatsverwaltung für Arbeit und Frauen, 1994.

"Frauenförderung in den Hochschulen der Neuen Länder." *Hochschulrektorenkonferenz: Drucksachen—Nr. 1240/47*, October 6, 1992, 67–108.

Die Frau in der Deutschen Demokratischen Republik. Statistische Kernziffernsammlung. Berlin: Statistisches Amt der DDR, 1990.

"Die freie Wissenschaft ist auch frauenfrei." *TAZ*, May 15, 1993, 11.

Fremdheit und Gewalt. Zur Diskussion von Rassismus und Antisemitismus in der Frauenforschung. Beiträge zur 4. Jahrestagung des Förderprogrammes Frauenforschung des Senats von Berlin. Berlin: Senatsverwaltung für Arbeit und Frauen, 1993.

"Geschäftsbericht des Bundesministers für Bildung." *Deutscher Bundestag. 12. Wahlperiode*, 1992. Drucksache 12/4133.

"Gleichstellung 2000?" *Forum Wissenschaft* 4 (April 1991): 2–10.

Merkel, Ina. "Frauenpolitische Strategien in der DDR." In *Soziale Lage und Arbeit von Frauen in der DDR*, edited by S. Gensior, F. Maier, and G. Winter, 56–70. Paderborn: Universität-Gesamthochschule Paderborn, 1990.

Mocker, Elke, Beate Rüther, and Birgit Sauer. "Frauen- und Familienpolitik: Wie frauenfreundlich war die DDR?" *Deutschland Archiv* 45, 11 (1990): 1700–5.

Nickel, Hildegard Marie. "Arbeitsmarktsegmentation: mentale Brüche und ambivalente Folgen." *ZiF-Bulletin* 4 (1992): 5–10.

―――. "Geschlechtersozialisation und Arbeitsteilung." *Weimarer Beiträge* 34 (1988): 580–91.

―――. "Women in the German Democratic Republic and in the New Federal States: Looking Backwards and Forwards." *German Politics and Society* 24–25 (Winter 1991–92): 34–52.

Penrose, Virginia. "Vierzig Jahre SED-Frauen-Politik. Ziele, Strategien und Ergebnisse." *Frauenforschung* 8, 4 (1990): 580–91.

Rosenberg, Dorothy J. "Shock Therapy: GDR Women in Transition from a Socialist Welfare State to a Market Economy." *SIGNS. Journal of Women in Culture and Society* 17(1991): 129–51.

Situation der Frauen in Berlin. Bildung, Arbeitsmarkt. Kurzfassung—Zwischenbericht. Berlin: Senatsverwaltung für Arbeit und Frauen, June 1994.

Scholz, Hannelore. "East-West Women's Culture in Transition: Are East German Women the Losers of Unification?" *Journal of Women's History* 5, 3 (Winter 1994): 109–16.

"200. Rufannahme." *Humboldt. Zeitung der Alma mater berolinensis*, 37, 7 (1992/93) [June 10, 1993]: 8.

3

Stasi at Humboldt University: State Security's Organizational Structures and Control Mechanism in the University

Hanna Labrenz-Weiss

In Berlin, as in much of Germany, discussions about the *Stasi*, the Ministry for State Security, have centered on the disconcerting public revelations of spectacular *Stasi* connections and collaboration with well-known, nationally and internationally respected personalities of the former German Democratic Republic residing in the city and, more often than not, associated with Humboldt University. There has seemed to be a never-ending flood of disclosures coming from those individuals who are finally able to view their own *Stasi* files. The tables are turned: The very people who were spied upon by the East German secret service could uncover the culprits and the reasons for their suffering. When reading their own files, these victims often experienced strong emotions; they felt violated, betrayed, and personally denigrated by the secret reports about all aspects of their personal life and about the defamation and denunciation of their political persona. Yet they had to go through this experience and must ultimately accept it, for "in order to get rid of the nightmares of history, one must first acknowledge the history," as Heiner Müller observed some time ago, "one must know history. Otherwise it may haunt you in a very old-fashioned way, as a nightmare. . . . One must first analyze it, then one can denounce it, and get rid of it" (Müller 1982, 85). This means that, in the interest of humanity and of preserving human dignity and human rights, the task at hand should not exclude anything or excuse anyone. By the same token, any attempt to mystify the *Stasi* octopus is to be avoided as much as possible; because of the emotional involvement in our individual experience with the *Stasi*, we should not be blind to the nature of the Ministry for State Security and to its global enterprise and structure. It is in this spirit that I will attempt to de-emotionalize in this article the debate, as a demystification of an experience.

ON THE PRESENCE OF THE MINISTRY FOR STATE SECURITY AT HUMBOLDT UNIVERSITY

It came as a shock to many professors and students that the Humboldt University had to be renovated; the University was, after all, considered an important and tradition-filled alma mater and the shining star of higher education in the German Democratic Republic. After the fall of the Wall in 1990, many scholars believed that the renovation of the University could take place with almost all of its professors and employees continuing in their jobs. Unfortunately, this was wishful thinking. The official *Stasi* files showed another picture: They contained proof that almost one-fifth of the academic personnel—of those still employed at the Humboldt University in 1990—had conspiratorial contacts to the *Stasi*. The University's professional stature and reputation could not hide the fact that the moral integrity of these academics had suffered greatly due to their activities for the secret police, and that the University's credibility had already come under suspicion during the days of Socialist Unity Party rule.

It must be noted that not all Humboldt professors were interested in pursuing an investigation into these matters. Actually only very few of them actively did. Rather, the academics were consumed by such matters as the imminent abolition and restructuring of departments, the dismissal of President Fink, and major personnel changes in the general restructuring of the university. As far as an investigation of the *Stasi* past was concerned, the involvement of individuals was taken into consideration and not larger structures and issues. This was also the case with the various University committees created for investigating the political past: the Hearing Panel, the Rehabilitation Commission, and the Honors Committee.[1] These committees concentrated on individual cases of collaboration. Three major groups helped to uncover the relations between the Humboldt University and the *Stasi*: first, individuals who inspected their own *Stasi* files; then the student research groups; and last but not least, the reports requested from the "Office of the Federal Commissioner for Documents of the State Security Agency of the former GDR,"[2] commonly called *Gauck-Behörde* (Gauck Commission) after its chairman Joachim Gauck, a Protestant minister from Rostock who was active in the opposition in the GDR before its demise.

THE GAUCK COMMISSION

On January 12, 1990, under pressure from the people of the German Democratic Republic, then prime minister Hans Modrow issued a statement before the *Volkskammer* (GDR parliament) disbanding the Ministry for State Security of the GDR. This came in response to the opposition of East German revolutionary groups, targeting *Stasi* buildings, who had been holding continuous demonstrations in front of local offices throughout East Germany. By early December 1989, when word spread that *Stasi* officials were destroying enormous numbers of documents, these groups had occupied regional *Stasi* centers. But it was not until January 15, 1990, that they stormed the national headquarters in Berlin. This gave the mostly high-ranking *Stasi* officers in Berlin six weeks longer than elsewhere to destroy important, incriminating documents. The oppositional groups formed citizens' committees, which posted guards to protect the documents and attempted to sort through the files and materials. A special parliamentary committee, appointed by the *Volkskammer* after the March 1990 free elections in the postcommunist GDR, was charged with supervising the breakup of the Ministry for State Security. Under the leadership of Joachim Gauck, the committee also drafted a bill dealing with the *Stasi* legacy that the East German parliament ratified in August of 1990. On December 29, 1991, following reunification, the newly elected all-German *Bundestag* passed the "Act Concerning the Documents of the State Security Service of the Former German Democratic Republic" (*Stasi-Unterlagengesetz*), which regulated the use of GDR secret materials for political, historical, and legal investigations into *Stasi* activities. Gauck was appointed director of the government commission in charge of all *Stasi* documents, now commonly referred to as the Gauck Commission.[3]

It is important to stress the legal avenues followed in the political developments that lead to the present policies of dealing with the *Stasi* past. The developments were the direct results of the conceptualization and activism of East German oppositional groups. These groups of citizens of the former GDR were successful in their demands concerning the *Stasi* archives and files. They would neither be destroyed nor would they be deposited in the Federal Archives of West Germany, for which some people had argued. Rather, they would be made accessible to the people. Every citizen was to be enabled to examine his or her own file and to find out what the secret police had collected about him or her and how the *Stasi* had operated. The oppositional groups had rightly considered the State Security Service the prime instrument of oppression, and they knew how important it was to preserve these documents and

to make them accessible, to "return the former rulers' instrument of knowledge to those it had ruled and oppressed," as Joachim Gauck remarked.
" 'Political reckoning with the past' " (*politische Aufarbeitung*) meant,
among other things, the right to investigate MPs and all elected bodies, as well
as public employees, to see if they had previously worked for the Mfs
(Ministry for State Security), either as *Inoffizielle Mitarbeiter*[4] (*IM*, undercover collaborators) or even as *Hauptamtliche* (full-time employees). Where
the vetting process revealed such collaboration, the MP or public servant was
to be dismissed from his post" (Gauck 1994, 279). Gauck now heads an
agency with more than three thousand staff members headquartered in Berlin;
it also has fourteen branch offices in the five new federal states in East
Germany. The Gauck Commission has the task of preserving and arranging
some 120 miles of file shelves and processing applications for access. (By
mid-1993, some 1.85 million requests had been made from over 650,000
individual citizens wishing to see their own files.)

SOURCES

The actual use of the *Stasi* files only became a reality more than a year
after the legal groundwork had been laid. The legislation (*Stasi-Unterlagengesetz*) had the following results with regard to Humboldt University:

1. Individuals could finally find out what and who had interfered with their
   academic careers and personal lives and why they had been destroyed, why they
   had not been allowed to travel, and so on as the case may have been.

2. Humboldt University employees could now be checked for former collaboration
   with the *Stasi*. Early on, everyone had agreed to such an investigation. The
   Senate Office for Scholarship and Research submitted the list of faculty and staff
   to the Gauck Commission for investigation. On principle, the Commission
   releases only such information as is found in files that are presently in its
   archives. It does not make any assessments nor does it give any recommendations. The University must decide on the basis of the information provided by
   the Commission which members of its faculty and employees to retain and which
   to dismiss. The Commission did not, and presently does not, have any influence
   on these personnel decisions.

3. The close collaboration between the Honors Commission and the Humboldt
   University Research Groups[5] in establishing a Division of Education and
   Research under the direction of Christian Ladwig was instrumental in coming
   to terms with the University's recent historical and political past.

4. Last but not least, the proximity to the seat of the Gauck Commission contributed
   to Humboldt University's rapid progress in the renovation of its University

faculty. The University was also the first one whose *Stasi* documents became available in large quantities for the historic investigation and renovation of its professoriate.

My own research is based on those materials from the archives of the Ministry for State Security that were made available to the Honors Commission and to the Humboldt University Research Groups by the Gauck Commission when it was still in its developing stages. I also used statements by individual Humboldt University professsors about the structural entanglements of the University.[6]

Personnel files on university employees that undercover collaborators (*IMs*) had assembled for the *Stasi* vary greatly in regard to the quality and quantity of the information gathered. They reveal very little about the structures of State Security and its infiltration of Humboldt University; rather, they provide information about the kind of cooperation, about cover names, about *Stasi* Command Officers (*Führungsoffiziere*), about the administrative units and chain of command, as well as about the duration of collaboration with the *Stasi*. Where huge amounts of data have been collected, they concern, as a rule, mostly specific information from individual departments as well as reports about individuals. Materials of Department XX/3 of the Administrative District of Berlin (*BV*), which the Citizens' Committee seized,[7] contain additional information about the activities of university administrators and the Socialist Unity Party's functionaries (District Officers) within Humboldt University. I was also able to analyze working papers and planning documents developed by the SED District Administration for the institutions of higher education in Berlin.

STASI STRUCTURES AND ORGANIZATION FOR HUMBOLDT UNIVERSITY

A major division of *Stasi* (*HA*, *Hauptabteilung*) was responsible for the Ministry for Higher Education and its main institutions and objects; district administrations were in charge of individual universities and colleges. We estimate the number of *Stasi* units directing Humboldt University professors to be approximately forty.[8] Full-time employees, officers with a special mission (*OibE*, *Offiziere im besonderen Einsatz*), as well as undercover collaborators carried out the operations. It was their task to prevent "political diversion" and "infiltration." The *Stasi* defined infiltration as "the penetration of foreign thoughts into the consciousness of citizens of the socialist states in order to further the subversive goals of political-ideological diversion."[9] On principle, any critical thoughts were considered as revisionism controlled by outside forces; "diversion" was looked upon as a crime against the state. According to *Stasi*'s definition, "political-ideological diversion" was an important component of subversive attacks launched by the secret service agencies of the West and by other agencies of NATO against the very foundations of the socialist system of the GDR. "Political-ideological diversion" was supposedly aimed at destroying the socialist consciousness of the people and sought to establish political underground activities within the GDR.

The close connection between "political-ideological diversion" (*PiD*) and "political underground activities" (*PUT, politische Untergrundtätigkeit*) was brought home in the slogan: "Ohne PiD kein PUT" (without political-ideological diversion, no underground activities). This accurately represents State Security's concept of "the enemy." An implicit contradiction becomes apparent in this simplistic, formulaic slogan, which is also essential for the official, ideological self-concept of GDR society as a whole: "Ohne PiD kein PUT" reveals a *weltanschauung* which rests on a simple friend-foe dichotomy as it existed on the inside and outside of the socialist state. In its simplicity, it was especially dangerous.

Having been specifically created for this mission, an administrative *Stasi* unit planned and coordinated extensive activities to supervise and influence persons at Humboldt University (Department XX/3; after the January 1989 restructuring of the Administrative District of Berlin: Department XX/8).[10] In this unit some seventeen active members were responsible for Humboldt, five of them especially for Charité hospital, the major medical complex and teaching hospital in East Berlin. Only those Humboldt faculty and staff who had already been employed by the *Stasi* before signing on with Humboldt were supervised by other *Stasi* sections; the majority of these were supervised by the Reconnaissance Division (*Hauptverwaltung Aufklärung, HV A*). Department XX/3 was in charge of controlling all institutions of higher education in Berlin, but Humboldt University was its main target as is evident from the personnel files. Of secondary importance was the supervision of institutions serving the universities and colleges, such as the *Deutsche Staatsbibliothek* (State Library), the Museum for German History, or the *Fachschule für Information und Dokumentation* (School for Information and Documentation). Department XX/3 was unable to control all of the nonmedical colleges of the University. Therefore, *Stasi* targeted only specific areas with direct supervision: Education and Teacher Training, Earth Sciences, Asian Studies, Special Education, Communications, the Law School, Language and Area Studies, Mathematics,

Physics, and Electrical Engineering. In sum, there was a direct supervisor in ten academic departments.

Within Department XX/3, the assignments and responsibilities were as follows: The Department Head was Chief Lieutenant Mentschke who was in charge of fifteen "operative members," three "officers on special assignment" (*OibE*), and two "officers supervising undercover collaborators" (*hFiM, hauptamtliche IM führende Mitarbeiter*). His deputy, Major Simonis, was the official *Stasi* representative in Humboldt University. He led discussions with the president, vice-presidents, the SED District Office, and representatives of mass organizations.[11] Major Schneider who, among other duties, was in charge of keeping all "operations" secret and supervising the departments of Education and Development and of Geology also had constant contacts with the vice presidents. Chief Lieutenant Hannawald was likewise in charge of ensuring secrecy. He also recruited undercover collaborators from among the math and natural science faculty. Keeping their activities secret and undercover was considered to be an especially important task; thus two more *Stasi* officers, Captain Stallbaum and Second Lieutenant Hagen, had the mission of ensuring the secrecy of all operations. In addition, Hagen controlled the departments of Mathematics, Physics, and Electrical Engineering.

Captain Zöllner and Chief Lieutenant Kopelke supervised the social and behavioral sciences. Zöllner also had the task of controlling the "Fighting Squads"[12] and "Civil Protection"[13] at Humboldt University; he had the same functions at the State Library, the Museum for German History, and the School of Library Sciences (*Fachschule für Bibliothekswesen*). Chief Lieutenant Heinrich attended to the professors in languages and literatures, Major Nöschel to international visiting professors and lecturers. Nöschel also supervised the international relations of Humboldt University, as well as three academic departments: Asian Studies, Special Education, and Media Studies. The Law School was controlled by Chief Lieutenant Brunk, who was also in charge of the surveillance of the University's student body, their recreational activities, dormitories, the *FDJ*[14] District Administration, and the Society for Sport and Technology (*GST*), the students' paramilitary training group. Department XX/3 (and later XX/8) was also responsible for secretly procuring copies of University documents under the direction of Major Scheiner who additionally was charged with exit visa problems and who collaborated with the Director for Cadres and Qualifications.[15] As late as November 1989, there were still twelve leading officers actively engaged in controlling Humboldt University and recording some two hundred ongoing "operations" of surveillance and interference.

STASI ACTIVITIES AT HUMBOLDT UNIVERSITY

State Security influenced decisions by Humboldt University administrators in many ways; each of the presidents openly and officially collaborated with the *Stasi*, as was the case with the entire higher administration, that is, with the provost and vice presidents.[16] For example, the Directorate for International Relations (*DiB*) controlled cooperation with foreign universities, preparing visiting lecturers and professors for their mission abroad and international instructors for their visit in Berlin. It procured visas and official paperwork as well as travel money; it gave permission for scholarly work to be published in a foreign journal; it inspected all mail coming from a foreign country; it supervised all foreign visitors; and it established and controlled the rules and regulations for study abroad. Humboldt University maintained contractual relations with dozens of foreign universities, an activity the Directorate sought to intensify as one of its main objectives. The Ministry for University and Technical Colleges considered Humboldt University the leading institution for international university relations.[17]

Western technology, science, and politics were of special interest to the Main Intelligence Division (*HVA*)[18] when preparing international missions for Humboldt University scholars. The following groups and institutions were prime targets:

- U.S. citizens living permanently or for some length of time in Western Europe;
- biotechnologists, microbiologists, physicists, chemists, computer scientists, mathematicians, and journalists;
- secretaries, independent tax advisors, and industry and business consultants;
- students, especially of electronics, electrical engineering, telecommunications, and mechanical engineering;
- military personnel and civilian employees of the military;
- members of professional peace movements;
- interpreters, employees of West German public administrative institutions.

Industrial and research institutions of "operative interest" were, among others:

- Elektronik-System-Gesellschaft, Munich;
- Flug-Elektronik, Munich;
- Fraunhofer Gesellschaft für Festkörperphysik, Stuttgart;
- Max-Planck-Institut für Festkörperphysik, Stuttgart;

- AEG Telefunken Heidelberg, Backnang, Heilbronn, Wedel, and Ulm;
- Siemens AG, Munich, Erlangen, Bad Hersfeld, Braunschweig, and Berlin (West);
- SEL AG, Stuttgart, Pforzheim, Mannheim, and Berlin (West);
- Philips AG, Kiel and Hamburg;
- IBM Germany, Böblingen and Sindelfingen;
- Carl Zeiss AG, Oberkochem.[19]

On principle, State Security had to approve all travel, and it is a fact that the *Stasi* had access to all official travel reports. According to the "Instruction by the President of the Council of Ministers of the GDR of 1-13-1982 Concerning the Selection, Confirmation, and Training of Travel and International Cadres and the Implementation of their Travel,"[20] eligible directors (among others: ministers, directors of industrial combines, university presidents, national chairmen, directors of public institutions) were obligated to get security clearance for their employees slated to travel to the West.[21] Travel reports containing "operative" information would be forwarded to the Main Intelligence Division (*HVA*), which usually forwarded a copy to the "friendly organ," that is, the *KGB*, a rather common practice.

The intertwinement and cooperation of the Party (SED District Administration of Humboldt University) with *Stasi* units was even stronger than the University administration's ties to the *Stasi*. We can cite as an example the security manager of the SED District Administration, who was always an employee of State Security and had considerably more authority than the Humboldt University Security Officer. Because cooperation between the SED District Administration and State Security could take place officially, with few exceptions there were no undercover collaborators (*IMs*) among their ranks. If a Party functionary had previously been an undercover collaborator, this operation was "closed."[22] State Security was considered the "shield and sword" of the Party, an organ that was to protect and support the SED's power.[23] The Party usually supported State Security in releasing and retiring undercover collaborators. This was done, according to *Stasi* documents, with the help of the Party Secretary or one of his deputies.[24]

Occasionally, the Main Intelligence Division and the SED District Administration obstructed each other. For instance, Intelligence protected its undercover collaborators, who had been sent to the West and had been unmasked there, by a travel ban. For example, Intelligence put into place such restrictions on international travel by Humboldt University professors after the defection of Lieutenant-Colonel Werner Stiller of the Main Intelligence Division. Such measures were not always agreeable to the SED District Administration,[25] but the SED was nevertheless generally supported by all arms of State Security in most activities such as supplying propaganda material, training a security officer, and safeguarding certain research projects. The security officer had a special position, for he was informed of all extraordinary events such as the defection of professors to the West, border violations, contacts of Westerners with East German scholars, criminal activities, accidents with physical injuries, and the failure of technical equipment. He passed on such information to the SED District Administration, to State Security, and to the University president.

The ideological and political surveillance of scholars was one of the most important assignments of State Security in order to enforce the SED party line. Here undercover collaborators played a vital role. Their activities, which were viewed as a struggle against "political-ideological diversion" (*PiD*) and "political underground activities" (*PUT*) require further research. We know from the work orders of *Stasi* employees[26] that at Humboldt University as late as the end of 1989, thirty-two cases of "operative personnel controls" (*OPK*) were still being conducted, and ten "operative processes" (*OV*) were still actively being pursued. Such "controls" and "operative processes" sought to establish a person's criminal actions and/or "hostile-negative" opinions in order to act upon them.[27]

Of prime importance for such investigations were any contacts and connections with foreign nationals—especially from the West—who had lived for some time in East Germany, if it was apparent from their qualifications, their social status, and their connections that they would be assuming influential positions upon returning to their native countries. If they were undercover collaborators of the "defense" (i.e., all units of State Security), *Stasi* informed the Main Intelligence Division (*HV A*) or the lower-ranked Department XV of the District Administration[28] about their departure from the GDR. Intelligence then decided on its own whether any collaboration abroad with the returning visitors would be feasible and in the interest of the GDR.

In 1992, some 780 academic employees at Humboldt University were checked for collaboration with the *Stasi*. The Gauck Commission and the Humboldt University Honors Commission came up with the following figures: Of the 780 professors and lecturers investigated, 155 had *Stasi* involvement; only 67 were still active by the end of 1989. Three departments had more than 10 undercover collaborators (*IMs*) among the teaching staff according to presently available information: Business Administration (with a total of 61 professors on the staff), Physics (with 40 professors), and

Asian Studies (with 33). There were less than 10 undercover collaborators in each of the following areas: Biochemistry, Chemistry, and Agriculture/Horticulture. In Veterinary Medicine, the Social Sciences, German, Foreign Language and Literature, History, and Library Science departments, there were from 4 to 6 undercover collaborators per department. These figures suggest that in the area of liberal arts and social sciences, the SED's direct influence and control was rather extensive. Here the collaboration took place officially; my own interviews with members from these fields also support this. On the other hand, technical and scientific fields were not so highly politicized, so that more undercover activities were needed. What was aimed at in these fields was action against "political underground activities"; also in these areas there were important research projects associated with Humboldt University treated as state secrets. State Security controlled and monitored the Law School with special attention; this is also apparent from numerous depositions which officers on special assignment (*OibE*) gave to the Honors Commission's chair, Dr. Bert Fleming. The field of legal studies was especially important for State Security. A student wishing to apply to the Law School had to get political clearance because most graduates in this field would later become members of State Security or the police, so it was vital to investigate them thoroughly before and during their course of studies. While the legal studies section of the Law School enrolled large numbers of students who would later become prosecutors, judges, or attorneys, students in the criminology section were overwhelmingly assigned there by the Ministry for State Security, the Ministry of the Interior (*MdI*), and the Customs Offices. In this way, respective future employers could control the pool of graduates and thus ensure that they could employ only persons of their own choice.[29]

STATUS AND MOTIVATION OF UNDERCOVER COLLABORATORS (*IM*)[30]

The lowest level of collaborator with the *Stasi* was called an "Associate for Security" (*GMS, Gesellschaftlicher Mitarbeiter für Sicherheit*). This category comprised approximately 8 percent of the undercover collaborators at Humboldt University who until now have been positively identified as having had ties with State Security, but the actual numbers must have been significantly higher. The Main Intelligence Division's destruction of almost all of their own papers before the agency's demise makes an exact accounting difficult, since collaboration with Intelligence can no longer be documented from their files. The "Associates for Security" distinguished themselves, among other things, by an especially loyal attitude toward the state and the SED. They served as valuable and useful agents for operations at the grassroots level and as a pool for the recruitment of undercover collaborators, as well as for the selection and training of party cadres for State Security.

Over 53 percent of undercover collaborators recorded at Humboldt University had the status of "Unofficial Employee for Political-operative Penetration and Security" (*IMS, Inoffizieller Mitarbeiter zur politisch-operativen Durchdringung und Sicherung des Verantwortungsbereiches*).[31] It was the task of an "Unofficial Employee" to assist in uncovering and forestalling opinions that deviated from the prescribed party and state leadership line. These agents were instrumental in the comprehensive surveillance of the University. Nine percent of the undercover collaborators recorded among Humboldt University faculty were classified as "Unofficial Employee for Defense with Enemy Contacts, i.e., for the Direct Investigation of Persons Suspected of Espionage" (*IMB, Inoffizieller Mitarbeiter der Abwehr mit Feindverbindung bzw. zur unmittelbaren Bearbeitung im Verdacht der Feindtätigkeit stehenden Personen*). The majority of them had previously served as *IMs* and had been selected and trained with special care. As a rule they had befriended "dissidents" and had contacts with oppositional groups. Had the papers of the Main Intelligence Division survived, this group would, no doubt, be better documented and much larger in number.

A little under 12 percent of the Humboldt University professors who served as undercover collaborators were termed "Unofficial Employees for Securing Conspiracy and Communication" (*HIM, Inoffizielle Mitarbeiter zur Sicherung der Konspiration und des Verbindungswesens*). These professors placed their apartments, their addresses, or their phone numbers at the *Stasi*'s disposal. They usually were continuously involved in political undercover activity and had signed a written statement of commitment. Such a commitment contained the professor's express agreement to collaborate with State Security, his duties, instructions about secrecy and about contacts, and his undercover name.[32]

Of the academic personnel identified as undercover collaborators, the majority were full professors (44 percent), followed by tenured lecturers (37 percent) and by teaching assistants and administrative-professionals (7 percent). Their collaboration with State Security extended over a time period of one to five years. (It must be remembered, however, that German unification abruptly ended this collaboration in many instances.) Cases of thirty years of undercover collaboration have been established for seven individuals. Only a few genuine dropouts can be identified who terminated their cooperation with the *Stasi* on their own initiative. It was almost always State Security who ended the collaboration. Possible reasons for a termination on the part of State Security were the likely or imminent discovery of the agent (though given as a reason only in a few cases) and the "lack of perspective" (*Perspektivelosigkeit* was the term for an ideologically useless individual) for the work to be assigned.

More than two-thirds of the undercover collaborators at Humboldt University had been recruited during the seventies and eighties, the reason being that, after the international recognition of the GDR, the state intensified its exchange with diplomats and scientists from non-socialist countries. Reconstructing the reasons for collaboration with the *Stasi* using the agent files reveals that political conviction was the basis in the vast majority of cases. We must take into consideration that 85 percent of Humboldt University professors were members of the SED. Thus it is only natural that many willing collaborators would come from this pool of party members.[33] This may also explain why the majority of university professors received no monetary compensation from State Security aside from an occasional present. Of course, all professors received a good salary as university employees. Only in a few cases were additional monetary incentives decisive for cooperation. Top compensation was given to an area specialist with an emolument of 100,000 marks, an economist with approximately 50,000 marks, several other area specialists with approximately 10,000 marks each, and a scientist with a monetary compensation of approximately 9,000 marks.[34] In ten instances medals were given for the collaboration. As a rule, in order to preserve secrecy, collaborators were only verbally informed of such honors; the actual medals remained in their *Stasi* files.

CONCLUSION

State Security considered Humboldt University as the most prestigious and important institution of higher education in the GDR and thus strove for a broad presence, tight control, and consistent influence.[35] The fact that Department XX/3 (later XX/8), which was responsible for Humboldt University, was the largest in the administrative district of Berlin with regard to the number of personnel supports the importance of the operations at Humboldt.[36] State Security's influence was exerted in official as well as unofficial ways.

The president, vice-president, and the SED district administrators of Humboldt University were official contact persons for State Security. Using their influence on the higher administration and the SED functionaries of Humboldt University, the *Stasi* had the power to effect the employment of individual *Stasi* officers and undercover collaborators, the release (*Freistellung*) of such persons from academic duties for undercover activities, the identification of special cadres for State Security, the support of Main Intelligence Division's operations, and, last but not least, the admission or dismissal of students.

Undercover activities were so effective because State Security had been successful in placing at least one undercover agent in each key position at Humboldt University, as an analysis of *Stasi* personnel folders kept for each of these individuals clearly bears out. Thus it was ultimately possible to influence important central areas, such as the Directorate for Cadre and Qualification, the Directorate for Continuing Education, the Directorate for International Relations, and the Inspection of Laborers and Farmers.[37] The intensity and effectiveness of such collaboration could only be guaranteed by maintaining secrecy. If there was any sign that such activities were being discovered, State Security would routinely terminate such collaboration immediately.

The close network of undercover agents (*IMs*) among Humboldt University professors enabled and guaranteed the influential position of State Security and of the Main Intelligence Division in Humboldt University's academic and political activities. This network was especially strong in departments with important research projects and where the international recognition of the GDR played an important role. There was no clearly definable line of demarcation between the political-ideological interests of State Security and the leadership of the university. The decisions of the SED leadership were, in fact, binding for State Security as well as for the University and set their course. There was relatively little friction between these organizations because the president, the first vice-president, and all directors of key departments were members of the SED—in actuality 85 percent of Humboldt University faculty belonged to the SED.

The files show further that the University administration and many faculty members welcomed the support of State Security.[38] Without this support resulting from the political conviction of the university leadership and nearly all of the undercover agents,[39] *Stasi* would not have been able to occupy this position at Humboldt University. There were instances in which Humboldt University professors refused to collaborate with State Security. These cases show that a refusal to do undercover activity for the *Stasi* did not always result in disadvantages, crimination, or persecution. Of course, State Security was not responsible, as is sometimes assumed, for all the professional difficulties, obstructions, or failures in academic careers at Humboldt University. But for many it was. Thus the role of the SED District Administration at the University in career obstructions should also be investigated. It is an established fact that State Security watched over Humboldt University intensively and extensively and that a large number of professors joined in this surveillance as undercover collaborators. The attempted renewal of Humboldt University after 1989 occurred at first with these very same scholars still in their positions and thus was rather superficial and lacked credibility. Only when the former *Stasi* files were consulted at the Gauck Commission's archives and the official reports requested and received could Humboldt University succeed in the process of renovation of its academic personnel.

Translated by Barbara Becker-Cantarino

NOTES

BStU = Behörde des Bundesbeauftragten für die Unterlagen des Staatssicherheitsdienstes der ehemaligen DDR (Gauck Commission).

1. After its constitution in November 1990, the Honors Commission (*Ehrenausschuß*) established the following guidelines for its deliberations: 1. decreasing the mistrust among colleagues; 2. weighing the accusations of "collaboration with the *Stasi*," "professional advances based on political pressure" (*dienstliche Vorteile aufgrund politischer Einflußnahme*), and "malfeasance in office and corruption" (*Amtsmißbrauch und Korruption*); 3. taking up cases only with the agreement of the individuals involved (see *Geschäftsordnung des Ehrenausschusses 1990*).

2. *Behörde des Bundesbeauftragten für die Unterlagen des Staatssicherheitsdienstes der ehemaligen DDR* (BStU); *Gauck-Behörde* has replaced the laborious official designation.

3. The planning stage lasted into the summer of 1992. From October 1990 (the creation of the commission) to December 29, 1991 (when the *Stasi* legislation went into effect), the commission was called: *Der Sonderbeauftragte der Bundesregierung für die personembezogenen Unterlagen des ehemaligen Staatssicherheitsdienstes*; since January 1992, it's named: *Der Bundesbeauftragte für die Unterlagen des Staatssicherheitsdienstes der ehemaligen Deutschen Demokratischen Republik*.

4. Translator's note: *Inoffizieller Mitarbeiter* (always referred to as *IM*) literally means "inofficial employee"; it was State Security's covert designation for "undercover collaborator"; the translation was authorized by Gauck for the *Daedalus* article and which I will employ likewise. Gauck clarifies:

The IM undertook to collaborate with the Mfs [Ministry for State Security] by means of a written or oral statement. But, in the case of a small group of intellectuals and churchmen, the *Stasi*'s rules allowed for a more circumspect recruiting method. "Confidential talks" were arranged which, after a time, were held in secret ("adhering to the rules of conspiracy," as State Security termed it) by agreement between the two parties. . . . They fully accepted long-term contact with a *Stasi* officer, kept the relationship secret, acquiesced in a role rejected by others in comparable positions in the East. . . . The *Stasi* . . . pursued its own interests in processing the data gleaned from the IM, [and] such information was used, regardless of the supplier's motives, to support the regime's hold over its subjects. ("Dealing with a Stasi Past" 1994, 282–83)

5. These research groups (*HUB-Forschungsgruppen*) were the first external petitioners who received access to *Stasi* documents concerning Humboldt University. This occurred during the very early phase when the Gauck Commission was being established. The material in question is that of the former District Administration of the Ministry for State Security, which is now housed in the "*Außenstelle Berlin*" of the Gauck Commission Archives (*BstU*), carton 1-200. On the activities of these groups, see Richter, "Humboldt-Universität war fest im Griff."

6. While the investigation of Humboldt University professors was in progress, a number of academics had personal conversations with me. They reported about their experiences, which helped me in gaining insights into the structural entanglements.

7. By contrast to other regional offices, the Berlin district offices were not stormed. Instead, on December 12, 1989, members of the civil liberties movement (*Bürgerrechtsbewegung*) decided to reorganize the Berlin offices together with representatives from the Modrow government, in a "partnership for security." The basic idea was to eliminate certain sections of the district offices (e.g., Dept. XX) and to retain others (e.g., Dept. XV and II). While certain sections could continue their work, some quarters of Department XX were opened to the public. For the first time, outsiders could gain insight into "operative actions" (*Operative Vorgänge, OV*) and "operative control of persons" (*Operative Personenkontrolle, OP*). Members of the meeting on December 17, 1989, were, among others: Ibrahim Böhme, Dr. Wolfgang Ullmann, Reinhart Schult, Dr. Kummer, Mr. Erdman, and Wolfgang Wolf. In conjunction with the press, radio, and television, a "consensus" was announced. A poster at the district building proclaimed: "A citizens committee is working in this building." When the Ministry for State Security was occupied on January 15, 1990, the Berlin district offices were spared, because a citizens committee was already at work there.

8. See *Die Organisationsstruktur des Ministeriums für Staatssicherheit*, p. 112. When checking contacts between Humboldt University professors and the *Stasi*, the Gauck Commission investigation always lists the respective *Stasi* unit, if known. Thus we could establish the existence of 42 units; but the number must have been much larger, because the documents of the Main Intelligence Division (*Hauptverwaltung Aufklärung, HV A*) were destroyed. These key documents are no longer available for investigating contacts or for scholarly research.

9. "Politisch-ideologische Diversion" (*PiD*) is the official term used; see *Das Wörterbuch der Staatssicherheit*, p. 171.

10. As late as the beginning of 1989, restructuring took place within the Ministry for State Security; section XX/3 was divided so that section XX/8, with twelve members, was responsible for Humboldt, excluding the Charité hospital; the previous five Charité supervisors joined section XX/6, which was in charge of the entire medical and public health field in Berlin.

11. Mass organizations were, among others, the *FDJ* (Free German Youth), the *DSF* (Society for German-Soviet Friendship), and the *Kulturbund* (Culture League).

12. The GDR established Fighting Squads (*Kampfgruppen*) in industry and important institutions originally as protection against "the invasion from the West" in order to prevent "acts of sabotage" and "criminal activities." Later these units became less ideologically oriented and served more like a national guard. Members were usually army reserves. Universities, which had an SED District Administration of their own, also had Fighting Squads.

13. A type of national guard, the *Zivilschutz*, was established in the late sixties to serve the civilian population in case of foreign military aggression and invasion, air raids, and during catastrophic events.

14. The *Freie Deutsche Jugend* (Free German Youth) was founded in 1946 as the official youth organization to mold East German youth into ideologically fervent socialists; membership (from ages fourteen to twenty-four) was required for career tracks considered important to the state. Of all students at Humboldt University, more than 95 percent were members in 1985 (Keiderling 1987, 423).

15. The Director for Cadres and Qualifications supervised the selection, screening, and training of those students who were chosen for important positions in the SED and the government.

16. The assignment plan for employees of Department XX/3 of the Berlin District specifies that the Deputy Director, Major Simonis, was the official representative at Humboldt University; he had regular appointments with the president, vice-presidents and all administrators in key positions (See BStU, Arch. der ASt. Berlin, Simonis Uwe, KS II 852/91).

17. See Schreiben des Direktorats für Internationale Beziehungen der HUB, Vorlage für das Sekretariat der SED-Kreisleitung. BStU, Archiv des Ast Berlin, Karton Nr. A 107–109, Nr. 01.

18. *HVA* for *Hauptverwaltung Aufklärung* is the *Stasi* division in charge of espionage abroad; see also note 8, *supra*.

19. See Städteübersicht BRD—Schwerpunkte für die Aufklärung; BStU, Archiv der Ast. Berlin, Karton 107–9, Nr. 03.

20. "Anordnung des Vorsitzenden," VVS B2-1034/81 [State Security call number], BStU, Zentralarchiv (ZA).

21. "DA Nr. 4/85 über die politisch-operative Sicherung des Reiseverkehrs von Bürgern der DDR nach nicht sozialistischen Staaten und Westberlin," VVS MfS 0008–59/85 [State Security call number], BStU, ZA.

22. See a report of July 16, 1982 of the *HVA*, Abt. IX/AG; BStU, Archiv der AST. Berlin, Karton A 107–9, Nr. 04.

23. This touches on basic questions of the relationship between the SED and State Security that need further research. For example, the ABI-committee (for the "inspection of workers and farmers") was constituted in mid-1975, a cooperative effort of State Security and SED; the Party nominated the candidates, State Security investigated them; 60 percent of this committee consisted of undercover collaborators from State Security. See Dienstanweisung Nr. 1/75 des Leiters der Verwaltung Groß-Berlin, 3-18-1975, BStU, Archiv der AST. Berlin, Karton A 107–9, Nr. 05.

24. See, for example, document of February 8, 1983, BStU, Archiv der AST. Berlin, Karton A 107–9, Nr. 09.

25. See, for example, the document of the Berlin District Administration, Dept. XX, to the Director of the Main Intelligence Division of October 27, 1987, concerning the travel ban for a Humboldt University undercover collaborator; discussions took place at SED district administration. BStU, Archiv der AST. Berlin, Karton A 107–9, Nr. 09. Concerning Stiller's defection, see Stiller, *Im Zentrum der Spionage*.

26. See Arbeitsplan der Abteilung XX der BV Berlin 1989, BStU, AST. Berlin, Karton A 80.

27. See the definition for "operative Personenkontrolle" (*OPK*) and "operativer Vorgang" (*OV*) in *Das Wörterbuch der Staatssicherheit*, pp. 286–87.

28. Division XV of the Berlin District had the same tasks as the *HVA* as far as the district level was concerned; see Gill/Schröter, *Das Ministerium*, p. 55.

29. See Eckhart, "Die Berliner Humboldt-Universität," p. 776; see the entry of Department XX/3 of the Berlin District of February 2, 1985, about a conversation between the department's director Major Mentschke and the chair of Criminology at Humboldt University, Prof. Stelzer, BStU, Archiv des ASt. Berlin, Karton A 107–9, Nr. 10.

30. We count among the *IM* (*Inoffizieller Mitarbeiter*) those individuals whose written "statement of obligation" (*Verpflichtungserklärung*) is on record and who visited places of undercover activity and/or provided written or oral reports for the *Stasi*.

31. These numbers refer only to those who collaborated with State Security; those who worked for the Main Intelligence Division remain undocumented because of the destruction of files, as noted above.

32. There were a small number of professors working in three additional classifications: *HIM* (*Hauptamtliche Inoffizielle Mitarbeiter*, full-time undercover agents); *IME* (*Inoffizielle Mitarbeiter für besonderen Einsatz*, undercover agents for special missions); and until 1979, *IMV* (*Inoffizielle Mitarbeiter mit besonderem Vertrauensverhältnis*, undercover agents with a special trustworthiness), who became *IMB* thereafter.

33. In recruiting professors for collaboration, portraying the "danger of the enemy of socialism" was used as a persuasive tool; see *Das Wörterbuch der Staatssicherheit*, p. 190.

34. Money was often provided for financing undercover work; if apartments were used for such work, the *Stasi* would usually pay for the rent and furnishings. See the directives by the Head of Department XX of the Berlin District Administration, Colonel Häbler, of February 22, 1983 about "planning, usage, accounting and control of financial means for the establishment of conspiratorial apartments and bases." BStU, Archiv der ASt. Berlin, Karton Nr. A 107–9, Nr. 11.

35. See the Minister for State Security's order no. 1 of January 10, 1968, VVS Mfs 008-63/68 [old *Stasi* call number], BStU, Archiv der ASt. Berlin, Karton A 107–9, Nr. 11; working orders of Department XX of the Berlin District from 1980 to 1989, BStU, Archiv der ASt. Berlin, Karton 80; and see Flocken and Jurtschitsch, "Mielkes Argus-Augen."

36. See Stein, *Die Charité*, p. 220. Stein's statistics are based, in fact, on information supplied by me.

37. The "Inspection of Laborers and Farmers" (*ABI, Arbeiter- und Bauern-Inspektion*) was a means of controlling and educating the people for their role in the socialist state; see *DDR Handbuch*, vol. I, p. 33.

38. See Fuchs, "Der Abschied," pp. 30–32.

39. There were cases in which undercover agents entered *Stasi* employment without such political convictions; as the files document, in all of these cases *Stasi* terminated the collaboration with a remark of "unsuitable" or "lack of perspective."

REFERENCES

DDR-Handbuch. Bundesministerium für Innerdeutsche Beziehungen. Cologne: Verlag Wissenschaft und Politik, 1985.

Eckert, Rainer. "Die Berliner Humboldt-Universität und das Ministerium für Staatssicherheit." *Deutschland-Archiv* (July 1993): 770–85.

———. "Die Diskussion um die Staatssicherheitsverstrickungen an der Berliner Humboldt-Universität zwischen 1989 und 1993." *German Studies Review* Special Issue (1994): 147–56.

Flocken, Jan von, and Erwin Jurtschitsch. "Mielkes Argus-Augen an der Universität." *Der Morgen*, (November 6, 1990): 6.

Fuchs, Jürgen. "Der Abschied von der Diktatur." In *Aktenkundig*, edited by Hans Joachim Schädlich. Berlin: Rowohlt, 1992.

Füller, Christian. "Der rigorose Blick zurück." *Süddeutsche Zeitung*, November 14/15, 1992, 17.

Gauck, Joachim. *Die Stasi-Akten. Das unheimliche Erbe der DDR*. Reinbek: Rowohlt, 1991.

———. "Dealing with a Stasi Past." *Daedalus. Journal of the American Academy of Arts and Sciences* 123, 1 (Winter 1994): 277–84.

Geschäftsordnung des Ehrenausschusses des akademischen Senats der Humboldt Universität. Berlin, 1990.

Gill, David, and Schröter, Ulrich. *Das Ministerium für Staatssicherheit, Anatomie des Mielke-Imperiums.* Berlin: Rowohlt, 1991.

Keiderling, Gerhard. *Berlin 1945–86: Geschichte der Hauptstadt der DDR.* 2d edition. Berlin: Dietz Verlag, 1987.

Labrenz-Weiss, Hanna. "Die Beziehungen zwischen Staatssicherheit, SED and den akademischen Leitungsgremien an der Humboldt-Universität zu Berlin." *German Studies Review* Special Issue (Fall 1994): 131–46.

Müller, Heiner. *Rotwelsch.* Berlin: Merve, 1982.

Die Organisationsstruktur des Ministeriums für Staatssicherheit 1989. Berlin: BStU, 1993. BStU, Reihe A, Nr. 2/93.

"Pressekonferenz der Präsidentin der Humboldt Universität zu Berlin, Prof. Dr. Marlis Dürkop, und der Ehrenkommission." Berlin, August 7, 1992.

Richter, Christine. "Humboldt-Universität war fest im Griff der Stasi: Studenten erforschen in der Gauck-Behörde die MfS-Strukturen." *Berliner Zeitung,* October 31, 1992, 5.

Stein, Rosemarie. *Die Charité 1945–1992. Ein Mythos von innen.* Berlin: Argon Verlag, 1992.

Stiller, Werner. *Im Zentrum der Spionage.* 5th ed. Mainz: Hase & Köhler, 1986.

Das Wörterbuch der Staatssicherheit. Berlin: BStU, 1993. BStU, Reihe A, Nr. 1/93.

4

Berlin: A New Kaleidoscope of Cultures

Carol Aisha Blackshire-Belay

At a subway station in Berlin-Kreuzberg. "The Turkish train is coming." You know what that means. The smell of garlic, loud children, pregnant Turkish women, dirt and noise everywhere. Many people see it that way. Many people say that. On the bare walls of the train station: "Foreigners out!" You get used to it. You ignore it. It's not like that. So I am told.[1]

MULTICULTURAL GERMANY

Signs of a multicultural society in the new Germany are everywhere. Although this situation is more obvious in some German cities than in others, the fact remains: Germany is ethnically, culturally, and linguistically much more diverse than ever before in its history. During the past thirty-five years, two separate and different streams of migration brought large numbers of foreigners into the former Federal Republic of Germany and the former German Democratic Republic. In contemporary Germany, most discussions of the "foreigner issue" have mainly focused on foreign workers and asylum seekers. However, there are other groups of foreigners that should not be overlooked: the *Aussiedler* (ethnic Germans) from the former eastern bloc countries, foreign students, foreigners with German spouses, students from Third World countries who come to learn a trade, and employees of foreign companies in Germany. Although they are in a separate class, we must also include the many thousands of people of color of German descent, i.e., Afro-, Asian-, and Arab-Germans. The official policy of the German government maintains that Germany is "not an immigrant country," but this position has become inadequate for the situation that has arisen since the end of World War II. In reality, the importation of foreign labor during periods of economic boom is deeply rooted in German tradition extending back over many decades.

While an in-depth look at the historical side of immigration of foreigners to Germany is necessary to fully understand the serious dilemma that foreigners face in the new Germany, this would extend far beyond the scope of the present paper.[2] My focus here will be on the situation of foreign populations in East Berlin and West Berlin prior to the fall of the Berlin Wall on November 9, 1989, and prior to the German government's modification of the asylum laws, which have affected foreigners throughout Germany.

Berlin's political situation has been crucial to the foreign population in a number of ways, among them:

1. After World War II, there was a shortage of workers in most of the urban industrialized cities, but Berlin was hit hardest; the shortage became even more severe after the building of the Berlin Wall in 1961.

2. The German government established a recruiting campaign with a number of attractive incentives to lure workers, both German and non-German, to West Berlin.

3. In comparison to other major German cities with traditional culture and conventional life-styles, the novel (counter-) culture of alternative life-styles and beliefs was most prominent in West Berlin; it was *the* German city that initiated and disseminated new trends.

4. Because of the Wall, foreigners were less mobile in Berlin in comparison to other cities, which made it easier for them to find their place and feel a sense of home in city boroughs such as Kreuzberg, Neukölln, and Wedding. The visibility of the foreigners truly added to the "international" character of the city.

THE SITUATION OF FOREIGN WORKERS
AND REFUGEES IN WEST AND EAST BERLIN
PRIOR TO UNIFICATION

After the Second World War, East and West German industries were both rapidly reconstructed, albeit at a different pace. Soon it became quite apparent that neither country could supply the labor force needed for its industrial growth. Thus "guest workers" (*Gastarbeiter*) were recruited based on agreements signed with foreign countries. West Germany recruited workers from the relatively poor Mediterranean countries to help rebuild its economy. Despite the fact that the GDR mainly recruited workers from socialist countries (i.e., Mozambique, North Vietnam, and Cuba) and the FRG from non-socialist countries, the similarities of the two systems are very apparent. Even though later unemployment problems in Germany caused the official recruitment programs to be discontinued, the immigration flow did not stop. Foreign workers continued to feel they would earn a better living in Germany than in their home countries. In general, however, the workers did not see themselves as immigrants; they considered their stay a temporary one and planned to return to their native countries when circumstances would permit. However, the children of these foreign workers, who grew up in Germany and who speak German, do not intend to return to the country in which their parents were born and raised. This migration pattern is obvious in most urban industrialized cities in Germany, but for many reasons Berlin offers an excellent subject for the discussion of past and recent developments in the employment of foreign workers and for the investigation of the lives of the foreign workers as a whole.

Long before the Second World War, the city of Berlin, the German capital since 1871, had become the economic center of the country. In the Federal Republic, West Berlin was the city with the largest population. Similarly, East Berlin was the largest city in the German Democratic Republic and was also its capital. While the number of the incoming foreigners varied, and the reasons for their immigration into East and West Berlin differed, they now represent the largest concentration of foreigners in the reunited Germany. To fully grasp the present situation of these groups and the dilemma that confronts them in German society, we should be fully aware of why the foreigners came to Berlin, and why they are still there.

Because of the continued shortage of workers in the former GDR, the East German government recruited foreign workers on the basis of agreements with the governments of selected countries, first from the socialist states of Hungary and Poland, and later from Algeria. But the employment of the workers from Algeria, a nonsocialist country that did not require that worker's rights be strictly regulated in the GDR, led to friction between different foreigner groups. As a result, the contract between the GDR and Algeria was terminated at the end of 1970. In 1980, the GDR signed agreements with Vietnam, Angola, Mozambique, and Cuba. The Ministry of Labor made this decision at the governmental level and did not inform the people about the details. By the end of the 1970s, there were approximately 18,000 Algerians, in the 1980s over 1,000 Chinese, a few hundred Libyans and North Koreans, as well as a sizable number of Bulgarians, Namibians, Hungarians, and Iranians. In late 1989, shortly after the Berlin Wall was opened, there were some 88,100 foreign workers living in East Germany. They included 59,000 Vietnamese, 15,100 Mozambicans, and over 8,000 Cubans. Surely, the biggest contingent of foreigners were Soviet soldiers and their families. In addition, of the approximately 2,000 Jewish Soviet citizens residing in the GDR who decided in 1990 to go to Berlin, only a few went to West Germany. Of the Rumanians who sought asylum, 80 percent were Roma. Their numbers grew to 1,200 in 1990 (Stach 1991, 4–5).

Before 1989, the exact number of foreigners living in the German Democratic Republic was not available. This was considered a state secret, so that it was only after the fall of the Berlin Wall that the official numbers could be assessed. Of course, these numbers are inaccurate for several reasons; for example, several thousand Vietnamese sought refuge in West Berlin or in other parts of Germany, other foreigners left for their own countries, and many are no longer legally registered. There are numbers, however, available to us of foreigners in the territory of the former GDR after the fall of the Wall.[3]

In the GDR the government had established the following conditions for foreigners:

1. The workers were not entitled to social services and benefits.
2. Twelve percent of their earnings had to be sent to the country of origin.
3. There was strict control on the individual through GDR organizations and consulates.
4. Reuniting with family members in East Germany was strictly forbidden.
5. Women workers were deported in case of pregnancy unless they agreed to an abortion.
6. Membership in foreign organizations and in political parties of the GDR was not allowed.
7. Membership (with the payment of dues) was mandatory in the one official labor union (Hussain 1991, 27).

The GDR sent workers back to their countries of origin as soon as employment ended. If a foreigner married a German national, which allowed him or her to remain in the country after termination of employment, the foreign worker was obligated to pay the government varying sums of money. For a normal factory worker the sum of 8,000 marks had to be paid to the East German government; for an academic 30,000 marks; students had to pay 22,000 marks; and job trainees 12,000 marks (Stach 1991, 13).

The GDR government provided foreign workers with housing. A large percentage of the workers lived in the so-called *Ausländerwohnheime* (housing for foreigners), many of which have become the target of violence recently. The housing situation of foreign workers living in East Berlin was very similar to that in West Berlin, but little, if any, documentation has been provided about the lives of the foreigners in these housing projects before the fall of the Wall. Based on my own experience of living in a housing project as a field-worker in West Berlin, I can attest to the fact that housing has had a direct impact on foreign workers and their families.

West Berlin was also affected by the changes that took place in the rest of the Federal Republic. The industrialized West German economy had definite needs for imported labor, particularly in the areas of construction, mining, and heavy industries. The influx of foreign workers into the Federal Republic began in response to a recruitment campaign initiated by the government in the 1950s. Its intent was to meet the shortfall in labor that was becoming obvious as economic growth moved steadily forward. Between 1959 and 1965, the number of foreign workers rose by one million. In March 1960, Minister of Labor Blank signed recruitment agreements with Spain and Greece patterned after an earlier agreement with Italy. This was followed by a series of additional agreements: with Turkey on October 30, 1961; Portugal on March 17, 1964; and Yugoslavia on October 12, 1968.[4] By the autumn of 1970, the foreign labor force totalled over 2 million. By the time recruitment officially stopped in 1973 and tighter immigration restrictions were introduced following the economic decline of the early 1970s, almost 4 million new foreigners lived in the Federal Republic. The number of foreign residents increased six- to seven-fold between the early 1960s and the late 1980s, from 0.7 million or 1.2 percent in 1961 to 4.9 million or 7.8 percent in 1989.

When the Berlin Wall was built on August 13, 1961, West Berlin lost 60,000 skilled workers because they lived in East Berlin and were no longer allowed or able to commute to West Berlin. There was indeed a shortage of workers within the city. To bridge this gap, West Berlin launched a campaign to recruit workers from West Germany. In addition, the Federal Republic allocated special funds to Berlin. In 1961, the Bundestag passed a Berlin Aid Law that gave people working or investing in West Berlin various tax breaks and other incentives. These soon showed positive results.

In 1987, nearly 260,000 foreign nationals lived in West Berlin; there had been 128,000 in 1970, and for 1991, the number of foreigners in all of Berlin was estimated at 341,000.[5] They made up 12.7 percent of the population in 1987 (6 percent in 1970, about 10 percent in 1991). By the late 1970s, West

Berlin had the largest non-German population of any German city. For example, 114,000 Turks lived in West Berlin, more than in any other West German city. Additionally, there were 31,000 Yugoslavs, nearly 12,000 Poles, just over 8,000 Italians, and 7,000 Greeks in West Berlin. More than one in five West Berlin children under six years of age had non-German parents. Newcomers from the Mediterranean and the Balkans mainly lived in Kreuzberg, Neukölln, and Wedding boroughs. Kreuzberg still has the largest proportion of foreign residents, 31 percent in 1991, followed by Wedding (24%), Tiergarten (22%), and Schöneberg (20%). Turkish shops and markets give these districts an exotic, Oriental feel. By comparison, residential districts in East Berlin have relatively few foreigners, between 0.6 percent (Treptow) and 5 percent (Lichtenberg).

Berlin was not known to have a "foreigner" problem. However, it is not always easy for people with different traditions, customs, and cultural backgrounds to live together without friction. Even before the most recent incidents of violent right-wing extremist attacks against foreigners, there were signs that foreigners did not live in complete harmony in the city. Ultimately the integration of the foreign workers and their families in West Berlin became a hot topic of debate. To encourage integration, at the end of 1981, West Berlin became the first federal state to appoint a commissioner for the affairs of foreign residents; Barbara John filled this position.

PROBLEMS OF ADAPTATION
FOR THE FOREIGN WORKERS

By German standards integration generally means total assimilation of the foreigner into the German way of life. Foreigners are often viewed in the negative: They are associated with violence, ghettoization in certain parts of the city, and abuse of the German social system. On the other hand, these healthy, adult human beings who were recruited by Germany had desires and aspirations for a better life for themselves, their spouses, and children. Life in a foreign country is not an easy one for the newcomers. But their situation is rarely portrayed from the point-of-view of the foreigner. Therefore, I would like to take the opportunity to view this difficult, new situation from the perspective of the foreign workers themselves.

One of the causes of the difficult situation that arose was the fact that immigration to Germany was initially regarded as a transitory phenomenon. West Germany's policy was directed toward providing workers for industry who could easily be sent away in the event of an economic crisis. For this reason the residence rights of the foreign workers were limited and the entry of dependents was discouraged. The enactment of the Foreigners Law (*Ausländergesetz*) of 1965 did little to improve this situation.[6] During the 1966–1967 recession, the foreign labor force dropped rapidly, but nearly one million foreign workers remained in Germany, even though many Germans lost their jobs. After this first major economic recession of the postwar period was over, large segments of the West German public realized that foreign workers were not going to vanish from the scene in the same inconspicuous way that they had been recruited. It became evident that many of them would settle permanently in West Germany. This realization led to a reorientation of policies and, unfortunately, to negative attitudes toward the foreign population.

Almost overnight issues raised by the presence of foreign workers in Germany were overwhelmingly regarded as social problems, urgently demanding social solutions. The situation of the foreign workers—and the policy toward foreign workers of successive West German governments—moved to the forefront of public attention. In public discussion concerning foreign workers, West Germans questioned the expansion of recruitment from southern Europe, demanded a halt to immigration, contested the right to bring family members, worried about the second and third generations of foreigners, about problems of integration and assimilation, about low-level qualifications and ghettoization. When large numbers of Turkish workers were brought to Germany at the beginning of the 1970s, even more criticism appeared on the scene. There was talk of foreign infiltration (*Überfremdung*), xenophobia, and hatred of Turks that, in essence, was directed toward all foreigners.

In considering the present situation in Germany, it becomes obvious that the so-called foreigner question (*Ausländerfrage*) involves more than just problems of social and economic adaptation. German nationals have had very little experience or success with the practice of cultural pluralism; prejudice and discrimination abound. Many Germans resent the foreigners' presence in Germany, particularly during times of economic recession and rising unemployment. Traditionally, Germans are reserved toward foreigners, which has caused the foreign worker population to feel unwanted there. Furthermore, Germany was a country with a very homogeneous social and cultural life-style that made it more difficult for foreigners to settle and become integrated. Germany's official policy is called "aliens policy" (*Ausländerpolitik*) rather than "immigration policy," reflecting the official position that Germany is "not an immigrant country." Since foreign workers are not regarded as immigrants or potential immigrants, their children born in Germany do not automatically get German citizenship.[7] The German government was not prepared for the migration of families and is still trying to cope with problems in the areas of housing, employment, and education.

The foreign workers recruited to Berlin (as well as to Germany in general) faced a multitude of problems. Among the major ones were the problems of adaptation, housing, and most of all the difficulties with the new language. In many cases, the foreign workers and their dependents share a subordinate status both socially and economically in Germany. Confronted with discrimination, language barriers, low incomes, and housing shortages, many foreigners have become concentrated and isolated in urban slums in the older sections of cities. Moreover, their presence has created an added strain on the cities' infrastructures by placing heavy demands on housing, schools, and day-care centers. Since unification, the structure of Berlin in particular has drastically changed. The areas of the city where the foreigners once felt secure were the city boroughs closest to the Wall (Kreuzberg, Wedding, Neukölln). Since the fall of the Wall, these areas of the city have now become the territory of many right-wing groups and neo-Nazis, groups that violently oppose foreigner presence in Berlin and in the rest of the country. Many foreigners simply do not feel safe any longer.

On the whole, many foreign workers suffer deeply from isolation due to marginalization in private housing complexes. The only German nationals who might possibly live on the same floor belong to marginal groups themselves, like students or the Alternatives (members of the counter-culture), and have a social life which is quite different from that of immigrant families, thus offering little ground for contact. On the other hand, since many foreign workers regard their stay abroad as temporary, they have not been interested in social contact and integration. The outside world may seem cold and hostile to them, and they prefer to spend their time in personal conversation and games with their compatriots. But there are others who are interested in their new surroundings, who want to make friends and learn the language. Many of the workers whom I interviewed indicated that upon their arrival in Berlin, they made attempts to establish friendships with German nationals, but most of those relationships were short-lived.

Foreigners have great difficulty in finding housing. One reason for this is discrimination: Many landlords simply refuse to rent accommodations to foreigners. In addition, foreigners often have special needs and problems that put them at a disadvantage on the housing market. Particularly in West Berlin, which attracted workers with families in very high numbers, the search for housing on the private market was (and still is) in direct competition with the native German population—or at least its lower income groups. Very few foreigners live in the fashionable, high-minded district of Charlottenburg or Grunewald, while large segments reside in Kreuzberg, Wedding, or Neukölln. Discrimination against foreign workers is widespread as is indicated by numerous advertisements for furnished accommodations in local papers carrying stipulations such as *Gastarbeiter unerwünscht* (foreign workers not desired), or *nur für Deutsche* (Germans only). And recently buildings housing foreigners have become targets of attack, an indication that this situation has grown worse. Paradoxically, the present circumstances have provided German landlords with yet an additional reason for not renting to foreigners.

During the post–World War II recruitment period, most group accommodations provided by employers for the foreign workers were dormitories usually shared by up to six or eight men, often sleeping in double-decker bunks. Furniture generally included little more than a table, a few upright wooden chairs, and wardrobes. The communal cooking (hot plates) and washing facilities (two showers for 35 people) were often primitive and did not meet modern sanitary standards. In 1962, approximately two-thirds of the newly recruited *Gastarbeiter* lived in communal hostels maintained either by the firms employing the foreigners, the municipal authorities, welfare associations, or private individuals.

My fieldwork conducted in the mid- to late-1980s in Berlin revealed that a very large percentage of foreign workers still lived in the housing built immediately after World War II. I lived in a residence in Berlin-Tegel; many such residences were also located in the districts of Wedding and Tiergarten. When the foreign workers were allowed to reunite with their families in Germany, the factory responsible for the housing ultimately rented these units to entire families. A typical family shared two to three rooms depending on the number of family members. The rooms were bare and inhospitable, lacking even the simplest things that could make them more pleasant, such as lampshades and curtains. Immigrant workers spent nearly all their non-working hours in these surroundings, because they lacked the money or were too tired to go out in the evenings or on weekends. To fully grasp and understand the difficulties of the foreign workers living under such conditions, one has to live within the walls of such a dwelling with the workers themselves. In the former West Berlin, the largest concentration of foreigners was precisely in those parts of the city where buildings were older and unrenovated, and often had substandard conditions with no running water in the living unit and a shower and other facilities shared by several families on one corridor.

Language is the first and foremost problem for most foreign workers. Many of them do not succeed in overcoming their language difficulties throughout their stay in Germany. Regardless of the number of years in the Federal

Republic, most of the workers have not acquired the necessary linguistic tools to function well in their second language environment. They have developed a rudimentary knowledge of German used at the workplace, for encounters with the native population, and for cross-national communication among themselves. Known to many as Foreign Workers' German (FWG), it is a contact language in progress that is not yet clearly understood. It is an unwritten, oral form of communication and is not the mother tongue of any of its speakers. Foreign Workers' German is spoken by approximately five million or more foreign workers and their family members residing in Germany. It is often referred to by many names, such as *Gastarbeiterdeutsch* (guest workers' German) or *Fremdarbeiterdeutsch* (alien-workers' German), a term seldom used because of its association with Nazi terminology.

SURVIVAL IN THE PROMISED LAND

I had the opportunity to conduct extensive fieldwork in the foreign worker community in Berlin, observing the workers' daily lives in order to gain a better understanding of the role that foreign workers' German played in their lives in intimate surroundings, namely in the home environment. To do this, I obtained a room in one of the foreign housing units in West Berlin. This residence was occupied by foreign workers, all of whom worked in the same textile factory. Approximately eighty-five people, adults and children, of different nationalities lived there, and the majority of their time, when they were not at the workplace, was spent in the residence (evenings, weekends, holidays, etc.) It worked to my advantage that prior to this study I had lived in Germany for many years as a foreigner at the university. As an African-American woman, a member of a minority within the United States, I was able to understand and relate to the workers' problems. This fact also helped the foreign workers to accept this "outsider" into their community and to involve her in their personal lives.[8]

It is clear that I would not have been allowed to participate in many of the foreign workers' personal affairs had I not won their trust. Ultimately I established a bond with the foreign worker community, a bond that has remained and enabled me through study of the inner dynamics of the foreigner situation in Berlin to gain additional insights into the crucial changes in Germany affecting foreigners.

The serious dilemma that the foreigners faced when they were recruited to Germany and the problems that they continue to face is illustrated in the following excerpt from an interview with Mehmet, a Turkish worker. "We were told that Germany is paradise. Beer flows from the water tap, and you get money everywhere for everything: money for child support, unemployment money, and money for your vacation—so we were told at that time. But not that you had to work extremely hard in paradise, they didn't say that. Even my fellow countrymen always want to present everything better than it truly is. So that they can appear as big people and not be viewed as little workers. And we came to Germany, and everything was different."9 The overwhelming majority of these workers came from rural areas. Even if their country of origin has made considerable progress towards industrialization, the migrants were brought up in regions that have remained predominantly agricultural. The foreign worker coming to Berlin for the first time may never have seen a factory before, let alone worked in one. Typically, he or she lived all his or her life in a peasant community, using traditional production methods and preindustrial technology. Urban life consequently proved difficult and confusing. It must be recognized that people coming from small villages have to adapt to new forms of housing and accustom themselves to new modes of transportation, and to different methods of exchanging and distributing goods.

In personal interviews I gathered firsthand insights into the personal lives of the foreign workers. It is interesting to note that during the time of this particular fieldwork project Günter Wallraff published a book revealing some of the hardships of the workers living in Germany. Wallraff, a German national, disguised himself as a Turkish worker in order to show just how difficult life in Germany was for foreign workers. He was criticized and attacked from all sides of the German populace, something that ultimately convinced him to leave Germany. Ironically Wallraff's book appeared at the very same time that I was an observer in the residence in Berlin. The foreign workers there became aware of Wallraff's book and his actions. Their reaction was quite simple: Why would a German want to do such a thing?10

In order to illustrate the difficulties that individual workers encountered in settling in their new environments, I have selected information from 1986 and 1993 interviews of three individuals who reside in the city of Berlin.

Case Study 1: Vladimir (Yugoslav Moslem from Bosnia)

Vladimir came to Germany in 1970 and had been living in West Berlin for 14 years. He was forty-one years old at the time of the first interview. In Yugoslavia he had worked in a coal mine. He was recruited to work in a textile factory in Berlin. At the time of recruitment he was newly married and his wife was pregnant, but he came to Germany alone. His wife Marija arrived in 1972 to be employed in the same factory; two more children have been born since that time. Their hopes of returning home are no longer a reality because of the civil war in the former Yugoslavia. After unification the factory closed, and unemployment became a problem for them for the first time. Fortunately Vladimir was able to find a job in the steel industry and remains employed there today. Their three children are all adults, married with their own families, and they all now reside in Berlin. During the time of the interview, this family lived in a residence in Berlin-Reinickendorf. In 1993, the family lived in private housing in Berlin-Spandau, a section of the city with a smaller concentration of foreign workers. Due to the fact that they are further away from the workplace and thus from their colleagues and friends, they live in relative isolation. Any attempt to develop new friendships with their German neighbors is extremely difficult for them.

Case Study 2: Dmitris (Greek from Valos)

Dmitris came to Germany alone in 1964 although he had also recently married. He was forty-five years old at the time of the first interview and had been living in West Berlin for twenty-two years. He was recruited to Berlin to work for Siemens. His wife remained in Greece, but he had the opportunity to visit on two separate occasions and as a result two daughters were born. Ultimately that marriage ended in divorce, and several years later Dmitris married a German national. They have two children of their own. In 1993 Dmitris was unemployed due to a plant closing and supported his family on unemployment benefits. There was no longer enough money to send back to Greece for his family there. He had no intention of returning to Greece. He resides with his German wife and children in Berlin-Tegel.

Case Study 3: Hasan (Turk from Anatolia)

Hasan had been living in Berlin for twenty-one years at the time of the first interview and was fifty years old. He was recruited to Germany from Turkey in 1965 to work in the nursery industry. Hasan was a farmer in Turkey but left his farm and his family in order to accept work in Hamburg, Germany. His wife had just given birth to their first daughter. Several years later Hasan responded to an offer from a shoe factory to relocate in West Berlin. There he received a better salary and better working conditions. This worker lived alone in Germany until 1973, when he was reunited with his family. He was the sole supporter of his family. All of his six children have married and live in different parts of the city of Berlin. He lives in the borough of Berlin-Wedding.

It is extremely difficult at this point to predict the future of the foreigners who were brought to the country to work but are now no longer needed. Many are close to the age of retirement, so their presence in Germany and in Berlin is not as critical as that of their children who represent the second and third generations. It is quite apparent that many of the decisions that will be made on behalf of these groups lie more or less in the hands of the policymakers in the German government. However, no long-term policies toward foreign nationals in the united Germany are visible on the horizon. The dispute over foreign workers who send for their children and relatives to join them has not yet been resolved; the problems with language and schooling for foreign children remain staggering despite the introduction of various assistance programs. Ghettoization as a result of neighborhood colonies of foreigners has intensified and continuing massive unemployment has led to the increased incidence of preindustrial forms of foreign labor exploitation, so-called *Leiharbeit* (hiring out). As a consequence of the increase in the number of applicants seeking political asylum, the problem of foreigners in the Federal Republic has taken on new dimensions.

By the late 1960s, it became increasingly clear that the attitudes of certain segments of the native German population toward their foreign colleagues was very negative, for example, the rise in right-wing extremists, young neo-nazi groups, and skinheads. Since *Ausländeranwerbestopp* (halt to recruitment of foreigners) in 1973 and most recently since the rising amount of unemployment among German nationals in East Germany, tensions toward foreigners have escalated in many quarters. Since unification, xenophobia has taken on a new magnitude and explosive force. The seriousness of this situation is reflected in the new asylum restrictions that went into effect as of July 1, 1993. The restrictions state that asylum-seekers who come to Germany through neighboring countries or whose countries of origin have been deemed secure under German asylum law will no longer be accepted. The new law also affects ethnic Germans and foreign workers in Germany, but it is primarily intended to reduce the number of foreigners who enter the country to claim asylum. Agency officials widely publicized the fact that immediately after the restrictions went into effect the daily number of those seeking asylum decreased by half ("Fewer Asylum-Seekers" 1993).

Since unification the increase of hostility toward foreigners and attacks on foreigners have certainly been obvious and alarming in many German cities. Even in the city of Berlin, which once had the reputation of accepting strangers, a climate of rejection, even hostility, seems to prevail. To what extent this hostile climate will deepen and expand is difficult to assess. Signs of hostility could already be noted even toward Germans who resettled from the former German Democratic Republic to the west, whose numbers have likewise risen sharply over the last several years. This phenomenon became apparent in West Berlin in the 1989 elections to the Berlin Senate, in which the right-wing radical Republikaner party was able to win several seats for the first time. It is the far right in Germany that is agitating against foreigners and other minority groups. A sizable portion of the general public does not distinguish between *Gastarbeiter*, *Aussiedler*, political refugee, foreign student, etc. In the end they are all *Ausländer* (foreigners), and the xeno-phobic mood is directed equally against all individuals who do not "look" German, in particular those of color.

It has long been a tradition in German history to attempt to prevent the permanent settlement of foreigners and to define and regulate their stay as temporary. But it is now evident that this state of affairs has come to an end. The more than five million foreigners and their families recruited as workers during the past three decades will remain in Germany, no matter what policies are pursued by successive German governments.

As has been the case in many western countries, large numbers of foreigners are often viewed as the "other," as a threat to the majority society. Often overlooked are the opportunities to create a society in which *every* individual involved can be a full participant. Many people, both Germans and non-Germans, had mixed reactions about the redesignation of the city of Berlin as the German capital. It means that Berlin must set an example for the rest of the country. It can begin to play a leading role by demonstrat-ing that the country's capital is an ideal for the whole: unified Germany following the example of Berlin. Reunited Berlin with its "new" kaleido-scope of cultures, a multicultural society in which all groups, individually and collectively, can prosper, may be a testing ground for the future of Germany.

NOTES

1. From Bermel-Rodominsky (1981, 9), my translation.

2. I am presently engaged in the study "Transformation, Identity and Dis-course in a Unified Germany: The Mutual Impact of Foreign Workers and Ger-mans on Language and Society" (forthcoming in 1996).

3. In 1989, a total of some 191,200 foreigners lived in the GDR. The distribu-tion according to the country of origin was as follows: Vietnam 60,100 (31.4% of all foreigners); Poland 51,700 (27.1%); Mozambique 15,500 (8.1%); Soviet Un-ion 14,900 (7.8%); Hungary 13,400 (7.0%); Cuba 8,000 (4.2%); Belgium 4,900 (2.6%); Czechoslovakia 3,200 (1.7%). There were also foreign workers from Yugoslavia (2,100) and from Angola (1,400).

4. For the German-Spanish Recruitment Agreement, concluded on March 29, 1960, see *ANBA* 1960, 269 ff; for the German-Greek Recruitment Agreement of March 30, 1960, see *ANBA* 286 ff; for the Agreement with Turkey, dated October 30, 1961, see *ANBA* 1961, 587. The German-Turkish agreement initially contained a "rotation stipulation" limiting length of stay to two years. However, this clause was revoked effective September 30, 1964. Agreements with Portugal were concluded in March 1964 and with Yugoslavia in October 1968.

5. Source: *Berliner Statistik* June 30, 1991. Numbers are rounded up.

6. A useful collection of the many regulations governing the position of foreigners in Germany is to be found in Weicken et al., *Ausländer in der Bundesrepublik Deutschland* and its regular supplements. The enactment of a new foreigners' law in 1990 has modified these conditions considerably.

7. Unlike the United States' policy of *ius soli*, whereby the child automatically receives U.S. citizenship when born in the United States, Germany's policy is that of *ius parentum*, whereby the children of foreigners born in the Federal Republic obtain their parents' citizenship. The new foreigners' law of 1990 has changed the rules for citizenship; it stipulates the conditions under which children of foreigners have a right to German citizenship (Wilpert 1993, 75).

8. After approximately three months of living in the foreigner housing unit, I was visited by a teenage daughter of one of the families. When the teenager commented to me that *dein Herz klopft mit unser* (your heart beats with ours), it was obvious that my goal to be fully accepted and integrated into the foreign worker community had been achieved.

9. "Uns hat man erzählt, Deutschland ist ein Paradies. Aus den Wasserhähnen fließt Bier, und man bekommt überall für alles Geld: Kindergeld, Arbeitslosengeld, Urlaubsgeld—wurde gesagt, damals. Nur nicht, daß man auch schwer arbeiten muß im Paradies, das hat man nicht gesagt. Auch meine Landsleute wollen immer alles besser darstellen, als es in Wirklichkeit ist. Damit sie als große Menschen und nicht als kleine Arbeiter gesehen werden. Und wir kamen nach Deutschland, und alles war anders." (Böseke 1981, 61).

10. Wallraff's book reminded me of the book *Black Like Me*, written by John Howard Griffin, who, as a white American, took pills to darken the pigmentation of his skin, and traveled to the deep South to experience the racism against blacks in the United States.

REFERENCES

ANBA. Amtliche Nachrichten der Bundesanstalt für Arbeitsvermittlung und Arbeitslosenversicherung. Nuremberg: Bundesanstalt für Arbeitsvermittlung, 1960–1969.

"Ausländer 1989." *Wirtschaft und Statistik* (August 1990): 540–44.

"Ausländer in der DDR." *Wirtschaft und Statistik* (August 1990): 544–45.

Berger, Frank. *Thyssen gegen Wallraff.* Göttingen: Steidl, 1988.

Bericht der Bundesregierung über die Beschäftigung ausländischer Arbeitnehmer in der Bundesrepublik. [Report of the Federal Government on Employment of Foreign Workers in the Federal Republic.] Deutscher Bundestag, December 21, 1962, IV/470, 6.

Berliner Statistik 1989–1993. Berlin: Statistisches Landesamt, 1993.

Bermel-Rodominsky, S. "Ich bin nach Deutschland gekommen." In *Zu Hause in der Fremde*, edited by Christian Schaffernicht. Hamburg: Rowohlt, 1981.

Blackshire-Belay, Carol Aisha. *The Germanic Mosaic: Cultural and Linguistic Diversity in Society.* Westport, CT: Greenwood, 1994.

————. *Language Contact: Verb Morphology in German of Foreign Workers.* Tübingen: Gunter Narr, 1991.

Böseke, Harry. "Deutschland, ein Land voller Wunder." In *Zu Hause in der Fremde*, edited by Christian Schaffernicht, 61–62. Hamburg: Rowohlt Taschenbuch Verlag, 1981.

"Fewer Asylum-Seekers in June, but More Overall in 1993. New Asylum Restrictions Have an Effect." *The Week in Germany.* New York: German Information Center, July 16, 1993.

Griffin, John Howard. *Black Like Me.* Boston: Houghton Mifflin, 1961.

Hussain, Saleh. "Die Situation der Ausländer vor der Wende (1989–1990)." In *Ausländer in der DDR*, 26–32. Berlin: Ausländerbeauftragte des Senats, 1991.

"Official Tolerance Seen as Abetting German Violence." *New York Times*, December 31, 1992, 3.

Stach, Andrzej Waldemar. "Ausländer in der DDR: Ein Rückblick." In *Ausländer in der DDR*, 4–25. Berlin: Ausländerbeauftragte des Senats, 1991.

Statistisches Jahrbuch der Deutschen Demokratischen Republik. Berlin: Staatsverlag der DDR, 1989.

Wallraff, Günter. *Ganz Unten.* Cologne: Kiepenheuer & Witsch, 1985.

Weicken, H. *Ausländer in der Bundesrepublik Deutschland.* Frankfurt: Verlag für Wirschaft und Verwaltung, 1969.

Wilpert, Czarina. "Ideological and Institutional Foundations of Racism in the Federal Republic of Germany." In *Racism and Migration in Western Europe*, edited by John Solomos and John Wrench, 67–81. Oxford/Providence: Berg, 1993.

5

Art and Money: Cultural Innovations within the Urban Setting of Prenzlauer Berg

Friederike Eigler

The relatively young history of the Prenzlauer Berg district is marked by rapid urban development, an increasingly diverse population and, more recently, by a thriving local culture, the so-called *Kiezkultur*. Daniela Dahn, a writer from the GDR, has been most successful in capturing the local culture and everyday life in Prenzlauer Berg in the pre-*Wende* era of the mid-1980s. Today, Dahn's portrayal of Prenzlauer Berg in *Kunst und Kohle*[1] reminds us of a multifaceted culture in an East Berlin neighborhood that existed despite the GDR's attempts to regulate and control its cultural institutions. This local culture was by no means limited to the relatively small group of writers and intellectuals who made headlines in Western newspapers in the winter of 1991–92 when Wolf Biermann revealed the *Stasi*-activities of the poet Sascha Anderson, a leading figure of Prenzlauer Berg's literary avant-garde.

In retrospect, one can read *Kunst und Kohle* as documenting a moment of historical transition in a local Berlin neighborhood: it displays the fissures and cracks of the socialist system in the GDR without yet indicating any of the new perspectives or major changes that Gorbachev's *perestroika* would encourage and that, in the late eighties, would lead to the emergence of a broad-based citizens' movement and, ultimately, to the collapse of the GDR.

Since the unification of Germany, Prenzlauer Berg has faced more severe economic, social, and urban problems than other parts of Berlin and former East Germany. Yet its rich local culture offers unique opportunities that can help to combat the general disorientation and the ensuing destructive and xenophobic tendencies that we have witnessed since 1990. While people involved in local cultural activities agree that Prenzlauer Berg's *Kiezkultur* can play a positive role amid the social and economic upheavals in the post-unification era (cf. Tebbe 1990), the very existence of many cultural institutions and projects depends on the overall economic situation and on the priorities of the city council.

This chapter assesses the opportunities some cultural projects in Prenzlauer Berg offer and the challenges that they face. The first part of the chapter serves as a preface to the discussion of the cultural innovations in that it presents a brief urban history of Prenzlauer Berg. This historical perspective illuminates the particular cultural and social identity of the district and thus helps to clarify the current situation. Later in the chapter, I discuss recent developments in Prenzlauer Berg against the backdrop of Dahn's portrayal of Prenzlauer Berg in the preunification era.

THE URBAN SETTING OF PRENZLAUER BERG

The (in)famous Berlin *Hinterhöfe* are most frequently found in the Berlin districts of Kreuzberg and Prenzlauer Berg; these paved backyards shape the particular urban atmosphere of both districts and are testimony to the extremely dense construction in these neighborhoods. It is therefore hard to imagine that until well into the nineteenth century, the somewhat elevated Prenzlauer Berg was a popular location for windmills.[2] Until the mid 1800s, the area was located outside the city limits of Berlin. Used as farmland, it provided produce for the city population. Industrialization and the ensuing influx of the rural population into the city caused Berlin to grow in the early nineteenth century beyond its city limits, but Prenzlauer Berg remained almost entirely undeveloped until the 1860s. Thus its urbanization arose comparatively late in Berlin's 750-year history.

In an 1861 census, the department for hygiene initiated a survey of living conditions in the inner city of Berlin. The survey revealed substandard living conditions (compared to other large cities like Vienna or London).[3] Consequently, the police department put James Hobrecht, an engineer, in charge of planning the development of the previously rural area of Prenzlauer Berg. Since the blueprint for development was based on the size of the fields in this area, most of today's streets coincide with the delineation of the rural properties.

The most extensive development of Prenzlauer Berg took place in the 1870s and 1890s, during the so-called *Gründerjahre* (founding era). Prussia's war against France and the ensuing unification of Germany under Bismarck in 1871 was followed by an era of economic prosperity. Because of the city's steadily increasing population, urban developers added more and more buildings to the relatively small district of Prenzlauer Berg. The rising property value encouraged the construction of densely built rental units and the development of even those areas that the original blueprint had preserved for squares and parks. This resulted in a doubling and tripling of tenant houses that were accessible only through small paved courtyards, the Berlin *Hinterhöfe* (there are a total of 3,000 *Hinterhöfe* in Prenzlauer Berg). During the harsh recession in the 1920s, many of the larger apartments were divided and rented out to two different parties.[4] This defeated the original plan to ensure some social mix within the neighborhood by combining larger units in the front house (the *Vorderhaus*, often built with nicely decorated exterior walls) with smaller units in the modestly built houses in the back (the *Hinterhaus*). Generally speaking, the rapid urban construction took place with little consideration of social needs or of overall city planning.

THE SOCIALIST ERA (1949–1990)

The emergence of East Berlin's first citizens' group sixty years later serves as a postscript to the urban history of Prenzlauer Berg and as an example of how the socialist bureaucracy exacerbated existing urban planning problems. In 1981, a number of Prenzlauer Berg residents came together to promote the creation of a much-needed small park and playground in one of the few unused squares. The local group eventually succeeded despite obstacles from two rather different camps: the city administration on the one hand and a group of teenagers and punks on the other. (The punks lost their hangout place due to the park and consequently tried to block and partially destroy the park project.) Among the local activists who had promoted the park project was a woman who experienced a curious encounter shortly after the park had been completed and before one of the local elections: she witnessed a number of city workers uprooting the plants in the park, claiming that they were told to build a playground instead. The woman protested and pointed out the playground—recently completed by the citizens' group—just around the corner. When the men told her that a local resident had put in a request to the city for a playground, she realized that she had personally made that request ten years earlier. But only after fighting her way through the city administration and ascertaining the appropriate instruction did the workers eventually stop dismantling the park (Dahn 1987, 67–74). This account seems symptomatic of more general problems concerning urban planning in the GDR. But the modest and localized goals of the first citizens' group in the history of East Berlin also highlight the very different political and social situation in the early eighties when compared with the large-scale protest movements of the late eighties.

In many respects Prenzlauer Berg was the Eastern counterpart to the West Berlin district of Kreuzberg. After World War II, Prenzlauer Berg came under Soviet control and ultimately part of East Berlin, the capital of the GDR; Kreuzberg became part of West Berlin and, after 1961, was cut off from the historical city center by the Berlin Wall. Due to the relatively little damage Kreuzberg and Prenzlauer Berg had incurred in the World War II Allied bombardment of the Nazi capital Berlin,[5] most of the old buildings in both districts remained; few renovations and modernization were done in the postwar era. Consequently, rents stayed relatively low and both districts continued to attract mostly low-income people.

Traditionally, the majority of residents in these neighborhoods were blue-collar workers. During the early 1900s, the working class district of Prenzlauer Berg was Berlin's most overcrowded area—with an average of 300 people per hectare (Dahn 1987, 40). Today, this figure has dropped by approximately 50 percent, but Prenzlauer Berg and Kreuzberg continue to be the two most densely populated sections of Berlin.[6] During the last decades, the number of older long-time residents and the influx of foreign workers has been growing (the latter applies especially to the large number of Turkish residents in Kreuzberg). Low rental costs and vacant buildings that were used for various cultural and social projects also attracted an increasing number of young people including students, artists, dropouts, and the unemployed. The social makeup of these districts resulted in a thriving local culture. Similar to Kreuzberg, during the 1970s and 1980s, Prenzlauer Berg became a neighborhood with a high concentration of young painters, writers, musicians, and artists, many of whom were also involved in social or political activities.

Due to general neglect and lack of repairs since World War II, Prenzlauer Berg has more severe building structure problems and dated sanitary installations than Kreuzberg. Since the fifties and well into the seventies, the East Berlin administration seriously considered tearing down large parts of Prenzlauer Berg. Although the city never acted on this radical plan, it continued to do little to stop the steady deterioration of the neighborhood. Several new apartment complexes and public housing projects were built on the outskirts of Prenzlauer Berg.[7] But, for the most part, they lack the social and cultural infrastructure which, in the historic part of Prenzlauer Berg, facilitated the integration of social, cultural, and commercial life (Guhr 1991, 24).

An example of the living conditions of two longtime residents in the historic part of Prenzlauer Berg may help to explain the reasons for the large-scale deterioration of building structures. An old couple who had lived in the same building since 1926 initially paid forty-two marks a month for rent on a two-bedroom apartment. The rent was raised to forty-nine marks by 1939, the year World War II began, and more than four decades later they were still paying the same amount.[8] This minuscule—from a Western perspective—rent came at the expense of poor living conditions. The building in which the old couple had lived for sixty years had aged with them: similar to many houses in Prenzlauer Berg, the exterior and the staircase were in urgent need of repair and the sanitation facilities were outdated.[9] The socialist government subsidized housing heavily. But the only way to keep rents so extremely low was to keep costs for repairs and general upkeep to an absolute minimum. It seems that the GDR pursued this policy on a large scale, not only in the area of construction and housing but in areas of industrial modernization and the general infrastructure as well. Mismanagement of this kind ultimately contributed to the GDR's economic collapse.

URBAN TRANSFORMATIONS SINCE UNIFICATION

The districts of Prenzlauer Berg and Kreuzberg were separated by the Berlin Wall from 1961 until 1989. While both districts were centrally located before the division of the city (with Prenzlauer Berg just north of Berlin *Mitte* and Kreuzberg just south), during the postwar era, they became literally and figuratively "marginal" districts in their respective parts of the city. In fact numerous streets in both districts turned into dead ends, leading up to and ending at the Berlin Wall. The unification of East and West Berlin has reconnected the two districts to the historical and commercial centers of Berlin.[10] Yet the multiple effects of the marginalization of Kreuzberg and Prenzlauer Berg cannot be undone merely by reopening streets and public transportation.

Prenzlauer Berg continues to face severe problems including high unemployment, rising rental costs, and generally run-down tenant houses. In many ways, the situation in Prenzlauer Berg is a microcosm of the challenges that still exist in large parts of the former East Germany. Since unification some buildings in Prenzlauer Berg have been renovated, mostly with public funds from the city. In light of the severe housing shortage in Berlin, funds were primarily channeled into the redevelopment and modernization of damaged vacant houses (*Vorbereitende Untersuchung*, 6).

In the summer of 1992, the Berlin city council appointed independent advisory committees to assess the need for redevelopment plans in 39 residential areas, six of them located in the district of Prenzlauer Berg. The city council decided to put two of the Prenzlauer Berg areas on its priority list, among them the residential area surrounding the Kollwitzplatz which includes a total of 6,500 rental units. Kollwitzplatz is one of the few larger squares in the center of Prenzlauer Berg and is named after the artist Käthe Kollwitz who lived there for over fifty years.[11] The square is one of the liveliest in the area and has a number of coffee houses, bars, art galleries, and other artistic projects that are run by locals. The goals of these redevelopment plans are to improve living conditions and to revitalize the area's dire commercial life while keeping the social makeup of the area alive, that is, avoiding the displacement of its residents. Considering the high unemployment rate, rising rental costs, and the unclear property status of many buildings in Prenzlauer Berg,[12] this is going to be a most difficult task.

CULTURAL TRADITIONS

Amid major political, economic, and social upheaval, the existence and continued public support of a thriving local culture in Prenzlauer Berg has assumed new significance. The new political and economic structures that came with the unification of Germany had dramatic effects on the cultural life in the five new states (Ohlau 1993, 193–96). The quickly rising rental costs meant the end of many local projects and semi-private studios, galleries, etc. Furthermore, the complete reorganization and streamlining of most state-run cultural institutions meant the loss of an entire infrastructure and its subsidies. Some institutions have "survived" unification, albeit in a changed form, while several new cultural projects have emerged in Prenzlauer Berg since 1989.

A good example of continuity in Prenzlauer Berg's local culture is *Jugendklub Erich Franz*. Until 1990, the "Franz Klub," located in the former Schultheiß brewery, was the largest and most popular youth club in Prenzlauer Berg.[13] While GDR youth clubs served an important social function for teenagers, they also helped to keep young people in check. Teenagers who were unwilling to conform with the political norms were often excluded from the state-run youth clubs. In *Kunst und Kohle*, Dahn mentions her encounter with two teenage punks who were not permitted into Prenzlauer Berg's "Franz Klub." These teenagers appear alienated in a society that left little room for individual development. They express, for instance, their contempt for the hypocrisy of a state that prevented them from individually acknowledging the victims of fascism in the concentration camp Sachsenhausen on May 8 because antifascism was part of the official state doctrines.[14] At first sight, it seems ironic that these two punks are children of accomplished socialists. Yet their alienation was perhaps symptomatic of the state of the country in the mid 1980s: while the punks' "anti-establishment" attitude is somewhat naive and immature, their family background may have put them in a good position to assess the discrepancies between state ideology and everyday life in the GDR.

Since 1989, many publicly funded youth clubs have undergone considerable change or have been closed. A number of full-time positions have been cut and those employees who remain had to undergo retraining from politically oriented educators to social workers (Pißarek 1993, 387). The popularity of the Franz Klub and its reorganization have contributed to the fact that it is one of the youth clubs to have survived unification (Rau 1993, 183). The integration of the Franz Klub into the newly founded cultural center Kulturbrauerei exemplifies a successful transition from the pre-Wende to the post-Wende era. The club continues to attract a lot of young people by offering frequent live concerts (Jazz, Blues, Classical Music), music workshops, and other cultural events. The Franz Klub receives no city funds but supports itself through ticket-sales for music events. Despite or perhaps because of its changed outlook, the Franz Klub thus provides some cultural and social continuity for the local youth—which is of particular importance considering the widespread discontent and social unrest among teenagers.

The history of the Prenzlauer Berg's theater *Mime Centrum Berlin* founded more than thirty years ago illustrates some of the obstacles that local cultural projects faced in the GDR. During the formalism debate in the 1950s, representatives of the official party line attacked any kind of avant-garde art, including mime, as bourgeois, decadent, and thus "counter-revolutionary." Only after the art and architecture of the Bauhaus had been "rehabilitated" in 1961 did some individual initiatives succeed in establishing artistic projects like the mime theater in Prenzlauer Berg. Initially, the mime group performed in vacant factory rooms that they rented and renovated at their own expense. Shortly afterward, the *Kreiskulturhaus*, the state-run local cultural agency, started subsidizing and regulating the performances of the mime group (Dahn 1987, 15). The example of the mime theater demonstrates that on the one hand private initiatives could create some space for local cultural projects and activities, but that on the other hand those initiatives could be maintained in most cases only at the expense of making compromises with the state authorities.

Until 1989, the mime theater was one of only seven semi-independent art projects in Prenzlauer Berg. Since unification, approximately 45 independent artistic groups emerged, but many of them lack affordable rental space and thus struggle for their existence (Pißarek 1993, 389). Due to its long and successful history and its uniqueness in the city of Berlin, the mime theater not only survived unification but has expanded to the more comprehensive "Mime Centrum Berlin." The city of Berlin provides funds for particular projects but does not subsidize the center on a regular basis. Today, the Mime Centrum functions as a professional art school for actors and directors; it also includes a center for information, communication, and documentation that organizes seminars, workshops, and conferences related to mime theater (Tebbe 1990, 217).

In *Kunst und Kohle*, Dahn keeps a critical and sometimes ironic distance to the Prenzlauer Berg literary avant-garde, to the "dropout" attitude of a group of writers and artists she encountered there. Some of them invited her to a privately organized art exhibit and reading that seemed to her accessible only to a select group of insiders. Dahn admits that she could not relate to their artistic "games" seemingly detached from any social reality. She quotes a line from a poem, *"Berührung ist nur eine Randerscheinung"* ("contact is merely a marginal event") and reads this phrase as describing the artists' lack of contact with society (Dahn 1987, 227).

Dahn's skepticism foreshadows the criticism of the artistic circles in Prenzlauer Berg in the aftermath of the *Stasi*-scandal involving two of this group's leading representatives in 1991–92. Both Dahn's critical remarks and the more recent wholesale dismissal of the Prenzlauer Berg artists' circle as elitists and state collaborators prevent a more complex assessment of the flaws and achievements of these artistic groups.[15] For instance, Dahn does not mention or is unaware of the fact that the line she quotes ("Berührung ist nur eine Randerscheinung") is also the title of an impressive anthology published by the East German poets Elke Erb and Sascha Anderson in 1985 in the West. This anthology includes contributions by approximately thirty mostly younger writers who, because of their "deviant" attitudes concerning art and politics, were generally excluded from the GDR's official cultural life.

Many of these writers and artists lived in Prenzlauer Berg, including the editors Anderson and Erb. They were part of the alternative cultural groups that emerged in numerous East German cities during the late 1970s. Most of them rejected what they perceived as politically and socially determined art (including officially sanctioned and dissidents' art). Instead, they sought to withdraw from society and to focus entirely on the aesthetic and linguistic dimensions of art (Emmerich 1989, 422–38; Thulin 1990). A number of anthologies published since unification provide a cross-section of literary and theoretical texts written in the 1980s that for the most part differ significantly from the GDR literature as most of us in the West knew it until 1989.[16]

Contrary to their own political and artistic stances, at least some of these artists worked as informers for the East German state police (*Stasi*). Indeed, two of the "counterculture's" main representatives, Sascha Anderson and Rainer Schedlinski, had—for different reasons and to different degrees— informed the *Stasi* on many of their friends and fellow artists (cf. Biermann 1991; Fuchs 1991). Considering their ability to conform to the political structures of the GDR, it perhaps does not come as a surprise that Anderson and Schedlinski were among the quickest to adapt to the new conditions of a free-market society. In 1990, they opened a private publishing company in Prenzlauer Berg, called "Galrev"—the reversal of *Verlag* (publishing house). They have published not only works by local writers and artists but also contemporary British and American literature. Part of this small business is a café in the Lychener Straße frequented by local artists. So far this private enterprise has survived despite the public scandal following the discovery of the long-term *Stasi*-activities of the "entrepreneurs" Anderson and Schedlinski.

Considering the media attention given to Schedlinski and Anderson, it is important to note that there were many artists in the Prenzlauer Berg avant-garde circle who did not work for the *Stasi*; in fact several writers learned that they had been the "objects" of Anderson's and Schedlinski's activities as informers. While Schedlinski and Anderson have shown little interest in entering a debate about their involvement with the *Stasi*, other writers and artists—Peter Böthig, Kurt Drawert, Elke Erb, Jan Faktor, Uwe Kolbe, Klaus Michael, and Gabriele Stötzer, among others—have begun to engage in a long-overdue internal debate about issues of complicity and resistance within the socialist society (Böthig 1993).

NEW CULTURAL PROJECTS

The dramatic changes since unification also made room for new ideas and new projects, some of which had existed as blueprints but could not be realized within the rather rigid structures of the GDR. Four of these projects deserve discussion in more detail: *Frauengewerbezentrum*, a commercial complex run by and for women; *EWA*, a women's center offering cultural and educational programs and counseling services; *Kulturbrauerei*, an association of artistic and cultural groups working in the former Schultheiß brewery; and *Pfefferwerk*, a loose organization representing eighty different cultural and social projects that unsuccessfully tried to obtain a long-term lease of another former brewery in Prenzlauer Berg.[17]

These four projects have some striking features in common: in different ways, they all integrate cultural activities with local social and commercial concerns. Thus these multi-functional projects play an essential role in improving the current situation in Prenzlauer Berg, which continues to be economically and socially unstable (Rau 1993, 188–89). Although all of these projects initially require the support of public funds, they are—with the exception of the women's center—conceived in such a way as to create an internal system of subsidies that will lead to self-sufficiency.

The first two projects serve quite different functions, but they are both predominantly designed by and for women. In each case, the planning phase started before the unification of Germany and thus involved mainly women from East Berlin. Both projects were originally designed to respond to the professional, social, and cultural needs of women in general, but they have assumed a particularly important role given the well-documented fact that women in the East have been affected dispro-portionately by the adverse social and economic effects of unification.[18] Both projects respond to the current situation by providing a variety of social services and cultural programs and by creating at least some additional job opportunities for women.

Frauengewerbezentrum WeiberWirtschaft

Traditionally, *Weiberwirtschaft* is used as a pejorative term to describe an all-female household. In this instance, women have reclaimed the phrase to describe a business complex (second meaning of *Wirtschaft*) run by and catering predominantly to women. *WeiberWirtschaft* is a coopera-tive founded in 1987, that is, two years before the opening of the Berlin Wall, and is currently supported by 500 investors. After long negotiations with the *Treuhandanstalt*[19] and the procurement of considerable financial support from the city, *WeiberWirtschaft* managed to purchase a building complex in Prenzlauer Berg that previously housed the largest cosmetics factory in the former GDR. Major renovations were completed by 1994; approximately 100 small businesses, most of them run by women, re-ceived access to relatively low-cost office space in the building complex. The businesses will include a midwife center, a fitness center, a variety of stores, law offices, and a consulting firm for women in business (*Frauenunternehmensberatung*). Ironically, only 10% of these businesses are run by women from the East, presumably because many women in the

East simply cannot afford the start-up costs under present conditions (*Reine Frauensache*).

EWA Women's Center

EWA is an acronym for *Erster Weiblicher Aufbruch* (First Female Departure) and is phonetically reminiscent of the female name "Eva." This name captures the general goal of this center, namely, to encourage and enable women to go beyond the limits society has traditionally set for them. *EWA* assists women in the search for new avenues in the social, professional, and cultural realms (*EWA e. V. Infoblatt*). *EWA*'s beginnings go back to the brief time between the opening of the Wall in November 1989 and the elections in March 1990, followed by the unification of Germany in October of the same year. A number of women from the local citizens' group *Neues Forum* in Prenzlauer Berg founded *EWA* in December of 1989 with the intention of creating a politically oriented center for women. They received support from the East German interim government of Hans Modrow and from the advisory "round table" (*Runder Tisch*) that represented a variety of citizens' groups. In April 1990, *EWA* was thus able to open the first women's center in East Berlin. It is housed in buildings previously occupied by a "*Stasi*-emergency center" (*Bereitschaftszentrale*) in Prenzlauer Allee.

Since 1991, *EWA* has been fully funded by an agency of the unified Berlin Senate administration (*Senatsverwaltung für Frauen und Arbeit*). With these public funds *EWA* employs a full-time staff of four women to run the center and also employs a number of instructors and counselors with temporary or part-time contracts. *EWA* attempts to cooperate with women's groups in the Western part of Berlin—which may contribute to improving the strained relationships between feminist groups in the East and the West. The regular services and courses *EWA* offers, however, clearly serve the educational, cultural, and social needs of women in the local neighborhood of Prenzlauer Berg. The courses include foreign language classes (most prominently English), computer classes, and a variety of classes in crafts, sports, and self-defense. Free-of-charge services include psychological, legal, and educational counseling. In addition to these services, the center offers a variety of round tables and cultural events, ranging from movie showings to photo exhibits. A small library (*Hex-Libris*) includes practical reference books and journals, and the center is in the process of building a collection focusing on the women's role in the forty-year history of the GDR. While many of these services can be found in women's centers elsewhere in Germany, *EWA* differs from similar centers in the West in that it offers a number of activities for women with children, including child-care services.[20]

Kulturbrauerei

The *Kulturbrauerei GmbH* (a semi-private corporation) represents five different cultural organizations that started operating in the vacant buildings of the former Schultheiß brewery shortly after the opening of the Wall. Among these organizations are the popular youth and music club *Franz Klub* (which I discussed earlier), a theater company working with handicapped children, and a group of artists who run small exhibits. *Kulturbrauerei* managed to negotiate special conditions with the *Treuhandanstalt*: any future buyer will have to pay for the urgently-needed renovations and will have to guarantee low rents to approximately one third of the complex used by the nonprofit organizations of the *Kulturbrauerei*. While it is laudable that the *Treuhand*—which drew strong criticism for transactions that ignored human and social concerns—agreed to many of the *Kulturbrauerei*'s requests, this is only the first step toward assuring its future existence. In 1993, for instance, a French real estate corporation that in the previous year had shown serious interest in purchasing the complex withdrew its offer, arguing that the high cost of renovations would not be outweighed by the anticipated profit (reduced by the rent-control agreement for part of the complex). Although new takeover bids are coming in, the favorable conditions negotiated with the *Treuhand* ironically have complicated the sale of the large building complex and have thereby threatened the future existence of the organizations located in the *Kulturbrauerei*.

Pfefferwerk

Pfefferwerk e.V. is a nonprofit organization representing eighty different groups that were interested in using the large building complex of another former brewery, Pfefferberg, named after its first owner Pfeffer. *Pfefferwerk e.V.* was founded in 1990 and emerged from a number of social and cultural groups that had been active since the early 1980s (*Pfefferwerk-Broschüre*). While the Kulturbrauerei's goal is to make possible "cultural and artistic work through its ties to powerful investors" (Rau 1993, 188), *Pfefferwerk* aimed at integrating a number of commercial enterprises in the overall user-plan for the building complex. Most specifically, the available space was supposed to be used by social, cultural, and commercial projects in equal parts, with the understanding that the latter would help to subsidize the former by allowing them to pay lower rents.

The implementation of this plan eventually failed due to the complicated status of ownership of the brewery and due to the lack of support by the city.[21] Since 1990, a number of groups represented by *Pfefferwerk* had started to work in the complex even though many of the buildings were in a state of disrepair. The city had granted these groups temporary rental contracts, but the buildings continued to deteriorate over the two years of negotiations. Despite continued efforts by *Pfefferwerk* to come to an agreement with the city council, in October 1993 the city declined to renew the rental contract, effectively terminating the entire *Pfefferwerk* project. While the threat to the *Kulturbrauerei*'s future will most likely subside with the assistance of state and city agencies, the lack of support by the city has jeopardized the future of *Pfefferwerk*. The contrasting prospects of the two multi-functional new projects in Prenzlauer Berg, which have been described as *Wendekinder* (offspring of the *Wende*), exemplify the potentials and the problems of local cultural institutions since the unification of Germany.

The situation in Prenzlauer Berg demonstrates the difficult balancing act between the demands of a free market system on the one hand and government intervention in the interest of social equity and cultural diversity on the other. Considering the harsher economic realities of the 1990s that some see as the crisis of the social market system (*soziale Marktwirtschaft*) affecting all Western democracies, cultural projects such as the *Kulturbrauerei* and *WeiberWirtschaft* deserve special attention: the idea of combining social, cultural, and commercial interests by creating an internal system of subsidies could serve as a new model for a viable local culture. Prenzlauer Berg thus illustrates the cultural potentials of the unified city of Berlin beyond the limelight of the new German capital and its heavily subsidized "high culture" or *Repräsentationskultur*.

NOTES

I would like to thank Almut Finck, Matthias Rau, Birgit Schneider, and Joyce Mushaben for their assistance in providing information and documentation about Prenzlauer Berg and Berlin.

1. Daniela Dahn's book *Prenzlauer Berg-Tour* was published in 1987 in East Germany; in the same year, it appeared in the West as *Kunst und Kohle: Die 'Szene' am Prenzlauer Berg*.

2. From the mid 1700s to the mid 1800s approximately thirty windmills were built in this area as part of corn-producing farms (Guhr 1991, 14).

3. In Berlin, almost 25 percent of the half-million inhabitants lived in one-room apartments occupied by five to ten people each; 10 percent lived permanently in basement units.

4. When in 1920 the metropolitan area of Greater Berlin was created by incorporating numerous adjacent townships, Prenzlauer Berg became the twenty-first administrative district. Thereafter, Berlin's total population reached its all-time high of more than 4 million, and the city became one of the most densely populated in the world.

5. In Kreuzberg and Prenzlauer Berg only approximately 10 percent of all houses were destroyed and 7 percent were badly damaged.

6. Kreuzberg has the highest density—150 people per hectare—compared to 138 in Prenzlauer Berg. The total number of residents in Kreuzberg is 156,600; 145,700 live in Prenzlauer Berg. The total population of Berlin is 3,460,300. See *Einwohnerregister* of the city of Berlin, June 1993.

7. Two new high-rise complexes were built: one in the 1970s along the area bordering Weißensee in the North-East of Prenzlauer Berg; and another in the early 1980s next to Thälmann Park, at the site of a previous energy plant. In 1992, major environmental damages were discovered in the residential area of Thälmann Park. The soil and groundwater are heavily contaminated from the shutdown and incomplete removal of the energy plant in 1981. The only immediate measure city officials could take was the closure of a playground located above the former benzol installation of the plant. The exact assessment of the contamination and the clean-up procedures themselves are costly; see *Umweltschutzbericht*.

8. In 1985, the official exchange rate for forty-nine marks was approximately thirty dollars; the real buying power was considerably lower.

9. Like many apartment buildings in Prenzlauer Berg and in Kreuzberg, their apartment did not have a bathroom, and the toilet was located outside the apartment in the hallway. Furthermore, many apartments did not have a central heating system; instead, they were equipped with tiled stoves that were heated with coal stored in the basements.

10. While most streets were reconnected immediately following the events of November 1989, it took another four years until several Berlin metro lines were reopened and expanded: subway line U 2 now provides direct access from the East Berlin neighborhoods Pankow and Prenzlauer Berg to Potsdamer Platz (previously located in the no-man's-land of the border area) and to the districts Tiergarten and Charlottenburg in the Western part of Berlin. Subway line U 1 was altered and extended, and now connects Kreuzberg and Dahlem.

11. In her book *Kunst und Kohle*, Dahn incorporates excerpts from Käthe Kollwitz's diaries which comment on the quirks and hardships of everyday life in Prenzlauer Berg during the Weimar Republic; see Dahn 1987, 77–95.

12. A major obstacle to the commercial revitalization of Prenzlauer Berg (and other parts of former East Germany) resulted from the 1990 unification treaty, which left the status of property rights concerning many buildings unclear. The

complex regulations governing property rights favor return of property to private owners over compensation. The regulations have considerably hindered investment and the general economic recovery of the five new states; see *Vorbereitende Untersuchung* 6.

13. Until 1989, approximately ten youth clubs existed in the neighborhood of Prenzlauer Berg. Even for GDR standards, this was a large number of clubs for a relatively small area.

14. For a critical analysis of the GDR's instrumentalization of antifascism, see Eigler and Pfeiffer 1993, 23–41.

15. For a more detailed discussion of the relationship between art and politics in the Prenzlauer Berg circle, see the volume edited by Peter Böthig and Klaus Michael and my own two articles on the subject.

16. See the anthologies *Abriß der Ariadnefabrik* by Koziol/Schedlinski and *Vogel oder Käfig sein* by Michael/Wohlfahrt.

17. The only large commercial enterprises that were established in Prenzlauer Berg in the second half of the nineteenth century were a number of breweries. Since 1989, the large building complexes of these breweries have assumed an unforeseen role in the restructuring of Prenzlauer Berg's local culture.

18. Unemployment rates for women are twice as high as for men, and the prospects for re-employment are far smaller for women (see *Arbeitsmarktdaten*). Furthermore, the drastic reduction of affordable child-care facilities has created a vicious cycle especially for single mothers.

19. *Treuhandanstalt* was the state trust agency, acting under the responsibility of the Federal Ministry of Finance; it was in charge of privatizing public property and real estate previously owned by the socialist state.

20. Another recently founded organization in Prenzlauer Berg, *Netzwerk*, is entirely concerned with children's needs. It functions as a "clearinghouse" for local groups, projects, and events concerning children in Prenzlauer Berg, and sees its primary role in facilitating contacts, information, and cooperation among a variety of educational and cultural organizations and groups working with children. *Netzwerk* has contributed, for instance, to the creation of an adventure playground, a children's farm (in the area where the Wall used to be), and a children's museum, as well as to the organization of special events for children (Tebbe 1990, 213–14).

21. The unification treaty determined that the large building complex should belong jointly to the city of Berlin and the federal government. While the federal government was willing to sell its "half" to the city, the two parties were unable to reach an agreement about an adequate compensation for the property value.

REFERENCES

Anderson, Sascha, and Elke Erb, eds. *Berührung ist nur eine Randerscheinung*. Cologne: Kiepenheuer & Witsch, 1985.

1102   Berlin in Focus

1—————. Interview with Iris Radisch: "Das ist nicht so einfach." *Die Zeit*, November 1, 1991, 9.

Arbeitsmarktdaten in den neuen Bundesländern. DGB Bundesvorstand, Abteilung Frauen. May 1992.

Biermann, Wolf. "Über Georg Büchner: Der Lichtblick im gräßlichen Fatalismus der Geschichte." *Die Zeit*, October 25, 1991, 6–7.

Böthig, Peter, and Klaus Michael, eds. *MachtSpiele: Literatur und Staatssicherheit im Fokus Prenzlauer Berg.* Leipzig: Reclam, 1993.

Dahn, Daniela. *Kunst und Kohle: Die "Szene" am Prenzlauer Berg.* Berlin: Luchterhand, 1987. (*Prenzlauer Berg-Tour.* Halle, Leipzig: Mitteldeutscher Verlag, 1987).

Eigler, Friederike, and Peter Pfeiffer, eds. *Cultural Transformations in the New Germany: American and German Perspectives.* Columbia, S.C.: Camden House, 1993.

—————. "At the Margins of East Berlin's 'Counter Culture': Elke Erb's *Winkelzüge* and Gabriele Stötzer Kachold's *zügel los.*" *Women in German Yearbook* 9 (1993): 145–61.

Emmerich, Wolfgang. *Kleine Literaturgeschichte der DDR: 1945–1988.* Frankfurt am Main: Luchterhand, 1989.

EWA e.V. "Infoblatt." [Leaflet of the *EWA* women's center.] 1993.

Fuchs, Jürgen. "Landschaften der Lüge" [series of articles]. *Der Spiegel*, November 19 through December 23, 1991.

"Das Ganze ist mehr als die Summe seiner Teile." *VorOrt* [local paper in Prenzlauer Berg] 5 (1993).

Gaserow, Vera. "Reine Frauensache." *Die Zeit*, August 12, 1993, 12.

Gerhard, Ute. "German Women and the Social Costs of Unification." *German Politics and Society* 24–25 (1991–92): 16–33.

Guhr, Daniela (with the assistance of Thomas Schneider and Günter Wehner). *Berlin—Prenzlauer Berg: Straßen und Plätze. Mit der Geschichte leben.* Berlin: Edition Hentrich, 1991. [Catalogue of a local exhibit.]

Koziol, Andreas, and Rainer Schedlinski, eds. *Abriß der Ariadnefabrik.* Berlin: Galrev, 1990.

Liebmann, Irena. *Berliner Mietshaus. Begegnungen und Gespräche.* Halle, Leipzig: Mitteldeutscher Verlag, 1982.

Michael, Klaus, and Thomas Wohlfahrt, eds. *Vogel oder Käfig sein. Kunst und Literatur aus unabhängigen Zeitschriften in der DDR 1979–1989.* Berlin: Galrev, 1992.

Ohlau, Jürgen. "Challenges for Cultural Politics in the New Germany: The Example of Saxony." In Eigler and Pfeiffer, *Cultural Transformations*, 191–200.

Pfefferwerk-Broschüre. 1992. [Promotion material.]

Pißarek, Antje. "Stadtkultur und Kulturarbeit im Prenzlauer Berg." *MKF. Mitteilungen aus der kulturwissenschaftlichen Forschung* 32 (1993): 382–93. [Special issue on "Kultur in Deutschlands Osten."]

Rau, Matthais. "New Models of Local Cultural Projects: The Example of Pren-
    zlauer Berg." In Eigler and Pfeiffer, *Cultural Transformations*, 180–90.
Schedlinski, Rainer. "Die Unzuständigkeit der Macht." *Neue deutsche Literatur* 6
    (1992): 75–105.
Speicher, Stephan. "Ende der Nachkriegszeit. Berlin beginnt mit der Stadt-
    sanierung am Prenzlauer Berg." *Frankfurter Allgemeine Zeitung*, Sep-
    tember 6, 1993.
Tebbe, Krista, ed. *Kreuzberg—Prenzlauer Berg: Annähernd alles über Kultur.*
    Berlin: Kunstamt Kreuzberg, 1990.
Thulin, Michael. "Sprache und Sprachkritik. Die Literatur des Prenzlauer Bergs in
    Berlin/DDR." *Die andere Sprache. Neue DDR-Literatur der 80er Jahre.*
    Munich: text + kritik, 1990.
"Umweltbericht '92." *VorOrt* [local paper in Prenzlauer Berg] 6 (1993).
Vorbereitende Untersuchung: "Berlin-Prenzlauer Berg." Senat der Stadt Berlin:
    S.T.E.R.N., 1992.

6

The Woman and the Camera—Walking in Berlin: Observations on Walter Ruttmann, Verena Stefan, and Helke Sander

Anke Gleber

Charting the course of modernity involves tracing the steps of the flaneur as he appears in Heine's *Briefe aus Berlin* (*Letters from Berlin*), Baudelaire's poems on Paris, and Benjamin's *Passagen-Werk* (*Arcades Project*). As an overlooked, yet pivotal figure of modernity, the flaneur experiences city streets as interiors, traffic, advertising, displays, and the world of commodities as *Denkbilder*, images that evoke reflection.[1] A product and seismograph of his times, he represents the man of the streets in the cities of modernity. He is at once dreamer, historian, and artist, a character, reader, and author transforming his observations into literary, or more precisely, latently filmic texts. Surrounded by visual stimuli and confident of the all-encompassing power of his perception, the flaneur moves freely in the streets, intent solely on pursuing this unique, individual experience of the modern world.

   Within the domains of literature, film, and public culture, this unbounded, unrestricted pursuit of perception has been mainly ascribed to men, as their pleasure in the sights, views, and images of the street has seemed reserved to an experience of male spectatorship. Moving through and perceiving public spaces emerges as a uniquely gendered practice, one (almost) exclusively associated with male authors and protagonists. These flaneurs and their gazes are not limited in their subjectivity either by insecurity, conventions, modesty, anxiety, or assault, nor by restrictions erected through the controlling or commodifying presence of an other. The possibility of female flanerie, however, seems to be absent from the cities of modernity. In *Die Wiederkehr des Flaneurs* (*The Return of the Flaneur*,

1929), Benjamin does not acknowledge any awareness of the numerous women whom he passes by every day in the streets of Berlin. Kracauer, an eminent observer of Weimar culture, moves through his reflections of *Straßen in Berlin und anderswo* (*Streets in Berlin and Elsewhere*, 1925– 1933) without registering women as elements of the *Denkbilder* of his society. Their friend Hessel, formulating an aesthetic project of *Spazieren in Berlin* (*Walking in Berlin*, 1929), even cautions against walking with women who might present an obstacle to the flaneur's solitary wanderings.[2] This conspicuous absence in metropolitan culture moves me to search for traces of an alternate form of flanerie, one that might eventually inscribe the presence and potential of a female flaneur in the history of perception. The following scenes from both literary and filmic texts, proceeding on and describing the streets of Berlin, may suggest ways to rethink the status of a female flaneur. These speculations on an absence seek to conjure up an appearance—to (re)consider female scopophilia in movement, or in moving images—in order to theorize about the presence of women in public spaces, female spectatorship, and a more gendered definition of "modernity."

The female flaneur has been an absent figure in the public spaces of modernity, its media and texts, literatures and cities. Even if she is noticed, her experience in the streets is limited and circumscribed, her presence not understood in her own terms. In the texts and theories of flanerie mentioned above, we do not encounter a *flaneuse* in the street. The question of the public presence and representation of women, however, is neither a merely academic nor an accidental and marginal one. On the contrary, it suggests a pivotal constellation in prevailing structures of power and domination, a constellation that is a direct function of the—gendered—distribution of leisure, time and status, and of the economic, psychological, and physical autonomy of its society's subjects. Since the nineteenth century, flanerie has been not only the privilege of a bourgeois, educated, affluent middle class, but also, above all, of male society. Women's voices during the same period speak of a different approach to modernity, as they struggle first and foremost against their exclusion from the mobility reserved for men. Rather than indulge in specularity, women have only desired admission to the coveted realms of modernity and its spectacle. Only when chaperoned by companions, disguised as men, or covered by other subterfuge, was this entrance even tentatively possible. George Sand's efforts to overcome these obstacles give vivid evidence of the prohibitions facing women in the modern city. Sand realizes that she can never fully approach the outside world as long as she remains a woman who, in habit and behavior, adheres to contemporary conventions of femininity. She enters the world as a female flaneur in disguise, functionally outfitted in men's clothes, pants, and boots. She immediately revels in the first moments of her escape from the constrictions of a culturally constructed "femininity," a code used to control and restrict her attire and attitude: "With those little iron-shod heels, I was solid on the pavement. I flew from one end of Paris to another. It seemed to me that I could go around the world. And then, my clothes feared nothing. I ran out in every kind of weather, I came home at every sort of hour, I sat in the pit at the theater. No one paid attention to me, and no one guessed at my disguise. . . . No one knew me, no one looked at me, no one found fault with me; I was an atom lost in that immense crowd."[3]

This fiction of a male identity, constructed through its exterior trappings, grants Sand temporary entrance to a realm of considerable, if relative, freedom, opening up a previously utopian mobility as well as the promise of omnipresent experience. Many more women's lives during this period, however, were to remain determined and limited by rather different physical and psychological pressures. Many of these obstacles would remain in women's way long into the twentieth century. In texts and films from Weimar Germany, idle women are still regarded as prostitutes, and even feminists in the Berlin of the 1970s hesitate to enter streets at night and restaurants on their own (Stefan). Only since the end of the nineteenth century had the—bourgeois—woman even been permitted to walk the streets. As Anne Friedberg notes: "The female *flaneur* was not possible until a woman could wander the city on her own, a freedom linked to the privilege of shopping alone. . . . It was not until the closing decades of the century that the department store became a safe haven for unchaperoned women. . . . The great stores may have been the *flaneur*'s last coup, but they were the *flaneuse*'s first" (Friedberg 1991, 421). However, this conflation of shopping and strolling necessarily relativizes what is presumed to be the first instance of an "empowered gaze of the *flaneuse*," to the purposefully limited and economically promoted license of shopping (Friedberg 1991, 421). The early "department store *flaneuses*" only replicate forms of female presence that proletarian women, workers and housewives, had always presented in the streets without ever becoming female flaneurs in their own right: they would face the street in order to do the shopping rather than "go" shopping, to run errands rather than jog their imagination, to pick up children rather than experience free-floating impressions; they would take direct ways to the workplace rather than idle for a visual pleasure of their own. Less domestic manifestations of female presence in the street, such as the prostitute or the bag lady, only underline the disempowered status of female subjects in the public sphere.[4] The prostitute who has been driven to sell herself does not represent a self-determined female subject of the streets any more than the shopping *flaneuse* who has been mobilized by bourgeois consumption, or the bag lady who has been expelled into the streets after being consumed by the system. The question "To whom do the streets 'belong'?" pertains more to women than to underprivileged male subjects of any class, race, or age. Whether it belongs to the leisure or to the working class of society, to its dandies or demonstrators, pedestrians or flaneurs, the free and unimpeded movement of women undergoes additional peril under any of these constellations. Women cannot walk the streets without also expecting to be impeded by public judgments that prescribe their images and effectively render them objects of the gaze. Feminist sociology has outlined the tendencies toward a "basic asymmetry in the gendered distribution of physical and psychological power, unequal and inimical constellations that render women the more likely victims of rape, assault, intimidation, and physical and psychological harassment. Such latent and manifest factors must, as Shirley Ardener declares, have "a bearing on how women use space . . . and must be considered when the question of women's use of space is discussed" (Ardener 1981, 422). This epistemological situation is fundamentally inscribed into women's experience of public spaces as a continuing "containment" and resulting anxiety that rations their access to the ongoing life of the street (Pollock 1988, 63). The concomitant term and politics of a "women's movement," must so be understood in its very literal, immediately material implications, lifting the term beyond mere metaphor. In investigating women's dominant heterosexual socialization, Adrienne Rich asserts that the control of female movement is exercised as by patriarchal societies that have always, in one form or another, attempted to restrict women's ways to secluded and subdued positions: "Characteristics of male power include the power of men: . . . to confine women physically and prevent their movement by means of rape as terrorism, keeping women off the streets; purdah; foot-binding, atrophying a woman's athletic capabilities; haute couture, "feminine" dress codes; the veil; sexual harassment on the streets."[5]

Such material, physical, and economic obstacles are aggravated through forms of psychological containment that further impede the mobility of women's gaze and block their unrehearsed public presence. In the enduring and prevailing history of inequality, in the distribution of power and position on the other side of the gaze, these relations between the subjects of looking and the objects of this "being-looked-at-ness,"[6] between the spectator's subjectivity and his object's images, are not only gendered, but also neither reciprocal nor reversible. Women's presence in public is confronted with social environs into which she can never enter on her own terms.[7] She cannot occupy the position of an undisturbed observer, since it is she herself who is regarded as the "obvious" object of observation. The female flaneur is assumed to be absent, "invisible," and without a presence in the street.[8]

WOMEN IN *BERLIN: SYMPHONY OF A CITY*

From Berlin as a center of metropolitan culture and Weimar Germany as a formative phase of modernity comes Walter Ruttmann's 1927 film *Berlin. Die Sinfonie der Großstadt* (*Berlin: Symphony of a City*), the first significant filmic production that focuses on reflecting the metropolis and provides a promising point of departure in search of the absent female flaneur. While Ruttmann's metropolitan symphony is not a production of "feminist" modernism, it does present multiple images of "new" women on the screens and streets of modernity, illuminating the many facets of women's presence in the modern city. Highlighting the predicaments that a woman-as-streetwalker may encounter, one consequence in particular serves as a striking commentary on questions of female flanerie. It presents images of women who walk (on) the boulevards of Berlin and focus their gaze on men, that is, on other pedestrians. The position of these women in public and their assumption of an active gaze, their identity as urban women and spectators, defines their behavior as a possible visual manifestation of the female flaneur. Yet, in previous criticism of this film, not accidentally by male critics, these women walkers have unanimously been considered as professionals, as women who go after their business as "streetwalkers." In 1947, Kracauer describes the street scenes of the film in this way: "The many prostitutes among the passers-by also indicate that society has lost its balance" (186). Over thirty-five years later, William Uricchio still has not moved from this reading: "After several shots whose common element involves streetwalkers as a subject, a specific mating instance is presented. A prostitute and potential customer pass one another on the street" (1982, 209). Juxtaposing these prevailing accounts with a recent description by a female critic, one observes a striking case of gendered spectatorship. While Uricchio and Kracauer immediately interpret the scene as a site of prostitution, Sabine Hake only describes the action that can be ascertained: "The camera almost seems omnipresent . . . following several young women on the streets by themselves: one as she is being picked up . . . , another as she waits impatiently at a corner, and yet another as she window shops on elegant *Kurfürstendamm*."[9] The striking discrepancies in labelling these women and their activities might provoke a new reading of the *Sinfonie der Großstadt*, one that could envision the female "streetwalker" as a new figure of subjectivity that would be free of professional purposes, that would organize itself around a woman's own processes of walking, seeing, and recording the street: a *femme flaneur*. As the male reception of these female images in the film reveals, a woman walking the streets on her own will still appear the object of a male gaze and evaluations even in—and beyond—the presumably emancipatory era of Weimar Germany (Grossman 1983).

The establishing shots of the film set the scene for such a gendered view of the female image. After the camera defines the metropolis in spatial terms—trains, tracks, and telephone poles—it introduces a series of abstract, architectural, inanimate, and stationary shots, only to begin its move in tracking forward around a corner. First passing a shoemaker's shop—a foundational site of production for the film's ensuing fetishism—it then passes several facades in order to stop by a store-window and the first "human" figures that this camera has chosen. Its gaze comes to rest on a group of five women models, standing arranged behind a window, each frozen into a static pose in order to exhibit the one slip of underwear that partially covers their bodies. *Berlin. Die Sinfonie der Großstadt* revisits similar locations in many instances, focusing on window shots and the display of women's bodies as images. One of them presents a frontal view of the naked mannequins' plastic surfaces, as we see clearly inscribed in mirrored reflections on their motionless bodies, virtually imprinted in light, the store signs like markers of ownership. Artificial and simulated bodies of women are explicitly marked as both properties on display and circulating commodities on the market. A man is seen strolling by the window, maybe a flaneur, with sufficient leisure and visual desire to pause in his step, contemplate the display for a moment, consider it, dismiss it, continue walking. Many similar scenes of the city symphony follow this logic of public display and evaluation. On the runway of a fashion show—a small-scale model of an artificial "street"—women circulate within the confines of their modeled and modeling walk, a form of movement that sells—in more than an exterior sense—women's bodies and images. This fashion scene is preceded by the film's most desperate act, the spectacle of a woman's suicide, whose jump from a bridge in contiguity to the smiles from the runway suggests a narrative and causality of women's lives that connect their existence and demise in the city to the ways in which their images are exhibited and exploited in this society. The film runs the course from these scenes of women as models, instruments, and displayed commodities, to one crucial cluster of street scenes where a woman walking the street is herself perceived as an image, a commodity trying to sell herself.

Closer scrutiny of this scene, however, one more attentive to women's presence and existence in the street, reveals how these scenes of presumed prostitution are indeed composed of distinct instances of female figures, fashions, and habits in the street that allow a revision of our views on women in the metropolis. The first of these women is introduced as she looks out on the street, apparently surveying the scene. She is shown in profile, wearing a gray hat that leaves space next to her view for the spectator's gaze to take in the long shot of a street scene surrounding her image. This attentive character is not seen again, neither on her own nor as a companion to any of the men to follow in this sequence. Her striking image is but a glimpse of a potential female flaneur and her scrutiny of the city, as the symphony cuts from this gaze of the other to yet another other, the image of a black man surrounded by a group of pedestrians. Among these visual suspects of Weimar Berlin, the camera casts another woman who walks slowly under a different hat with a band. She arrives on the scene already in the company of a man, with no perceptible transaction marking their association as a commercial one. A third woman strolls on the far edge of the sidewalk, sporting a white hat and a curious gaze that she directs with interest upon her fellow pedestrians. No further signals define this specular intensity as one of either profession or leisure, prostitution or flanerie. Finally, a fourth woman emerges in a black hat, a figure whose swaying walk has elicited most often from male critics clichés of a "coquettish" stroll that is presumed to advertise her as a prostitute. She is an instant suspect who does not remain a female image and object but turns the corner and gazes back at another—male—pedestrian, mobilizing the 90-degree angle through the shopping window into a reflective mirror and transparent surface of specularity. Her interested gaze has been interpreted as so provocative that presumably it causes the man in the street to retrace his steps and return around the corner to join her. However, as we review this scene more closely, without attaching immediate labels of prostitution to this woman with her active gaze, we find that the woman with the black hat does walk off by herself after all. The man who subsequently walks by with a—different—woman at the far side of the window is part of a couple that only through careless, conventional viewing has come to be regarded as a successful transaction in "streetwalking."

Contrary to its previous readings, the scenes of this film prove to be open to a new presence of women in the street, revealing female images that confound rather than confirm preconceived notions of women walking and watching in the streets. Upon closer inspection, the *Sinfonie der Großstadt* represents fragments from the complex reality of Weimar women in the city.

Their walking the street opens a space for the female flaneur, one that is subject to continued containment and misrecognition by male interpretations of progressive women as prostitutes.[10] Yet, in the instance of one woman walker and determined looker, Ruttmann's film also captures a woman's pursuit of her own flanerie that goes beyond the mirror cabinet of mutually confining image values.[11] Female flanerie presents and enables acts of perception as resistance against woman's status as an image: it opens the space for a female gaze upon the exterior world, and makes way for women to partake and participate in *Berlin. Die Sinfonie der Großstadt*.

WOMAN AS (RE)VISITING IN THE MALE FANTASY OF A METROPOLITAN BERLIN: STEFAN'S *SHEDDING*

Upon closer scrutiny, another pivotal text of German culture in the late twentieth century also reveals itself to be a text about women, the gaze, the street, and Berlin. From the perspective of female presence and perception in public spaces, Verena Stefan's *Häutungen* (*Shedding*, 1975) can be (re)read as the foundational document of a feminist "movement" in the most literal and immediate sense.[12] The observations recorded by Stefan strikingly illuminate the ways in which the pursuit of women's uninhibited, autonomous presence in the street corresponds to a move toward female emancipation, one woman's move who continues to have to reflect and face the problems resulting from the predominant dynamics of the male gaze. While Stefan's account of this struggle reflects the central concerns of discussion within the women's movement of her time, her text can also serve to elucidate in exemplary ways an ongoing constellation of perception and the female image in public spaces. While the literature by male authors of this time is free to pursue a "Second Return of the Flaneur" with its move toward a "New Subjectivity," female subjectivity is still not established beyond the realm of speculation. The uncommented and uncensored presence of a female person in the street has, despite women's formal equality and democratic rights, in no way been acknowledged as an unquestionable phenomenon. Female flanerie continues to be an exception rather than any self-evident, everyday process and practice.

Stefan's text from the 1970s attests to the status of female experience of the outside world in encounters that represent the reality of discrimination against women in the streets of a possibly post-modern, yet by no means post-feminist, Berlin. As a woman on her own in the city, she feels consistently under surveillance, permanently gazed upon, hit upon (*angemacht*), checked out, commented on, in short, "constantly ogled and harassed"

(1978, 42). With neither time nor leisure to reflect on the pleasures of the street, she is as sensitive to the dynamics of the gaze as any flaneur, yet sensitized through and in an entirely different subject position. As a woman, her public perception has to negotiate her much more tenuous presence at the opposite side of this dynamics of the gaze. With every step she takes, she finds her own body and image serving as the objects of male scopophilia, a relation of power that denies her own gaze at the same time: "I am standing at *Wittenbergplatz* waiting for the traffic light. . . . I can sense two men approaching me from behind" (1978, 15). Their male gaze is shown to take the form of a sensory impact, a subtle yet persistent attack by male pedestrians who can choose to make a woman the object of their desires and perception anytime they wish: "Men's glances assault me . . . as I descend the stairs to the subway. . . . A lone woman, still an alien, and still up for grabs" (1978, 31).[13]

In understanding these relays of power and the gaze as historically gendered conditions that continue to objectify women to the present day, the uneasiness of this recent female flaneur has to be acknowledged as far more than an isolated incident, individual paranoia, or exaggerated insecurity. Stefan's character in her precarious state expresses an epistemological condition of female existence within the gendered dynamics of the gaze that Gertrud Koch explains as a constant of female experience: "Being looked at, I become the object of the Other who casts his judgement at me with his glance. Every woman knows this situation which Sartre describes as an ontological one: the domination through the appraising gaze which degrades into an object the one looked at, and subordinates her" (Koch 1979, 125). Seen from the perspective of woman, Sartre's "ontology" indeed describes a male epistemological position rather than an "objective" philosophical theorem. His view of the world marks itself quite strikingly as a partial and tendentious one when he exemplifies his definition of the "Other" first via his perception of a *woman* in the street: "Cette femme que je vois venir vers moi et autres passants sont pour moi des objets, cela n'est pas douteux" (1957, 310). No less doubtful is the consequence that many women who, along with Stefan, face such scrutiny and objectification on a daily basis—not only through the gaze of male philosophers—are left crippled and deprived of that self-evident self-confidence traditionally exercised by and attributed to their male contemporaries. As the dominant system of power and the gaze prevails, it is apt to render women insecure and passive objects, mere images devoid of the psychological and physical strength to return this gaze in kind by provoking male strangers. Women's scopophilia, along with their potential for female flanerie, has become subject to so many historical restrictions that they may wish to withdraw from the public sphere, no longer willing or capable of exposing themselves to the dominant and daily gaze of male evaluation. A potential female flaneur may disassociate herself altogether from an exterior world defined by the male gaze. Instead, she may retreat into domestic interiors, contemplate women's own bodies and psyches, assume her culturally prescribed presence as a man's companion, or take refuge with her family and friends, all in place of the pursuit of a flanerie on her own. As the conclusion and resignation of Verena Stefan's *Häutungen* demonstrates, the female flaneur's desire to explore the world is still likely to encounter its limits in male pedestrians and their fantasies, which assault, annoy, disturb, and at the very least evaluate her in the street. As a woman, the *flaneuse* can never expect to step entirely in the same unspectacular ways, to become the same respectable appearance in her own right that the male flaneur has always assumed. The woman that Stefan presents as victimized by a male gaze that exerts judgments is no longer inclined to participate in the prevailing rituals of specular evaluation, aggression, and control. Her eventual withdrawal into an interior world associated with women is also a way of disassociating herself from an exterior sphere that she perceives as inextricably defined by the scopophilia and specularity of the male gaze. While her own and other women's bodies and psychology become innovative and intense sites of exploration, the space of exterior public reality is still neither replaced nor redeemed in this text.

This futile pursuit of female flanerie occupies a pivotal position throughout Stefan's entire narrative. Even if her experience of Berlin only shines through these reflections in oblique ways, the desire for female flanerie represents one of the primary impulses of the *Erfahrungshunger* (hunger for experience) that moves this text: "Into the jungle of the cities, to be in the midst of it all!" (1978, 22). Yet, any female flaneur's step into the city and its exterior reality must be taken with an awareness of the (male) powers and structures of aggression that limit her mobility: "How could I get to know the world on my own? It was dangerous" (1978, 16). She cannot walk the streets solely to pursue her walking. Her movement is impeded by consistent harassment, conventions that she seeks to challenge but that remain beyond her control: "Why couldn't I travel without fear of being molested, why was this direct access to the world closed off to me?" Wherever she goes, she is made to realize that a woman in the street will not be "respected," that is, regarded as an equal to the male flaneur, as an aimless entity in her own right. An encounter with a male pedestrian testifies to the implied interests that her public presence arouses against her will, as he seeks to impose his expectations on the female traveller's singular presence: "That's hard to believe, a girl on vacation all by herself and not in the mood for it?" (1978, 18). Instead of pursuing this series of frustrating interactions, Stefan relinquishes her independent forays and retreats into the relative shelter of just one man's company: "Seeing no other way out, I fell in love with a guy who was bumming around the world. . . . To spend just one evening in this city with one of them instead of being hassled by all the rest, is that asking too much?" Female flanerie is shown to be effectively stopped short at every turn by the limitations and conventions established for female presence in public spaces. Stefan's character is left with nothing other than to reject this outside world in an ultimate denial of her own scopophilia: "I ride the subway only with my eyes closed" (1978, 31), she says. The woman in the street finds herself forced to remain a quasi-visitor to Berlin, the male fantasy of a metropolitan "Babylon" being incommensurate with her own experience: "This time, the city was closed to me. I felt myself being swept along through [its] streets, but the city itself remained inaccessible" (1978, 17).[14]

Under such limited and limiting conditions for women's free movement, Stefan's emerging feminist ultimately renounces her aspirations of flanerie and announces her retreat, in protest, from the city. Discontentedly, she feels pressured to proclaim a literal detachment from the urban promises and public potentials of flanerie: "There was nothing left for me to do in Berlin, nor was I looking to find anything" (1978, 93). Yet, this declaration comes not by choice and barely veils the acute awareness of a deficit that remains. One woman's *Erfahrungshunger*, to invoke the contemporary desire to partake in the immediate, material, public life that is regarded a key term of the discourse of—male—"New Subjectivity" in the 1970s, has been neither indulged nor satiated in this text.[15] Rather, Stefan's narrator resigns from the spaces of modernity, indulging their attractions in rhetoric even in the act of renouncing them: "The disquieting expanse of foreign lands, the stimulating space of the cities—all these needs were not yet satisfied, yet I did not long for those other places" (1978, 104). The residue of this desire rests with one of Stefan's first attempts to chart these experiences into a language of her own, in one of the early poems of her text. Her mournful reflection on the circumstances of "the first colonization in the history of mankind," that "of women by men" (1978, 33), is also an implicit, extended comment on the lack of female flanerie as it relates to the situation of women in the cities: "Who strung this fear in liana vines through the streets. . . . Our paths prescribed, fenced in. . . . Here we have access to our kitchens, . . . department stores, laundromats, a café and the movies—and yet during the day we cannot walk the streets without being annoyed, cannot go alone to the parks, and where do we eat when we're hungry at midnight alone?" (1978, 33).

The extent to which the rhetoric of Stefan's text is significantly defined by its optics becomes apparent as this little manifesto on the fundamental colonization of women's free movement makes its statement in terms of spatial perception, impeded movement, and circumscribed locations. The pivotal places of flanerie and its extensions—streets, stores, and the movies—are conjured as utopian sites alongside scenes of containment and exclusion—women isolated in kitchens, in fear in cities at night. The ongoing dilemma in these all-too-familiar, indeed pedestrian, scenes stands for neither an individual deficiency nor psychological incapacitation. Stefan's text, implicitly yet undeniably reacting to her experience of and defeat in the city, writes a crucial chapter from the everyday history of oppressed (and suppressed) female scopophilia that has in no way been redeemed or recuperated. However, an answer to the questions that she raises may still come from the streets of Berlin, from a medium that may be more conducive to female flanerie.

DIE MAUER MUSS WEG: TRANSCENDING THE BARRIERS TO WOMEN'S EXPERIENCE IN SANDER'S *REDUPERS*

The space of female flanerie has been prefigured in another realm, the scopophilia in the cinema. The store-windows of *Berlin. Die Sinfonie der Großstadt* through which the stroller sees her own objectification and beyond, if she dares, are replicated in the frames of the camera and extended to the images of the world. As the cinema releases the female spectator of her exclusion from exterior reality, scenes and sites of female flanerie have been inscribed in the medium of film since its beginnings. With its focus on and exploration of visual material and public images, cinema is able to institutionalize the participation even of women in processes of perception and scopophilia. The "spectatrix" in the movies is a figure apt to approximate the female flaneur who can be seen as a moving spectator in the streets.[16] Early cinema becomes one of the first sites in which this new freedom and position of the gaze is accessible to and exercised by women who until then have been excluded from scopic pleasures. Even a mediated view through the camera's eye grants the female spectator a relative autonomy of the gaze not known to her in other contexts. As Horkheimer and Adorno theorize: "In spite of the films which are intended to complete her integration, the housewife finds in the darkness of the movie theater a place of refuge where she can sit for a few hours with nobody watching, just as she used to look out of the window when there were still homes and rest in the evening" (1972, 139). The darkened space of the cinema removes her from the gaze, that is, the control, of others while at the same time allowing her unrestricted access, at an accelerated pace, to all the shocks and impressions of modernity, in this way approximating and even exceeding the experience of the street. As Heide Schlüpmann emphasizes, the new optical institution granted women a place to indulge their scopic desires while "the cinema finally accepted [them] as social and cultural beings outside their familial ties" (1990, 13). If women's move toward the movies encountered considerable resistance, they embraced all the more a medium that would liberate their scopophilia and open the first legitimate, protected forms of access to the spectacle and a perception of their own: "While the bourgeois theater-goer continued to reject [the movies], his wife already spent her free time in the cinema. For women, the cinema in general meant the only pleasure they would enjoy outside the house on their own, and at the same time also more than entertainment; they brought into the cinema the claim, not delivered by the theater, to see themselves [*sich selber zu sehen*]" (Schlüpmann 1990, 16). In the stationary, yet potentially infinite form of flanerie with which the cinema presents its spectators, the medium most focused on looking and recording has traditionally transmitted the images of exterior reality to the views of women and allowed them to relate to the world as unimpeded, invisible, respectable flaneurs in their own right.

In another example of female experience with the city, a cinematic record of walking and looking in Berlin links female flanerie to both the movement of women and the "women's movement" in Helke Sander's *Die allseitig Reduzierte Persönlichkeit* (*The All-Round Reduced Personality/Redupers*, 1977). The Berlin charted by this female "street film" is the terrain of a single woman who exhibits both self-confidence and self-consciousness in public and private spaces, but always the presence of mind of a decidedly visual, critical, scrutinizing woman. The film presents its female photographer as a flaneur who focuses unconditionally on the pursuit of her perception in the city, a character in such intense identification with Sander's theories and aesthetics that she is represented by the female director of the film herself. *Redupers* is, in every respect, an intensely self-referential document of a documented female flanerie, a "filmphotography of photographing women" (Berg-Ganschow 1979, 41).[17] In this expansive, ongoing perception of Berlin streets and public spaces, a female presence in the street takes decisive steps toward the utopian destination of female aesthetics, "to identify woman as the active looking subject rather than as the object of the male gaze."[18] Through(out) the film, the spectators' eyes can identify with a subjective camera that is directed by a woman's gaze on the city. This primacy of urban optics in a female perspective defines the film's aesthetic principles beginning with its establishing shots. Sander, the female flaneur as camera and director, immediately situates the place she will traverse in her following flanerie on film, as the very first frame signals the scene to be scrutinized: "Berlin, in March 1977." The name of the city is succeeded by the continuous movement of a camera that moves along facades at street level, takes in lengths of walls filled with graffiti, turns the corner at a pub. Unlike Ruttmann's *Berlin. Die Sinfonie der Großstadt*, however, this turn does not yield the commodification of female bodies in a window, but rather a multiplication of sensory stimuli linked to what Adorno has termed as "aural flanerie." The female director's seemingly aimless search for aural impressions on the radio dial—*AFN-News, Rias Berlin, Radio DDR*—underscores the significance of her camera's unfiltered reception of a continuum of signs in the city, her undivided attention directed toward the entire text of the street. For several minutes, Sander lets her flaneur-camera track along the street and into the film, absorbing explicitly political signs— "*KPD/ML*," reflecting implicit signals of an everyday Berlin—"*Die Mauer muß weg*," recording multiple markers of store windows, advertising, neon signs, and commercial inscriptions. This primacy of movement is established with the film's first shot as it scrutinizes the objects of the city, scans the details of streets and surfaces, and roams facades and structures in one extended tracking-shot. Taking in close images of walls covered with graffiti at the slow speed of flanerie, Sander's female flaneur registers with unparalleled attention the multiplicity of signs and sites, the many hieroglyphs of her city. The film gives us a female walker who finally asserts her presence in "reading the street."[19]

This freedom of perception assumed by a woman, previously perceived as an *All-Round Reduced Personality* in the patriarchal public sphere, is still a temporally and thematically circumscribed one. Beyond its punning on an "all-round developed socialist personality," the film's title could also refer to Sander's flanerie, a process that "reduces" the entirety of her presence of mind to the perception of urban "shocks" and stimuli in Benjamin's sense. Some critics have sought to depict even the multifaceted Berlin of the film as a "reduced" one: "The West Berlin that we see in the film is dingy, decrepit, cold and dreary" (Sandford 1980, 144). Others seem to understand these "reductions" as a more dynamic process, as Renate Möhrmann's statement indicates: "Geduldig zeigt [Sander] sowohl die Gewinn- wie auch die Verlustquoten auf dem Weg zu einer neuen weiblichen Identität" (1980, 90) and Elsaesser observes: "Here Berlin as divided city and the woman as artist-and-mother become the mutually communicating stages for the many divisions of the female self" (1989, 191). The woman's search for images is both motivated by and often limited through her professional and maternal roles—a photographer searching for motifs and a mother accompanying her child. Such pressures of domestic and economic expectations collide with the paradigmatic aimlessness, purposefree fascination, and timelessness of the flaneur. Sander's photographer is still forced to consider her affinities with the state of flanerie as professional liabilities: "She has difficulties to limit herself [to those images] that the papers will buy"—"She only learns slowly to be short and precise"—"She wastes too much time grasping situations." Those stereotypical limitations encountered by any female presence in the street, being subject to the gaze, evaluation, and aggression of men, continue to haunt even this courageous, professional woman of the street. Maybe in irony, maybe as allegory, the filmmaker presents an ostentatiously supportive bureaucrat of the Berlin art scene as the man who seeks compensation for his interest in the women's photography project through sexual favors in the street.[20] As a declared flaneur, however, Sander's filmic protagonist of the women's movement is able to put into perspective even this rape attempt in the night of the city. Though she is literally nauseated by the shocks that form an inextricable part of woman's experience in the street, she registers it, as one more discouraging experience of female presence in public, yet she does not accept it as the final comment on what is possible. "This is one of the ways in which I see my city," she concludes but continues, "so it goes on, step by step."

This primacy of the street renders *in nuce* the aesthetic project of this women's photography group, a loose association of female flaneurs who share and discuss their impressions recorded in the photographic medium. These women interpret the Berlin arts project—"Photographers see their city"—in their own idiosyncratic ways, challenging established views and revealing the secret city behind officially sanctioned facades. Their collecting images on and of their own is a subversive activity that creates a counter-public sphere of female perception, that makes visible and lets appear new contexts and connections—"Photos that you can never see like this anywhere else." These women's photographs pursue a view of the city that collects the marginal, redeems the everyday, retrieves the familiar, and subverts official sites and structures—in short, they pursue the project of (female) flanerie. Their gaze reveals and questions conventions of political and gendered dichotomies at once: one of their photographs traces eye-opening similarities in the everyday life of both Germanies, such as male conventions of the Saturday carwash routine. One by one, these images contribute to the mosaic of another imaginary and history, one that has long been overlooked as female and private, marginal and trivial. Shots from the photo-album of a forgotten aunt—"married to a tyrant"—are redeemed as glimpses from the private archives of German family history. They are juxtaposed with documentary shots tracking the passage of old women between East and West, "important ambassadors" who smuggle in their plastic bags a contraband of messages, stories, and news. These retired female flaneurs proceed in ways similar to this street film produced by a woman, director, and photographer: they seek acute and detailed descriptions of lives, "they record their observations and carry them fresh back and forth."

The female flaneurs of this film conquer new territory in the city and its public spaces; they overcome women's historically and socially "all-round reduced" personality through an "all-round alerted" persona's perception, one that is open to and "reduced" only by the shocks of the street, coming to transcend the barriers set to women's experience and imagination. Sander views her film as a decidedly programmatic text, one that aims at encouraging female (self-)confidence through the power of a perception that liberates prescribed roles and expands previous social maps. In doing so, it focuses primarily on reversing the force of the male gaze. As Sander notes: "Women have just begun to *dare* to see themselves and others, society, with their own eyes" (1988, 185). The "question about feminine imagery" (*weibliche Bildersprache*) corresponds to the question of women assuming a perception of their own. Any theory of a female aesthetics, gaze, or "women's movement" implies a quest for the freedom of female flanerie. No longer expelled from its scenes and streets, Sander's photographer not only participates in the "Symphony of the City," she conducts a "symphony" and perception of the city on her own terms and in her own right.

NOTES

1. I would like to thank Leslie A. Adelson for her suggestions on an early phase of this chapter.

2. A quasi "Second Return of the Flaneur"—to rephrase Benjamin's essay on Hessel "The Return of the Flaneur"—under the auspices of "New Subjectivity" in German literature and film since the 1970s, a movement characterized by a radically subjective turn toward the objective reality of exteriority, is also mainly discussed in terms of its *male* authors and directors.

3. George Sand, as quoted by Janet Wolff (1991, 148). A pivotal figure of female flanerie, Sand has remained influential in discussions of the women's

"movement"; cf. Ginka Steinwachs's evocative appropriation of her life as well as Sigrid Weigel's work on Steinwachs.

4. Cf. Susan Buck-Morss's discussion on the question of ownership of the street (1986, 114).

5. Adrienne Rich discusses these and other factors in her essay (1983, 183 ff). By extension, these restrictions result in the "horizontal segregation of women in employment" and the "enforced economic dependence of wives," and thereby contribute to the limitation of women's movement and range in an extended and immediate sense. Also cf. Ardener's observation: "Tight corsetting, hobble skirts, high heels, all effectively impede women's freedom of movement" (1981, 28).

6. Characteristically, Laura Mulvey's term was formulated in her seminal discussion of female spectatorship and film theory.

7. In a society organized around and dominated by the male gaze, "any presence of women" continues to be "sexualized." There is no representation of the female image that is neutral to and removed from issues of gender and power; cf. the discussion of related arguments in feminist film theory by Stam, Burgoyne, and Flitterman-Lewis (1992, 176 ff).

8. Cf. Wolff's argument in "The Invisible *Flaneuse*" and the impossibility of female flanerie.

9. Sabine Hake, unpublished manuscript, generously provided by the author.

10. "That the image of the whore is the most significant female image in the *Passagen-Werk*" remains a blind spot in the enlightening perception of a long line of Weimar critics and flaneurs. The absence of a genuine female flaneur typifies the history of male flanerie in its indifference toward female experience if prostitution—not a freely chosen form of flanerie—can indeed be considered, as Buck-Morss suggests it was, "the female version of flanerie."

11. As *Die Sinfonie der Großstadt* both reveals and celebrates, wherever woman goes and looks she finds her image surrounded by a (self-)critical gaze that subjects her image to continuous specular evaluation, valorization, rejection, and assessment. Buck-Morss explains: "Women make themselves objects. Even with no one looking, and even without a display case, viewing oneself as constantly being viewed inhibits freedom" (1986, 125). See also both Berger's and Weigel's distinction of the gaze under patriarchy, with a strategic "*schielende Blick*" as one of women's ways out of the predicament: "Für das Selbstverständnis der Frau bedeutet das, daß sie sich selbst betrachtet, indem sie sieht, *daß* und *wie* sie betrachtet *wird*; d.h. ihre Augen sehen durch die Brille des Mannes. . . . Ihr Selbstbildnis entsteht ihr so im Zerrspiegel des Patriarchats" (Weigel and Stephan 1983, 85); and Luce Irigaray's considerations of this constellation in a wider political and theoretical context: "Women no longer relate to each other except in terms of what they represent in men's desire. . . . Among themselves, they are separated by his speculations" (1985, 188).

12. Feminist criticism has frequently found fault with Stefan; see Classen and Goettle (1976, 4–5), and Marlies Gerhardt (1977), or focused on her critique of

language; see Schmidt (1982). Yet, Stefan's is indeed a "Bewegungstext," a text of female motions and the "women's movement," in even more ways than Weigel suggests in introducing this term in *Die Stimme der Medusa* (1987, 102).

13. Despite Weigel's assertion that Stefan's critique of the status quo is presented as obsolete, as part of a previous past, these experiences in the street and futile attempts at flanerie are, however, related in the present tense, testifying to an ongoing concern for women that has not been overcome (*Die Stimme der Medusa* 1987, 103).

14. For an extended exploration of city myths and male fantasies, see Scherpe (1988).

15. Cf. Rutschky's use of the term and investigation of this period.

16. For this term as well as a survey of diverse statements on and approaches to female spectatorship, cf. Bergstrom and Doane (1989).

17. Rich defines the narrative structures in *Redupers* as "discursive, self-interrupting, and non-hegemonic," in "She Says, He Says: The Power of the Narrator in Modernist Film Politics" (1983, 38).

18. Mayne analyzes the film as a "work in progress," a "collection of open-ended fragmented narrative structures" that circumvent elements of traditional narration in order to privilege the subjective formulation of women's every-day experience: "waiting, walking, figuring finances" (1981–82, 61).

19. Cf. Franz Hessel's term *"eine Art Lektüre der Straße"* (1984, 145).

20. Cf. Sander's indictment of the complex sexist and hypocritical practices that often determine funding for the arts, in "Frau K. und der berühmte Mann" (1987).

REFERENCES

Ardener, Shirley. "Ground Rules and Social Maps for Women: An Introduction." In *Women and Space. Ground Rules and Social Maps*, edited by Shirley Ardener. London: Oxford University Women's Studies Committee, 1981.

Berg-Ganschow, Uta. "wirklichkeit mit widerhaken. zu 'redupers.' " *Frauen und film* 20 (1979): 41–43.

Berger, John. *Ways of Seeing*. New York: Penguin, 1977.

Bergstrom, Janet, and Mary Ann Doane, eds. "The Spectatrix." *Camera Obscura. A Journal of Feminism and Film Theory* 20–21 (1989): 99–141.

Buck-Morss, Susan. "The Flaneur, the Sandwichman and the Whore: The Politics of Loitering." *New German Critique* 39 (1986): 119–32.

Classen, Brigitte, and Gabriele Goettle. *"Häutungen*, eine Verwechslung von Anemone and Amazone." *Die schwarze Botin* 1 (1976): 4–10.

Dudley, Andrew, ed. *The Image in Dispute*. Austin: University of Texas Press, 1997.

Elsaesser, Thomas. *New German Cinema: A History*. New Brunswick, N.J.: Rutgers University Press, 1989.

————. " 'It Started with These Images'—Some Notes on Political Film-making after Brecht in Germany: Helke Sander and Harun Farocki." *Discourse* 7 (1985): 95–120.

Friedberg, Anne. "*Les Flaneurs du Mal(l)*: Cinema and the Postmodern Condition." *PMLA* 106 (1991): 419–31.

Gerhardt, Marlies. "Wohin geht Nora? Auf der Suche nach der verlorenen Frau." *Kursbuch* 47 (1977): 77–89.

Grossman, Atina. "The New Woman and the Rationalization of Sexuality in Weimar Germany." In *Powers of Desire. The Politics of Sexuality*, edited by Ann Snitow, Christine Stansell, and Sharon Thompson, 153–71. New York: Monthly Review Press, 1983.

Hessel, Franz. *Ein Flaneur in Berlin/Spazieren in Berlin* [1929]. Berlin: Das Arsenal, 1984.

Horkheimer, Max, and Theodor W. Adorno. *Dialectic of Enlightenment*. Translated by John Cumming. New York: Herder and Herder, 1972.

Irigaray, Luce. "Women on the Market." *This Sex Which Is Not One*. Translated by Catherine Porter. Ithaca, N.Y.: Cornell University Press, 1985.

Koch, Gertrud. "Von der weiblichen Sinnlichkeit und ihrer Lust und Unlust am Kino. Mutmaßungen über vergangene Freuden und neue Hoffnungen." In *Überwindung der Sprachlosigkeit*, edited by G. Dietze. Darmstadt: Luchterhand, 1979.

Kracauer, Siegfried. *From Caligari to Hitler. A Psychological History of the German Film*. Princeton, N.J.: Princeton University Press, 1947.

Mayne, Judith. "Female Narration, Women's Cinema: Helke Sander's *The All-Round Reduced Personality/Redupers*." *New German Critique* 24–25 (1981–82): 155–71.

Möhrmann, Renate. *Die Frau mit der Kamera. Filmemacherinnen in der Bundesrepublik Deutschland*. Munich: Hanser, 1980.

Mulvey, Laura. "Visual Pleasure and Narrative Cinema." *Screen* 16 (Autumn 1975): 6–18.

Pollock, Griselda. *Vision and Difference. Femininity, Feminism and Histories of Art*. London: Routledge, 1988.

Rich, Adrienne. "Compulsory Heterosexuality and Lesbian Existence." In *Powers of Desire. The Politics of Sexuality*, edited by Ann Snitow, Christine Stansell, and Sharon Thompson, 177–205. New York: Monthly Review Press, 1983.

Rich, B. Ruby. "She Says, He Says: The Power of the Narrator in Modernist Film Politics." *Discourse* 6 (Fall 1983): 31–46.

Rutschky, Michael. *Erfahrungshunger. Ein Essay über die siebziger Jahre*. Frankfurt am Main: Fischer, 1982.

Sander, Helke. "Feminism and Film." In *West German Filmmakers on Film: Visions and Voices*, edited by Eric Rentschler. New York: Holmes and Meier, 1988.

————. "Frau K. und der berühmte Mann." *Die Geschichten der drei Damen K.* Munich: Frauenbuchverlag, 1987.

Sandford, John. *The New German Cinema*. Totowa, N.J.: Barnes and Noble, 1980.

Sartre, Jean-Paul. *L'être et le néant. Essai d'ontologie phénoménologique*. Paris: Gallimard, 1957.

Scherpe, Klaus R., ed. *Die Unwirklichkeit der Städte. Großstadtdarstellungen zwischen Moderne und Postmoderne*. Reinbek: Rowohlt, 1988.

Schlüpmann, Heide. *Die Unheimlichkeit des Blicks. Das Drama des frühen deutschen Kinos*. Frankfurt: Stroemfeld/Roter Stern, 1990.

Schmidt, Ricarda. *Westdeutsche Frauenliteratur in den 70er Jahren*. Frankfurt am Main: R. G. Fischer, 1982.

Stam, Robert, Robert Burgoyne, and Sandy Flitterman-Lewis, eds. *New Vocabularies in Film Semiotics. Structuralism, Post-structuralism and Beyond*. London: Routledge, 1992.

Stefan, Verena. *Shedding*. Translated by Johanna Moore and Beth Weckmueller. New York: Daughters Publishing, 1978. (*Häutungen*. Munich: Frauenoffensive, 1975.)

Steinwachs, Ginka. *George Sand: Eine Frau in Bewegung, die Frau von Stand*. Berlin: Medusa, 1980.

Uricchio, William. "Ruttmann's *Berlin* and the City Film to 1930." Unpublished Dissertation, New York University, 1982.

Weigel, Sigrid. "Flaneurin in der Welt der Schrift: Spuren Benjaminscher Lektüre in den Texten von Ginka Steinwachs." In *Ein Mund von Welt: Ginka Steinwachs. Text/s/orte/n*, edited by Sonia Nowoselsky-Müller, 62–69. Bremen: Zeichen und Spuren Frauenliteraturverlag, 1989.

————. *Die Stimme der Medusa. Schreibweisen in der Gegenwartsliteratur von Frauen*. Dülmen: Tende, 1987.

Weigel, Sigrid, and Inge Stephan, eds. *Die Verborgenene Frau. Sechs Beiträge zu einer feministischen Literaturwissenschaft*. Berlin: Argument, 1983.

Wolff, Janet. "The Invisible *Flaneuse*: Women and the Literature of Modernity." In *The Problems of Modernity. Adorno and Benjamin*, edited by Andrew Benjamin. London: Routledge, 1991.

7

Wim Wenders' Berlin: Images and the Real

Brigitte Peucker

Only film commands optical approaches to the essence of the city.
—Benjamin, "A Berlin Chronicle" (1978, 8)

According to Siegfried Kracauer, Carl Mayer, famous scenarist of the Weimar cinema, was "standing amid the whirling traffic of the 'Ufa Palast am Zoo' when he conceived the idea of the *City Symphony*. He saw a 'melody of pictures' and began to write the treatment of *Berlin* (1927)" (*From Caligari to Hitler* 1947, 182). As Kracauer also notes, Karl Freund, the cameraman who shot *Berlin: Symphony of a City*—perhaps tired of the virtuoso effects he had created for earlier films—longed to follow the lead of the Dziga Vertov group in making use of the camera in its recording function. Kracauer represents Freund as a man "starved for reality" and, indeed, Freund represents himself in the same way. "I wanted to show everything," he claims in an interview of 1939, "Men getting up to go to work, eating breakfast, boarding trams or walking. From the lowest laborer to the bank president" (1947, 185). To this end, Freund devised various means of taking candid footage while walking or riding through the city streets. But when—much to Kracauer's disgust—Walter Ruttmann, known for his work on abstract films, cut Freund's material on rhythmic movement and subjected it to principles of associational montage, in Kracauer's view this imposition of avant-garde techniques upon documentary images created a film notable for its visual surface rather than its recording character. From Kracauer's perspective, Mayer's "melody of pictures" had become a symphony of flashy images and cinematic self-display, at once a spectacle of modernity and a formalist exploration of cinematic technique.

For Kracauer, what distinguishes *Symphony of a City* from the work of Dziga Vertov is not a matter of what he calls "artistic intention": *Man with a Movie Camera* is, as Kracauer acknowledges, lyrical and highly self-conscious about technique. At issue is not the simple privileging of "realism" over "formalism," but resides, for Kracauer, in the complex interconnectedness of political realities and the aesthetic, an idea that marks Kracauer's work and is most interestingly worked out, perhaps, in "The Mass Ornament." What makes the work of Dziga Vertov preferable to *Symphony of a City* from Kracauer's perspective is not only the political attitude reflected there, but the "revolutionary energies" that permeate Soviet life and necessarily shape from within the images presented to the spectator's eye (1947, 185). The political realities available to the camera are different in the case of Soviet and German society, granted, but this observation in itself does not exhaust the matter for Kracauer.

The question of the camera's relation to the real is in itself a complex one, even when its proponents or theorists share a similar politics, and I have no intention of covering familiar territory here. But a few points of view concerning this relation warrant mentioning. From the work of Walter Benjamin to that of Susan Sontag, writers on the subject of photography often refer to Brecht's pronouncement that "the mere reflection of reality" does not reveal a great deal about the nature of that reality.[1] As Brecht goes on to claim, a photographic rendering of the Krupps works tells us little about the political relations that flourish there. According to Brecht, we can learn more about such matters from the composed image, the image subjected to artifice—and therefore susceptible to "unmasking"—than from its "documentary" counterpart. Brecht's attitude toward photographed reality is distinguished from Benjamin's sense of the way in which early photography lays bare an "optical unconscious." Stressing the technical capabilities of photography and film to present us with sights as yet unseen, Benjamin is fascinated with the physiognomic or topographical aspects of people, places, and things that the camera in the early period of photography—in the photographs, for example, of August Sander—is capable of revealing to the eye.[2]

A materialist aesthetics similar to that of Benjamin is promoted by Kracauer in his later work, *Theory of Film: The Redemption of Physical Reality*, which asserts film's unique capacity "to picture transient material life" (1960, ix). In Kracauer's view, films are proportionately more cinematic the more they cling to the surface of things—notwithstanding the fact that the notion of "surface" is a complicated one in his thinking. In *Theory of Film*, film's relation to reality is seen even more abstractly than in Kracauer's early essays, seeming almost mystically to extend beyond the merely mimetic: here Kracauer manifests a nearly Bazinian perspective toward the real in cinema. And indeed, *Theory of Film*, in conjunction with the work of Bazin, would seem to provide a source for Roland Barthes' contention in "The Photographic Message" that the photograph transmits "the scene itself, the *literal reality*" (1960, 16–17, italics mine).

For Barthes, the nature of the photograph lies in its doubleness, in the sense in which it is at once coded, susceptible to reading—and uncoded—or incapable of being read; in Barthes' terms, it is both cultural and *natural* (1977, 19). Barthes is even closer to Kracauer's notion of what makes a film cinematic in an essay generated by a look at some Eisenstein stills, where he claims that "the filmic is that in the film which cannot be described, the representation which cannot be represented" (1977, 64–65). Paradoxically, for Barthes the "filmic" is most accessible in the film still, by means of which film comes closest to the photograph and hence is most capable of revealing its "uncoded" or "natural" dimension—the presence of the "real."

In *Wings of Desire* (*Himmel über Berlin*, 1987), Wim Wenders approaches the issue of cinema's complex relation to the real from a number of avenues. With its gestures toward semi-documentary status, *Wings of Desire* takes Kracauer's—and Bazin's—perspective toward the real in cinema, suggesting with Bazin that cinema bears an "ontogenetic" relation to the real (Bazin 1967, 19). Though obviously not a documentary in any strict sense, *Wings of Desire* draws upon the genre of the city symphony in carrying out its complex project; a somewhat lyricized image of an as-yet-divided Berlin forms the backdrop for this film's meditations on a variety of representational systems, that of cinema among them.[3] The film's ubiquitous and intrusive camera reveals a strong urge to present a cross-section of Berlin's populace: it pursues a young girl half-heartedly playing at prostitution, artists contemplating their work, an alienated youth for whom rock music functions as a lifeline, aging workers, a Turkish woman doing her laundry, streams of pedestrians and, everywhere, the city's children. Wenders' probing camera with its aerial perspectives invades the spaces of Berlin and lays them open to the spectatorial view, voyeuristically pursuing pedestrians into the private spaces of their apartments with what resembles an erotic fervor. Like other films of its genre, the film presents its vision as totalizing: shots of a woman in labor complement shots of a dying motorcyclist and, like Ruttmann's *Berlin: Symphony of a City* (1927), *Wings of Desire* presents a suicide to our view. But the camera records a reality that remains in some sense impenetrable. Perhaps it is for this reason that Wenders' film exhibits, as I will claim, traces of a directorial desire to incorporate that reality, to penetrate it, and even to merge with it in the space of the text.

As though to highlight the real by aesthetic means, both Berlin films impose formalist techniques upon the images of the city. But if *Wings of Desire* appears to emulate the earlier film in its fascination with movement, in Wenders this fascination derives only in part from a preoccupation with cinematography, with the production of moving images. In this regard, Wenders' film seems to support Metz's dictum that "because movement is never material but *always* visual, to reproduce its appearance is to duplicate reality" (Metz 1974, 8–9). If Wenders represents his characters in every conceivable mode of transportation, it is also because these vehicles (cars, of "road movie" fame, are prominently featured) connect the various spaces of the city to one another, and evoke Wenders' typical manner of experiencing reality cinematically: a city for Wenders is a gridwork between landmarks. In *Wings of Desire*, there is a movement away from the internationalized world of *The American Friend* (1977), whose cities visually merge into one indistinguishable metropolis. The Kaiser-Wilhelm-Gedächtnis-Kirche, the Siegessäule, the Brandenburger Tor, the Kurfürstendamm, the Staatsbibliothek, and the Wall: images of Berlin's representative spaces mark the body of this text with the texture of reality.[4]

The problem of identity is central to the narratives constructed by Wenders and Peter Handke, his frequent collaborator, and their sustained interest in material reality, derived from the insistence on surface in the *nouveau roman* as well as from a Benjaminian interest in topography, relates to this concern (Geist 1988). Objects mediate between reality and the perceiving subject, both displacing and augmenting the search for personal identity. Photographs—which Wenders refers to as "monuments of moments" (Rayns 1974–75, 6)—are from this point of view particularly privileged objects in that they link the problem of identity to that of perception and memory, an idea that also recalls the theoretical underpinnings of the *nouveau roman* while alluding at the same time to Kracauer's 1927 essay on photography. For Wenders, polaroids, as unprintable photographs without negatives and hence not directly reproducible, more closely resemble paintings than ordinary photographs (Dawson 1976, 23). But as "instant objects," polaroids are also of interest to Wenders insofar as they—like other photographs in this regard—arrest the flow of time, "embalming" it, as Bazin has claimed.[5] Often photographs in Wenders' films are connected with the mother, as in *Kings of the Road*, or meditate directly upon the question of identity, as in *The American Friend*. In Wenders' films, photographs take on a totemic quality, as does the photograph of a piece of barren land in *Paris, Texas*: this image documents the place of the primal scene for Travis, the central character whose refusal of language is an attempt to reject that scene by a return to a pre-oedipal condition. In conjunction with the deathly stillness that is photography, this moment figures a merging of origins and ends. Anselm Haverkamp, alluding both to Kracauer's essay and to Roland Barthes, writes that "what photography is taking pictures of, in short, is Time itself" (1993, 264). The representation of time in its cessation: this is one significance that photographs hold for Wenders, whose early short films were shot without any cuts, recording the passage of time by means of what Wenders calls a "phenomenological approach" (Dawson 1976, 10–11). The "ghostly reality" of the photograph, as Kracauer puts it in his essay, is "unredeemed" (*unerlöst*, 32); its spatial configurations do not necessarily imply a whole. For Kracauer, the photograph kills off the person it represents, for "under the photograph of a person his story lies buried as under a blanket of snow" ("Die Photographie" 1963, 26, trans. mine). Already in this 1927 essay, Kracauer suggests that film, on the other hand, can redeem physical reality by telling its story. Similarly, in *Camera Lucida* Barthes' writing substitutes for the photograph of the dead mother in which it originates, but which it never brings to view.

As though in an effort both to frame and narrate the reality that the camera admits into *Wings of Desire*, the body of Wenders' cinematic narrative is bracketed by images of writing produced by the angel Damiel's writing hand that opens and closes the film. Since the film begins in black and white and only gradually acquires color, the initial black and white images are the more obviously presented as cinematic writing, as though to counteract a Bazinian realism with an allusion to the *nouvelle vague's* "caméra stylo." Connected with secondariness and absence, however, writing is doubly coded as "fallen" in the film: the angel Damiel is only capable of writing after he has literally "fallen"—after, that is, he has acquired a body and a history. The film's narrative, the whole of which exists as a flashback of sorts, is punctuated by Damiel's poetic evocation of an unfallen past, the repetition of which—"when the child was a child"—suggests that Damiel's written text, a product of experience like other stories, is governed by an elegiac desire for immediacy that the film represents as available only to the camera.

Wings of Desire contains a figuration of the narrative impulse in the character of Homer, "the storyteller," as he is usually called. This old man, in whom stories are said simply to "well up," is presented both as an allegorical figure, an ahistorical storyteller who has existed through the ages—whose "listeners" gradually became his readers at the point at which the oral tradition is superseded by the written one—*and* as a man with a specific German past dating from the early part of this century. Not surprisingly, one of the spaces in which the storyteller appears is the library, and in the delineation of this space allegiance is also divided between reference and self-reference: it is at once quite obviously Berlin's Staatsbibliothek and also a kind of Borgesian, allegorical Library. As the storyteller ponders a book of photographs of Berliners by August Sander, these photographic "memories" are replaced—in effect "animated"—by actual wartime documentary footage of the destroyed city with its dead. This movement from the Sander photograph to the moving picture also constitutes one of several allusions to Benjamin contained in Wenders' film,[6] suggesting the (historical) transition from the medium of photography as the mode appropriate to capturing the essence of the city to that of film as its proper medium. (The use of Curt Bois in the role of storyteller confirms the connection of this episode with the history of German cinema.) As Benjamin suggests in his "Berlin Chronicle"—another text that is a meditation on place, memory, and their representation—"the closer we come to [Berlin's] present-day, fluid, functional existence, the narrower draws the circle of what can be photographed" (1978, 8). Sanders' photographs, *Wings of Desire* implies, while "authentic" for their historical moment, are not adequate to the realities of war, which can only be gestured toward by the fragments of *cinema verité* that Wenders' film contains.[7] At the same time, however, this documentary footage is represented as constituting the storyteller's personal memories. As in the opening sequence of the film, where handwriting and the "writing" of the camera occur in concert with the narrating voice, in this moment the sense of the real conveyed in a genuinely documentary cinema is relativized—or redeemed—by appearing as the product of narrative desire and personal memory.

For Wenders, it would seem, as for Benjamin, "memory is not an instrument for exploring the past, but its theater. It is the medium of experience as the ground is the medium in which dead cities lie interred" (1978, 25). On another occasion, the storyteller as would-be *flaneur* hunts for the remembered places of a destroyed Berlin, for the Potsdamer Platz, site of the Café Josti where he had sat and of the tobacconist he had frequented. As the storyteller wanders aimlessly within a transformed cityscape, his fading voice mourns and is unable to evoke the places we do not see. Voice alone has lost its invocatory power; in the meantime, the camera exposes the rubble and rubbish of Berlin's "no man's land" to view. It reveals the odd chair and sofa, the detritus of another time that constitutes a topography of images around which memory may take shape. For Benjamin, such images, "like torsos in a collector's gallery," constitute the real treasure to be "unearthed" within this medium (1978, 25).

As in the example of the storyteller, memory, story, and history (the latter two joined in the word *Geschichte*) merge in the episode surrounding Peter Falk, who appears as an actor in a film concerning the Nazi past. In keeping with his interest in topography, Wenders focuses on the making of this film rather than on its subject: the camera lingers over the costumes, the set, and the actors as the material of which the film is to be constructed. Echoing Benjamin's project in the "Berlin Chronicle," stray memories that forge a fragile link to this period are more meaningful as evocations of the past than the film's narrative: Peter Falk meditates on the Berlin of the past via memories of his grandmother. In typical Handke fashion, these memories are cued linguistically through the words "spazieren" and "arbeiten" that evoke her image for Falk. Here the "Berlin Chronicle" resurfaces: memories are often generated, Benjamin notes, by words that—through the process of condensation—have attained the status of things. Benjamin's archaeological metaphor of the space of memory as an interred city is supplemented by a geological one: such words, like "a malleable mass that has later cooled and hardened" and preserve in him "the imprint of a collision between a larger collective" (1978, 14) and himself. In the scene involving Falk, language—expressive of its time and of those who share it—is given a material density—the word as fossil—that facilitates the conjuration of the past.

Another sequence in Wenders' film harnesses the invocatory power of language to the image while affirming the priority of that image: a visual montage illustrates a voice-over in which a creation myth suggests a land before time—and language. This spoken myth gives way to a brief evocation of "history," which in turn yields to images of the "present," swans floating on the river Spree that reveal the myth's romantic origins. Tellingly, the images that illustrate this narration are very much in the mode of Werner Herzog, while the intoning voice-over presents a disquisition on the origin of language and writing to which Herzog might also subscribe. It is at the end of this sequence that the main character, the angel Damiel, expresses his desire for embodiment and for a story—*Geschichte*—once again suggesting the merger of the personal narrative with the grander narrative of history. In "The Philomela Project," Geoffrey Hartman reads this merger as a productive one: "The Germans—but they are only an extreme case for

Wenders—must learn to experience their past without evasion, and this the film translates as *to experience for the first time*" (1991, 172).

For Wenders, Berlin is the sum of its subjectivities, and each man is indeed an island linked, however, by a network comparable to the roads connecting monuments and public places. Motion along these roads stands in not only for film language, but for language per se, for arteries of communication. *Wings of Desire* is a far cry indeed from the documentary without a voice that Ruttmann's Berlin film was originally intended to be, the kind of film that, according to Mary Ann Doane, "promotes the illusion that reality speaks and is not spoken" (1986, 344). Montage is the dominant structuring principle of Ruttmann's Berlin film and, given its historical moment, this is necessarily a voiceless montage, a montage of images alone that renders human bodies mechanisms continuous with their surroundings. In contrast, what is notable about Wenders' film is the montage of *voices* it comprises: its montage of interior monologues, so extensive as to dominate the fabric of the film and to compose its network, is unusual in film history.8 Presented by means of voice-overs, this montage of sound constitutes an aural equivalent of the film's montage of images, thus fulfilling what Lacan calls the invocatory drive, the spectator's drive to hear as well as to see (Doane 1986, 347). By imposing voice-overs upon the images of characters' bodies—rather than simply allowing them to speak their lines of dialogue—the film acts out its desire to penetrate the opacity of their bodily presence, perhaps precisely because the body belongs to the impenetrable real.

When the cinematic voice is not "anchored" or grounded in an imaged body, this detachment of sound from its source threatens simultaneously to reveal the voice as a signifier and the heterogeneity of film as a medium (Doane 1986, 340). In the case of the interior monologue, as Doane points out, "the voice and the body are represented simultaneously, but the voice, far from being an extension of the body, manifests its inner lining. The voice displays what is inaccessible to the image, what exceeds the visible: the 'inner life' of the character. The voice here is the privileged mark of interiority, turning the body 'inside out' " (1986, 341). In *Berlin: Symphony of a City*, the absence of an overarching narrative other than that of its own formalizing impulse suggests that this film is to some extent *about* the unavailability of personal narratives in an urban setting. Wenders' interior monologues, in contrast, impose personal narratives upon the characters that are more intimate than any that the spectatorial gaze alone can afford. But Wenders' control over the image is short-lived: through the separation of speech from its source in the speaking subject, a rupture is created between the revealed body—whose mouth does not move—and the personal voice of the interior monologue. This rupture, slight as it is, produces a split in point of view for the spectator, who cannot wholly reconcile image track with sound track.

Thomas Elsaesser has called the cinema "an apparatus designed by a Kantian epistemologist," basing this claim on Baudry's discussion of that "hidden third term" of the cinematic apparatus—the camera—which necessarily sets up "an unbridgeable subject/object division that renders the object forever unknowable" (1986, 536). In the films of Herzog, Fassbinder, and Wenders alike, Elsaesser has noted, both the place of the "self" and that of the spectator are effectively "empty" and the camera both unlocalizable and omnipresent. Indeed, *Wings of Desire*, like Ruttmann's film, is characterized at times by flashily subjective camerawork from a character's point of view, while at other times the camera is invasive and "disembodied." Unsuccessful though it may be, the use of interior monologue is one way in which *Wings of Desire* gestures toward a bridging of the gap between subject and object necessarily set up by cinema.

Most obviously, perhaps, the collapse of subject into object occurs on the level of the narrative, for Wenders's film allegorizes its desire for access to the seen. The narrative proper begins with a shot of clouds followed by an image of a great "transcendental eye" that cues a preoccupation with vision. It tells the story of the angel Damiel's desire to leave the realm of the spiritual for that of the material and for bodily sensations: he wants to feel pain, to take off his shoes under the table, to feed the cat—"like Philip Marlowe." Damiel wants an existence governed by temporality: he wants a story. A frustrated observer of life, Damiel is distanced by virtue of his spectatorial relation to the world: he can see and hear, but he cannot be seen or be heard in turn, and hence cannot participate in the narrative of life that unfolds before him. Although Damiel is necessarily visible to the film's spectator, within its diegesis he is visible only to children who, like him, are as yet unfallen.

During the course of the narrative, Damiel's desire for embodiment is fired by the female trapeze artist Marion who, as a circus performer, offers a lure for the eye. Although Damiel feels desire for Marion, she cannot feel his touch and he cannot be touched in turn; the frustration provoked by Marion, as spectacle, motivates Damiel to abandon his voyeuristic relation to the city and its inhabitants and to participate in its life. We might say, then, that Damiel's position closely parallels that of both the (male) spectator and the director of a film: he is caught up in narratives in which he cannot participate, which he must watch from a distance, and to which he exists in a relation of desire. Insofar as Marion is connected with the camera as well, Damiel's desire for her also figures the directorial preoccupation with the apparatus.[9] Wenders's coup in this film is to have narrativized the spectatorial and, somewhat more obliquely, the directorial position. During the course of *Wings of Desire*, the angel Damiel "materializes"—is rendered "real" in the context of the narrative—and thus metaphorically realizes the spectator's and director's entry into the text.

Wenders signals Damiel's embodiment through an ingenious use of color: before his "fall," Damiel had been able to "see" only in black and white. After his "fall" deposits him near the Berlin Wall, his head bleeding slightly, the scene gradually becomes suffused with color—the film is now "in living technicolor," as it were—and the Wall is revealed to be decorated with multiply reproduced images of cartoon men, graffiti by the artist Thierry Noir,[10] featuring the color red. Almost immediately, Damiel touches his wound, says of his blood "it is red" and tastes it, learning colors and physical sensations at one and the same time. Lest we should forget, however, that color retains the representational force that had been the exclusive province of black and white, the paint on the Wall is there to remind us of this, ironizing the success of Damiel's descent into the real. It is there as well to suggest a similarity between red paint and red blood, less ironically, pointing thereby to a mode of representation that seeks to collapse the distance between body and sign, despite remaining irreducibly a sign.[11] By means of this scene, the film gestures toward actualization, toward the attainment of the real, and in this way metaphorically infuses contemporary—reproducible, cinematic—representations with new life. As a gesture toward the real, it exists in opposition to a *trompe l'oeil* moment in Wenders' *Paris, Texas* (1984), in which the camera pulls back to reveal that the blue sky against which the Dean Stockwell character had been posed is actually a commercial, reproducible billboard representation.[12] In this moment, the irrefutably textual status of reality is gestured toward; *Wings of Desire* wants instead to focus its materiality.

In *Wings of Desire*, Wenders is fascinated with an impenetrable "reality" that enters film via the camera, and this fascination explains his concern with quasi-documentary images. Finding this "reality" to be inaccessible, Wenders inverts the problem by composing a narrative around the real by means of which he can then fictionally enter what has obviously become a text. By suggesting that he can be absorbed into the spectacle before him, Wenders stages a collapse of the subject/object relation implicit in cinema, attempting thus to resolve the narrative of desire at its most basic level. Wenders narrativizes this collapse in the sexual and spiritual union of Damiel with Marion, concerning which Damiel's voice-over claims, "I was in her and she was around me."[13] Tellingly, the desire for fusion with the film is figured not only as a desire for sexual union, but also as the regressive desire, not fully conscious in the film, to return to the womb (thus echoing the desire of Travis in *Paris, Texas*). Nevertheless, from a cinematic perspective, what Wenders' film effects is a metaphorical collapse with the "real," a collapse that is figured as a "becoming real" within the narrative and as an act of erotic appropriation. This strategy—which we might call Wenders' "solution" to the subject/object gap in cinema—is an "authentically" postmodern solution.

A brief look at Godard's *Two or Three Things I Know about Her* (1966), a film that conflates city and woman, may serve to bring Wenders' film into relief. In *Two or Three Things*, it is the director's voice—Godard's voice-over—that unites the various representational systems that are carefully separated and juxtaposed by the film's modernism. It is Godard's subjective, often whispering and intimate voice that binds the systems he has deliberately taken apart into a new whole. Indeed, his voice-over, unanchored by any visible body, suggests the presence of a muted but insinuating authority, and the controlling power of this voice, given the subject matter of the film (the city as prostitute), is connected with sexual control—over the woman whose story is told, over the city whose story the woman indirectly tells, and over the body of the film itself. Wenders' film, on the other hand, is marked by an even higher degree of self-consciousness about the directorial power to dominate the material of film than Godard's, a mode of self-consciousness (not without its own attendant blindness) that substitutes fusion for dominance.

The rhetoric of the postmodern aside, however, Wenders' allegory of fusion ultimately remains just that. Damiel, though granted a body and plunged into the city to which he had previously existed in the relation of voyeur, is nevertheless ultimately and ironically left in the position of writer and narrator. Distanced in the act of writing, at the end of the film Damiel's body is figured only in a gesture of loss as the writing hand that frames the film. While *Wings of Desire* does seem to suggest that cinema "embodies"—gives immediacy, life, and color to—the hopelessly distanced signs of the writer's medium, in its final frames the various subjectivities that the film had been at such pains to evoke collapse into the subjectivity of its authors after all, and its voice-overs stand revealed as Handke's text. Its "documentary" images acknowledged to have been shaped by human perception, Berlin itself stands revealed as the product of the authors' constructing view.

NOTES

This essay is for Marilyn Fries, who introduced me to the hold that cities exercise upon the imagination.

1. See Benjamin, "A Small History of Photography" (1979, 255), and Sontag, *On Photography* (1973, 23).

2. Benjamin, "A Small History of Photography" (1979, 243); he makes a similar point concerning film in "The Work of Art in the Age of Mechanical Reproduction." As far as later photography is concerned, Benjamin is in agreement with Brecht concerning the necessity of shaping the image.

3. Caldwell and Rea have commented on the fact that Wenders' film evokes *Symphony of a City*; see also Kolker and Beicken (1993, 144).

4. Undoubtedly they also mark Wenders' return from a self-imposed exile and his deliberate identification with a cultural context that is specifically German. As Wenders himself has said, the film reflects "the desire of someone who's been away from Germany for a long time, and who could only ever experience 'Germanness' in this one city" (as quoted in Donohue 1992, 13).

5. See: Rayns, "Forms of Address" 1974–75, 6; Bazin, "The Ontology of the Photographic Image" 1967, 14; Kracauer's essay on photography anticipates Bazin's thinking on a number of points. See Siegfried Kracauer, "Die Photographie" (1963).

6. As Vila and Kuzniar have pointed out (1992, 16), one reader in the library is shown reading Benjamin's reading of Klee's "Angelus Novus" in *Theses on the Philosophy of History*.

7. It should be noted, however, that Wenders' gesture of animating the photograph is also a gesture of rivalry with photography. In *Kings of the Road*, for example, the movie camera's images substitute for a torn-up photograph of the grandmother's house.

8. In literary history, of course, we associate it with the modernism of James Joyce and of Döblin's *Berlin Alexanderplatz*—to which Wenders' technique may be alluding. In my reading of Wenders' film I am indebted to one of my students, Kevin Affonso, whose senior essay on Wenders (May 1991) helped to shape some of my ideas.

9. Here Wenders plays upon the traditional conflation of circus trapeze acts with virtuoso displays of camera movement.

10. I am indebted to Karin Schroeter of Brown University for this information.

11. It is here that Wenders' film most clearly shows its Kleistian preoccupations. Indeed, this film gives expression to the position delineated in Kleist's "Letter of a Painter to His Son," in which a work of art—a painting—is seen as the union of body and mind, the vigorous offspring of both whose climbing about between heaven and earth—*zwischen Himmel und Erde*—(whose ontological status, as it were) will perplex philosophers and aestheticians. It is not surprising, then, that—as Kolker and Beicken put it—"Damiel . . . comes to Marion in a

dream, in full angelic armor—reminiscent of Eric Rohmer's *The Marquise of O*"
(1993, 156). Reminiscent also, I might add, of *Amphitryon*.

12. Pascal Bonitzer reads this moment as an example of Lacanian *anamorphosis* in cinema (1985, 36).

13. Although I am intrigued by this film's theoretical project, I am disturbed
by its sentimental, tendentious tone and even more by its ideology; it is regressive
and does nothing to redeem the role of women in Wenders' films, no matter how
much it claims the contrary.

REFERENCES

Barthes, Roland. *Image, Music, Text*. Translated by Stephen Heath. New York:
Hill and Wang, 1977.
Bazin, André. "The Myth of Total Cinema." In *What Is Cinema?*, vol. I. Translated by Hugh Gray. Berkeley: University of California Press, 1967.
Benjamin, Walter. "A Berlin Chronicle." In *Reflections: Essays, Aphorisms, Autobiographical Writings*. Translated by Edmund Jephcott. New York: Harcourt, Brace Jovanovich, 1978.
————. "A Small History of Photography." In *One-Way Street and Other Writings*. Translated by Edmund Jephcott. London: NLB, 1979.
Bonitzer, Pascal. *Décadrages: Peinture et cinéma*. Paris: Cahiers du Cinéma/Editions de l'Etoile, 1985.
Caldwell, David, and Paul W. Rea. "Handke's and Wenders's *Wings of Desire*: Transcending Postmodernism." *German Quarterly* 64 (1991): 46–53.
Dawson, Jan. *Wim Wenders*. Translated by Carla Wartenberg. New York: Zoetrope, 1976.
Doane, Mary Ann. "The Voice in the Cinema: The Articulation of Body and Space." In *Narrative, Apparatus, Ideology: A Film Theory Reader*, edited by Philip Rosen. New York: Columbia University Press, 1986.
Donohue, Walter. "Revelations: An Interview with Wim Wenders." *Sight and Sound* 12 (May 1992): 8–13.
Elsaesser, Thomas. "Primary Identification and the Historical Subject: Fassbinder and Germany." In *Narrative, Apparatus, Ideology: A Film Reader*, edited by Philip Rosen. New York: Columbia University Press, 1986.
Geist, Kathe. *The Cinema of Wim Wenders: From Paris, France to* Paris, Texas. Ann Arbor: University of Michigan Press, 1988.
Hartman, Geoffrey H. "The Philomela Project." In *Minor Prophecies: The Literary Essay in the Culture Wars*. Cambridge, Mass.: Harvard University Press, 1991.
Haverkamp, Anselm. "The Memory of Pictures: Roland Barthes and Augustine on Photography." *Comparative Literature* 45 (1993): 258–78.
Kolker, Robert Phillip, and Peter Beicken. *The Films of Wim Wenders: Cinema as Vision and Desire*. Cambridge: Cambridge University Press, 1993.

Kracauer, Siegfried. *From Caligari to Hitler: A Psychological History of the German Film*. Princeton, N.J.: Princeton University Press, 1947.

————. "Die Photographie." In *Das Ornament der Masse*. Frankfurt am Main: Suhrkamp, 1963.

————. *Theory of Film: The Redemption of Physical Reality*. London: Oxford University Press, 1960.

————. "The Mass Ornament." *New German Critique* 5 (1975): 67–76.

Metz, Christian. "On the Impression of Reality in the Cinema." In *Film Language: A Semiotics of the Cinema*. Translated by Michael Taylor. New York: Oxford University Press, 1974.

Rayns, Tony. "Forms of Address: Interviews with Three German Filmmakers." *Sight and Sound* 44 (Winter 1974–75): 2–7.

Sontag, Susan. *On Photography*. New York: Farrar, Straus and Giroux, 1973.

Vila, Xavier, and Alice Kuzniar. "Witnessing Narration in *Wings of Desire*." *Film Criticism* 16 (1992): 53–65.

8

The Ubiquitous Wall: Divided Berlin in Post-Wall Fiction

Siegfried Mews

During the slightly more than twenty-eight years of its existence, from August 13, 1961 to November 9, 1989, the Berlin Wall was one of the most conspicuous and infamous examples of a political boundary that, in the prevailing Western view, signified containment, isolation, and stasis rather than freedom of movement, communication, and change. The Berlin Wall provided the most visible manifestation not only of the post–World War II division of Berlin and Germany but also of the "iron curtain" that, in Winston Churchill's memorable phrase, split Europe into East and West. As a much discussed topic of contemporaneous *Realpolitik* and *Realgeschichte*, the Wall inevitably attracted the attention of writers of fiction. Generally speaking, German authors—inasmuch as they chose to acknowledge its existence in their fiction—tended to perceive issues related to the Wall in individualistic or nationalistic terms; authors of espionage thrillers, whose stock-in-trade was the world of political intrigue, the global East-West conflict, and the Cold War, supplied the international dimension and demonstrated that the Wall was by no means an exclusively German problem.

The end of the Cold War, the demise of the German Democratic Republic, and German unification on October 3, 1990, all of which were brought about by the fall of the Wall, signify changes of a magnitude virtually inconceivable before. These changes require an often painful adjustment to the post-Wall situation. Berlin, Germany's old and new capital, is now faced with both a singular opportunity and a singular challenge: the metropolis must engage in the formidable task of (re)constructing its center that was formed by the Wall (Schneider, "Chancen I" 1993, 54). According to longtime Berlin resident Peter Schneider, during the next five years Berlin's cityscape will witness changes of a virtually unprecedented magnitude ("Chancen II" 1993, 40).

The impending changes do not allow us to completely ignore the substantial body of fictional texts, explicitly written as contemporaneous responses to the Wall's existence, that may be read as attempts to question its legitimacy, to become accustomed to it, or even to justify it. Since most of the major texts have been analyzed in a monograph that seeks to chronicle the representation of the Wall as a literary subject in German fiction from the 1960s to the 1980s (Frech 1992; Mews 1990), the following discussion will center on noteworthy texts by well-established authors that were penned—for the most part—and published after its fall.

Perhaps not surprisingly, some of the post-Wall texts by Christa Wolf, Monika Maron, Jurek Becker, and Peter Schneider constitute a fictional revisitation of a construct that is no longer physically present but has impressed itself indelibly on the collective consciousness. Indeed, Schneider's adage in *Der Mauerspringer* (*The Wall Jumper*, 1982) has proven prophetic: "It will take longer to tear down the Wall in our heads than any wrecking company will need for the Wall we can see" (119). The survival of the ideological and psychological Wall manifests itself in post-Wall fiction: authors who locate their narratives in the historical context of divided Berlin and include implicit or explicit references to the Wall as the city's most ubiquitous and conspicuous phenomenon contribute via their texts to the ongoing debate of how to come to terms with the legacy of Berlin's and Germany's partition. The dimensions of this literary debate that entails the retrospective assessment of the public function of writers and their products in both parts of Germany on the one hand and attempts to chart the future course of literary endeavors in the united Germany on the other need not be explored here (see Williams, Parkes, Smith 1991; Mews 1993). Suffice it to state that the four different retrospective views of the Wall to be discussed are, to varying degrees, indicative of the difficulties German writers and intellectuals have encountered in coping with their recent past.

WOLF'S *WAS BLEIBT*

Among the four texts—Wolf's *Was bleibt* (*What Remains*, 1990), Maron's *Stille Zeile Sechs* (*Quiet Close No. 6*, 1991), Becker's *Amanda herzlos* (*Heartless Amanda*, 1992), and Schneider's *Paarungen* (*Pairings*, 1992)—Wolf's slim prose narrative is clearly the most controversial. Published in June

1990, *Was bleibt* has been called the first quasi pan-German publication (Schirrmacher 1990, 86). Yet apart from the fact that *Was bleibt* was published in post-Wall Germany, it is difficult to detect any pronounced "pan-German" tendency. Originally written in 1979 and revised in an unspecified manner in November 1989—an omission that was noted critically by several reviewers (Hage 1993, 197)—the autobiographical text deals with a disquieting event in the life of the narrating I (easily—albeit not exclusively—to be identified as Christa Wolf): she has become the object of surveillance by the omnipotent and omnipresent secret police, the dreaded *Stasi*, an organization that the narrator never mentions directly by name. Although in an essay of March 1990 Wolf alluded to the difficult process of redefining her social role as a writer in a postsocialist society (*Dialog* 167), *Was bleibt* can hardly be considered a valid attempt to tackle this task and to come to terms with her own long-held socialist convictions. Hence Wolf's prose narrative gained a degree of notoriety that is in inverse proportion to its artistic merit. Yet the debate about *Was bleibt*, which extended into the fall of 1990 and beyond, constituted the culmination of the probing of GDR literature that began after the dismantling of the Wall. Both friend and foe perceived Wolf as the foremost representative of GDR literature; as the title of a collection of essays put it, the central issue of the debate was not and is not Wolf (Anz). Rather, her case offered a prime example of GDR writers' strengths and weaknesses, their success and failure, and their uneasy hovering between opposition and accommodation.

Viewed in the context of that debate, Wolf's *Was bleibt* may be appropriately called an ambiguous farewell both to GDR society and to her own role as a GDR writer—however, without offering a new perspective (Lehnert 1991, 431). Although there is no explicit reference to the Wall, in one significant episode, which is fraught with intertextual references, the narrator faces the inescapable facts of Berlin's and Germany's division. She leaves her apartment in Berlin's *Mitte* district (the urban and administrative center of pre-1945 Berlin), walks in a southerly direction along the Fried

richstraße (which led to famed Checkpoint Charlie), and crosses the Weidendamm Bridge near the Theater am Schiffbauerdamm, home of Bertolt Brecht's and Helene Weigel's Berliner Ensemble. Upon noticing the announcement of the production of Brecht's *Galileo*, she reminisces about "poor old BB" (246) and his "purified dialectics" (246) that provided the playwright with the certainty to distinguish clearly between good and evil and have his figure Galileo proclaim the truth—albeit "fearful and cunning" (246). Such certainty is no longer available to Brecht's successors, including the narrator. She has experienced a sense of alienation from the socialist society that Brecht's figure and Brecht himself strove for. She is reminded of the "endless walks" she undertook more than two years ago. At that time, she was driven by "pure, raging pain" that turned her into an alienated being, "another person," who felt as if she were in "foreign territory," wandering through the "nameless streets of a nameless city" (246–47). We know from textual evidence that the narrator's walk across the bridge takes place on a day in March 1979 (231, 291); hence we may deduce that the highly disturbing events of more than two years earlier are related to the expatriation in November 1976 of poet/singer Wolf Biermann. This event sent cultural shock waves through the GDR (Lehnert 1991, 424); Wolf was among the first to sign an open letter, which was eventually signed by more than seventy prominent writers and intellectuals (Emmerich 1981, 188–89), protesting the expatriation and re-questing its reconsideration. As a consequence of her protest, Wolf was placed under open surveillance by the *Stasi*—precisely the procedure the narrator was subjected to (246 et passim). Rumors about Wolf's recanting and with-drawal of her signature under pressure (Schirrmacher 1990, 84) proved ultimately to be unfounded; the recantation rumor is attributable to a *Stasi* disinformation campaign designed to discredit Wolf ("Margarete" 1993, 165).

The passage that precedes the narrator's reflections on the turbulent events of November 1976 reads: "Leaning over the railing [of Weidendamm Bridge], I saw ducks and sea gulls and a barge with a black, red, and gold flag. . . . In the middle of the bridge hangs the cast-iron Prussian eagle, which stared at me mockingly and which I lightly touched in passing" (246). Herbert Lehnert (1991, 426–27) has suggested that the Prussian eagle alludes to Wolf's narrative *Kein Ort. Nirgends* (*No Place on Earth*, 1982) about the fictional encounter between Heinrich von Kleist (1777–1811) and Caroline von Gün-derrode (1780–1806) and to Wolf's essay on Günderrode (*Author's Dimen-sion* 1993, 131–75). Lehnert does not offer any explanation as to the function of the Prussian eagle as the connecting link between *Was bleibt* and Wolf's two previous texts; however, his argument that Wolf's interest in both Kleist and Günderrode (who as an impoverished aristocratic female was particularly disadvantaged) is attributable to her perception of them as representative alienated German intellectuals who engaged in the compensatory activity of writing is corroborated by Wolf. In interviews and essays during the 1980s (*Dialog* 1990, 142; *Author's Dimension* 1993, ix–x, 322) Wolf characterized her turning to the past as a reaction to her severely curtailed access to GDR media after her protest in the Biermann affair. Robbed of the possibility to address topical issues, she found some solace in the discovery of the kindred spirits of alienated intellectuals in literary history.

At the root of the narrator's alienation from society in *Was bleibt* is the issue of unfulfilled hopes and broken promises for sociopolitical reform. It remains open whether the barge in the passage cited above is flying the colors of the Federal Republic or those of the GDR—black, red, and gold in both cases; the GDR flag featured an additional emblem. Hence the reader may indeed associate the flag with the hope for the attainment of civil liberties and of unification under democratic auspices—the chief goals of the failed 1848 revolution during which the colors black, red, and gold were widely used (Lehnert 1991, 427). In contrast to the flag, the Prussian eagle is not emblematic of civil liberties in that it stands for both the authoritarian Prussian/German empire and the two contemporaneous German states (Lermen and Loewen 1987, 369). Yet Biermann in his well-known "Ballade vom preußischen Ikarus" ("Ballad of the Prussian Icarus," 1992) refashioned the Prussian eagle on the Weidendamm Bridge, the "hated bird" (47), and used it both as an identification figure and as a projection of his persona's ambivalent, conflicting desires: his wish to remain in "our half-country," the "island" held together by as well as surrounded by barbed wire, and his longing to become unfettered and to be able to move freely in both a literal and figurative sense—despite his realization that even limited flight must end in a precipitous fall (45, 47). Biermann sang the ballad on November 13, 1976 in Cologne, a few days before he was informed that he would not be allowed to return to the GDR. The fate of Icarus then prefigured Biermann's own fall, his banishment and exile (Lermen and Loewen 1987, 365). The ballad also provided the title for the first collection of Biermann's poems and songs published after his expatriation (*Preußischer Ikarus*, 1978).

In view of Biermann's famous tribute to the Prussian eagle, it is reasonable to expect that the narrator's reminiscences about her involvement in the Biermann affair were prompted by her encounter with the heraldic reminder of Berlin's Prussian and imperial past. In Biermann's ballad the eagle assumes symbolic significance and problematizes the existence of the GDR by drawing attention to its dependence on the Wall, a bulwark protected by "leaden waves" (1978, 45) or the bullets to be faced by transgressors. Another encounter provides the narrator with additional evidence of Berlin's and Germany's division. A "certain glass pavilion" (247) near the Friedrichstraße station, which served as a border checkpoint, induces her to invoke the *vox populi*. Her use of "tear bunker," the term given the pavilion in popular parlance because it witnessed so many heartrending farewell scenes, implies criticism of the highly restrictive and selective travel policies for GDR citizens without special privileges—the majority of the population. Although Wolf herself was largely exempt from such travel restrictions, the narrator's distinction between the appearance of the checkpoint as a "normal building" and her perception of it as a "monster" (248), an abomination, tends to intensify this criticism. Nevertheless, there is a noticeable difference between the topographical authenticity of her account and the vague and evasive formulations she uses in referring to the causes and human enforcers of the GDR's repressive policies. The absolute power of the "assistants" of the unidentified "master who controlled this city" (248) is alluded to in quasi-religious terminology (Lehnert 1991, 429). They are empowered "to bind and to release" (248); the characterization of "the lord who ruled my city without opposition" as "the ruthless advantage of the moment" (248) lacks any specificity and is hardly enlightening. Without going into further detail it may be argued that such vague phraseology highlights the narrator's inability to find her new language (246 et passim) and to overcome a state of dependency and subservience, her desire for "slavery" that, for privileged writers, also entailed a modicum of "pleasure" (246).

As one critic noted, the narrator's problematic timidity differs significantly from Brecht's precepts (Greiner 1990, 67)—although not necessarily from the notoriously unheroic playwright's actions. However, instead of dwelling on the great teacher Brecht who, after all, lived during a period in which good and evil were clearly distinguishable and making choices was simple, it is appropriate to refer to one of Wolf's fellow GDR writers. The narrator's (and Wolf's) cautious behavior and circumspect language differ strikingly from Biermann's courageous demeanor and provocative texts. Hence the Prussian eagle's mocking glance can be explained as an ironic comment on the narrator's lack of courage; her lightly touching the eagle may be interpreted as the gesture of a supplicant asking forgiveness for her inability to speak out more clearly. Faced with both the symbolic and concrete manifestations of one of the major causes of unrest in the GDR of the late 1980s, the travel restrictions, the narrator fails to take an unambiguous stand.

At the beginning of her literary career Wolf had incorporated the events of August 13, 1961 in her narrative *Der geteilte Himmel* (*Divided Heaven*, 1963). Although the Wall is mentioned only once, in both prologue and epilogue the threatening atmosphere caused by its impending construction is expressed in veiled fashion via weather metaphors. The epilogue reinforces protagonist Rita's acceptance of life behind the Wall and her permanent separation from her lover Manfred, who has left the GDR, and conveys her strong affirmation of such a life. Despite its alleged ideological shortcomings and formal deficiencies—for example, the use of "modernist" narrative techniques—GDR cultural functionaries and critics essentially praised Wolf's work for its affirmative stance, a view that is generally shared by present-day Western critics (Frech 1992, 36). If *Der geteilte Himmel* is ultimately concerned with the fate of GDR citizens rather than with the consequences of the Wall's construction for Germans on either side of it, the narrative anticipates the post-Wall *Was bleibt* in its tacit acceptance of confinement behind the Wall.

MARON'S *STILLE ZEILE SECHS*

Wolf's defense of the GDR and her veneration of its founding fathers who legitimized their Stalinist and post-Stalinist repression through their antifascism is implicitly called into question in Maron's *Stille Zeile Sechs*. Maron (born in 1941) began publishing longer works of fiction in the early 1980s, but she was only able to do so in the Federal Republic. In 1988 she obtained a visa that allowed her to leave East Berlin and the GDR. Unlike Wolf, Maron did not belong to the group of privileged writers; in fact, in a February 1990 essay, entitled "Die Schriftsteller und das Volk" ("Writers and the People"), she severely criticized her fellow writers for opposing unification on the grounds that at least some features of the GDR were worth preserving. Maron unequivocally endorsed the people's desire for unification and hailed "their victory over the Wall and State Security [*Stasi*]" (36). In the light of Maron's unambiguous pre-unification rejection of arguments favoring the GDR and her sharp repudiation of post-unification GDR nostalgia and claims for victim status on the part of segments of the former GDR population, it is not surprising that *Stille Zeile Sechs* strikes the accusatory note of a "bitter reckoning" (James 1992). An attempt to come to terms with the GDR past, the novel deals with the guilt incurred by the founding fathers of the GDR in terms of the human suffering they inflicted on those who grew up in the GDR and had no means of escaping. This older generation is chiefly represented by the former party functionary and professor Beerenbaum. During and after Beerenbaum's funeral, which signifies the passing of a generation, the first-person narrator, a female historian in her early forties, recalls in a series of perhaps "quaintly old-fashioned" flashbacks (James 1992) her involuntary cooperation with Beerenbaum. At the same time, she endeavors to present herself exclusively as a victim without admitting her own involvement.

Beerenbaum had dictated his memoirs that, in GDR terms, entailed a paradigmatic success story resembling the political career of Karl Maron, Maron's stepfather and GDR minister of the interior from 1955 to 1963. There is, then, a distinct similarity of author and narrator in terms of depicting the reactions of a "renegade daughter of a communist family"

(James 1992). Despite her resolve not to comment on the dictated material and to confine herself to passive notetaking and typing, the narrator's intense hatred of Beerenbaum, who reminds her of her own father, leads to frequent outbursts on her part. Although she feels cheated out of living a full and meaningful life by the Beerenbaum generation, in the end she is unable to sustain a dichotomous pattern of guilt and responsibility and feels implicated in causing Beerenbaum's death.

The novel's setting is East Berlin, specifically the district of Pankow, seat of the former GDR's prominent party and government functionaries. In the mid 1980s, as indicated by the novel's title, Pankow has become a tranquil haven for retirees. Pankow borders on West Berlin; hence the Wall, significantly called the "only, real Wall" (31), is obtrusively present and causes the narrator to feel being watched in almost Orwellian fashion (34). The Wall's political importance for the stabilization of the GDR is underscored in a heated exchange between Beerenbaum and the narrator. The former defends the construction of the "antifascist protection wall" as a defensive measure and invokes the image of pre-Wall West Berlin as a vampire sucking East Berlin and the GDR's lifeblood through the Brandenburg gate (107–8). In doing so, Beerenbaum unwittingly contradicts the official justification of the Wall, that is, to keep intruders out rather than the GDR population in. But the narrator, repulsed by the mere thought of having to write down the term that in official GDR parlance legitimated the Wall (107), is not attuned to subtle irony and fiercely counters with the argument that the Wall serves as a death trap for transgressors. These two positions represent irreconcilable extremes in the debate about the Wall and reveal the narrator's deep resentment.

This heated exchange gains poignancy through the presence of a writer— a character corresponding to GDR writer Christoph Hein (Hielscher 1992)—who serves Maron as a representative figure to be castigated for those views of GDR writers that she had attacked in her 1990 essay ("Writers"). The narrator's initial assumption that the writer shares her opinion about the inhumanity of the Wall is proved wrong when the latter defends its erection as a "necessary decision" (109). She perceives the writer's agreement with Beerenbaum, a "narrow minded apparatchik" (106), as spineless, opportunistic acquiescence; in Maron's perspective such acquiescence is indicative of the failure of writers to abandon their notion of the GDR, a repressive state with "a ruined economy and a demoralized population" as "the bulwark of their own utopia" ("Writers" 39) and to accept post-Wall, unified Germany as a viable option. There is merit in the suggestion that the novel is "very much a product of the state it is repudiating" in that its "propagandistic function" is allowed to dominate at the expense of "aesthetic merits" (James 1992). Such an assessment merely confirms the ubiquitousness of the mental and ideological Wall in post-Wall fiction.

BECKER'S *AMANDA HERZLOS*

Although Becker did not play a prominent role in the unification debate, he went on record as rejecting Martin Walser's claim in the latter's 1988 essay "Über Deutschland reden" (To Speak about Germany) that Germany's division was essentially a punitive act on the part of the victorious allies at the end of World War II (Parkes 1991, 201). Conversely, in a 1990 essay, entitled "Die Wiedervereinigung der deutschen Literatur" (The Reunification of German Literature), Becker claimed that GDR literature was essentially a result of the conditions imposed upon writers, notably censorship in its various manifestations, and that it would quickly disappear after the dismantling of the Wall. Becker's claim notwithstanding, it is doubtful whether his own novel *Amanda herzlos* does indeed constitute a radical departure from GDR literature.

Unlike the protagonists in Wolf's and Maron's narratives, the heroine of *Amanda herzlos* does not consider herself a victim. In contrast to Maron, who in her post-Wall essays took her former countrymen and countrywomen to task for not facing up to their complicity in sustaining the GDR regime, Becker, who has been living in West Berlin since 1977, does not look back at East Berlin in anger. After all, *Amanda herzlos* features, atypically, a happy ending. Needless to say, this ending was inspired by post-Wall events and would have been virtually inconceivable before the breaching of the Wall. Actually, Becker's novel anticipates unification on a private plane in that the much-loved Amanda is not only permitted to marry a West German radio reporter but also to leave the GDR legally. Becker's plot occasionally requires a hefty dose of suspension of disbelief. For example, Amanda's future husband succeeds in duping the Stasi in order to avoid becoming an informer—a feat that is hardly imaginable in the context of the Stasi's ubiquitous and dreaded role in *Was bleibt*.

Becker's lighthearted approach to the problems posed by the Wall's existence constitutes a significant departure from *Schlaflose Tage* (*Sleepless Days*, 1978), his fourth novel that he was not allowed to publish in the GDR. The novel evokes, albeit in a slightly Kafkaesque vein, "the daily grind of an authoritarian society: the psychic drabness of it all, the draining political rituals, the disenchantments" (Howe 1979, 7). Although the Wall is not a formidable presence and seems to have been implicitly accepted as an unalterable fact of life by the inhabitants of East Berlin, its very impenetrability inspires endeavors to circumvent it and to seek escape routes elsewhere. Tacit acceptance of the Wall turns into renunciation of the concept of *Republikflucht* (escape from the republic/GDR), a criminal offense according to GDR law, when the protagonist is faced with the incarceration of his female companion as a consequence of her unexpected attempt to cross the Hungarian-Austrian border. He becomes "convinced that she had every right to go wherever she pleased. . . . To want to prevent her [from doing so] . . . was an outrageous presumption" (95). Becker's text here assumes the function of articulating via the medium of literature sentiments shared by large segments of the population. In fact, Becker's novel anticipates actual developments, the escape, during the summer and fall of 1989, of thousands of vacationing GDR citizens to the Federal Republic via Hungary and Czechoslovakia.

The exceptional, extraordinary nature of *Grenzüberschreitung* (crossing the border) is not foregrounded in *Amanda herzlos*. Rather, at the conclusion of the novel, Amanda, not by any means a privileged *Reisekader* (a person allowed to leave the country on official business), explains to her son their impending, rather uncommon *Grenzüberschreitung* from East to West in terms of an everyday experience that has both advantages and disadvantages: "You have moved twice already and are still alive." In an effort to emphasize the common bonds between the two parts of Germany, she remarks: "Not even the language is different" (394). The novel ends with Amanda's words: "And do you know that you can buy bananas at every street corner? Truly, that's no disaster"—surely, as Günter de Bruyn noted, a satiric barb directed against GDR writers such as Stefan Heym and his West German counterparts. These writers had enjoyed easy access to consumer goods before the crumbling of the Wall, but during the weeks immediately following its opening they condemned the GDR populace for indulging in crass materialism and a buying spree rather than devoting their energies to another socialist experiment in the interest of preserving the GDR.

Before Amanda and her son are finally allowed to cross the Wall in January 1989, less than a year before its actual disappearance, two border crossings by the West German radio reporter offer contrasting experiences. The first crossing is depicted as a commonplace affair with a routinely jovial border official, whereas the second one entails a thorough search and dismantling of the reporter's car in a scene that is reminiscent of the last episode in Schneider's *Der Mauerspringer*. After all, the Wall remains, as Amanda formulates, "the most dangerous of all borders" (302) with an intricate security system, and she considers even planning to overcome it by unauthorized means as sheer folly. Yet Amanda thinks independently and does not succumb to a simplistic ideological pattern of interpretation: on the one hand, she condemns the shooting and killing at the Wall, on the other, she points out that the downing of an Iranian passenger jet by an American missile in the summer of 1988 cost more lives than had been lost at the Wall (353–54).

Other figures in the novel are far less prone to take a balanced view of the Wall, the Cold War adversaries, and their German allies. Notably Amanda's mother, almost a caricature in her ideological blindness, is impervious to rational argument. Buoyed by her conviction that she belongs to the "victors of history," she deems her daughter's planning to leave the GDR to be a mistake of utmost gravity: Amanda would step backwards "from the future into the past [of] the declining world of capitalism" (318). There is no point in belaboring the irony inherent in such a statement; the West German reporter's comment, "that is the craziest sentence I ever heard" (318), gains its poignancy from events that transpired after the narrated time. Amanda's first husband is an unprincipled opportunist. In order to further his career as a sports journalist he enlists the help of the Stasi in an effort to return ideologically wayward Amanda to the socialist flock. In addition, he seeks to prevent the *Republikflucht* (358) of Amanda and their son for egotistical reasons.

Amanda is rarely given a voice of her own. Therefore, she remains a somewhat shadowy and perhaps inscrutable figure who appears both as the object of desire and the narrated object in the three male narrators' accounts. Narrators number one and number three, who also function as husbands number one and number two, respectively, are following journalistic pursuits and choose the form of written communication to relate their experiences with Amanda. In a lengthy letter to his attorney, the sports reporter seeks to present valid reasons for his divorce; the radio reporter keeps a diary. Amanda's second lover Fritz Hetmann is a genuine writer, albeit a dissident. Not surprisingly, Hetmann uses his relationship with Amanda as the material for a novella; his account includes both his relationship with Amanda and his attempt to reconstruct the text file of the novella that has been erased. The novella's protagonist is a self-portrait of Hetmann who, following his model, is engaged in writing a book; as Hetmann remarks sardonically: "Writers cannot do anything else" (249). Hence there is in Hetmann's narrative the potential of "a story about the story in a story" (249). But Becker is not primarily interested in formal experimentation; rather, the figure of Hetmann serves him to deflate exaggerated notions about the purity of motives on the part of GDR writers presumed to be staunchly oppositional. The novel thus reflects on and participates in the post-Wall literary debate about the ambiguous role of literature under socialism in its aforementioned hovering between accommodation and opposition and examines, tongue in cheek, the privileged position of major GDR writers.

Paradoxically, the Wall does not pose an obstacle to communication that is carried on via the medium of literature. On the contrary, as Amanda explains, the GDR appears as a "bizarre country . . . in which all prohibited authors are celebrities and arouse lascivious interest" (182). For the sake of sustaining the novel's ironic mode, Becker may have indulged in oversimplifying the complex relations between censors and writers; clearly, Amanda's views correspond essentially to those of Becker ("Wiedervereinigung" 1990, 359–62). Instead of suppressing literature, Amanda avers, censorship exercised a salutary function: books prohibited in the GDR were immediately published in West Germany and returned "like a boomerang to the small country" (182). The Wall thus provides an intellectual sanctuary even for the dissident writer inasmuch as he is able to inscribe in his texts deliberate *Grenzverletzungen* or transgressing borders (213) that do not necessarily follow from the topic or structure of his work. Although the writer does so at the risk of expatriation or incarceration (cf. 213), such violation will automatically preclude publication of the respective text in the GDR and thus boost the writer's reputation. Hetmann, in fact, appears as a consummate artist in this game of self-promotion that, in order to succeed, requires a politically and ideologically divided city and country. As Amanda intimates, Hetmann uses interviews in which he makes daring statements as a publicity and advertising tool.

Becker provides further unflattering reflections on the role of GDR writers. In contrast to Hetmann, Amanda becomes involved in genuinely oppositional acts by joining church groups and by participating in the activities of the nascent civil rights movement that eventually became a major contributing force leading to the toppling of the Wall. Although not a typical representative of the GDR *Volk*—Amanda dabbles unsuccessfully in writing and has no profession—her engagement is indicative of the developing split between the people and their writers. As is well known, GDR writers were generally slow to join the civil rights movement, and the consensus between them and the people ceased when the latter opted for unification whereas the former wanted to retain some form of socialism.

Amanda's successive involvement with the three men in her life suggests her progressive distancing from the GDR: the conformist opportunist with the unflattering surname Weniger (Less) is followed by the dissident writer—who prospers because of his dissident status and has no intention of leaving the GDR—and, finally, by the West German radio reporter who enables her to leave East Berlin. Amanda's men do not exert any profound influence on her; although she remarries in the end, there is every indication that she will continue to think and act independently and will not succumb to the allure of Western consumerism.

According to one reviewer, much of Becker's "political comment" seems "irrelevant"; in the face of Becker's prediction of GDR literature's quick demise, this reviewer posits that especially the first and third books of *Amanda herzlos* represent the last of the genre of GDR literature. But in its anticipation of unification—if only on a private level—Becker's humorous and witty revisitation of the Wall is future-oriented in that it also implies a farewell to that ubiquitous phenomenon.

SCHNEIDER'S *PAARUNGEN*

Schneider's *Paarungen*, his first novel-length narrative, may be considered a counterpart to Becker's *Amanda herzlos* in that it takes place in West Berlin during the 1980s. At first glance, this evocation of a specific milieu, which is populated by the veterans of the student movement of the late 1960s and early 1970s, does not seem to be eminently political. Although the Wall is hardly mentioned in the discussions of the three male friends, the novel's protagonists, it has a palpable and uncanny presence: "[The Wall's] shadow reached far, . . . the Wall was present like the God of the Old Testament who does not have a name and of whom one is not allowed to make images" (99). The real Wall is then both precondition and reinforcement of the mental and ideological Wall whose existence Schneider discerned in *Der Mauerspringer* and whose persistence he discussed in his collection of essays, *Extreme Mittellage* (1990; translated as *The German Comedy*, 1991).

Der Mauerspringer, perhaps the most significant fictional text in terms of representing the Wall, challenges the prevailing tendency of the early and middle 1980s to accept the political status quo of a divided city and a divided country. Schneider's prose text provides instructive examples of such accommodation. On Berlin city maps, the Wall was presented in a contrastive pattern inspired by ideology. The desire to express self-sufficient containment was evident in the GDR version: "The world ended at the wall. Beyond the black-bordered finger-thick dividing line identified in the key as the state border, untenanted geography sets in." In contrast, the desire to suppress the unpleasant fact of the Wall's existence was predominant in the Western city map; merely a "small dotted band in delicate pink" (11) unobtrusively refers to the dividing line. Both methods of explanation—the attempt to legitimate the Wall and the attempt to deny or suppress its existence—fall obviously short, and the narrator introduces a perspective that transcends one-sided patterns of explanation based on ideology. On the one hand, the Wall is an unmistakable physical reality: "[I]t is the only structure on earth, apart from the Great Wall of China, that can be seen from the moon with the naked eye"(7). The Wall's elaborate fortification system is described in detail by the narrator, who states matter-of-factly: "The border between the two German states, and especially between the two halves of Berlin, is considered the world's most closely guarded and the most difficult to cross" (52). On the other hand, from the air, the Wall "seems more a civic monument than a border" (5). Such a monument unites rather than separates the "Siamese city" (5). The mirror motif does not only confirm West Germany's and West Berlin's fairness and superiority (12), it also denotes togetherness and common characteristics—albeit in a distorted image (9).

The five interpolated stories of Wall jumpers have in common that their protagonists simply do not accept the Wall's function of dividing the city into two halves. Precisely the absence of overt political motives on the part of the protagonists emphasizes the anomaly of the Wall that, by virtue of its existence, poses an incessant challenge: "The urge to master the Wall . . . would persist as long as the Wall remained standing" (59–60). The five stories offer variations of the narrator's main theme, "the story of a man who loses himself and starts turning into nobody. . . . Having come to distrust the hastily adopted identity that both states offer him, he feels at home only on the border" (22–23). The most extreme and almost farcical case of such loss of identity is offered by Bolle, the double agent, who no longer knows "for whom or what he was working: the East, the West, himself, or a united Germany" (86).

The loss of identity, which is also experienced by the narrator of *Der Mauerspringer*—his "national identity does not depend on either of the German states" (126)—is not the major issue in *Paarungen*. Rather, the title suggests that the novel is concerned with the love life of the former adherents of the free love, unfettered by bourgeois conventions, that the student movement had proclaimed. Now middle-aged, the emotional and sexual ties of Eduard, a molecular biologist rather than a writer, are in disarray: "[He] loves Klara, gets Laura pregnant and adores Jenny; he also gets Jenny pregnant, adores Klara and loves Laura, furthermore he loves Jenny" (Schreiber 1992, 277). Eduard's trials and tribulations are complemented by those of this drinking buddies, the Jewish musician André and the East Berlin poet Theo who apparently is allowed to travel freely to the West. This configuration—similar to that of Amanda's three men in Becker's novel—lends itself to the exploration of that which divides East and West as well as that which they have in common. As in *Amanda herzlos*, this exploration has been undertaken from the vantage point of the post-Wall situation; it lends the novel its slightly scurrilous features.

The physical construct of the Wall is put to some uncommon use in one particular scene. When Eduard and Laura meet in a West Berlin border café, the narrator's reference to the film version of John Le Carré's *The Spy Who Came in from the Cold* evinces the threatening nature of the Wall during the height of the Cold War (204); he further notes the anomaly of the Wall's "crazy course" (206) and remarks on the paradoxical fact that the border guards usually turn their backs to the West because "the enemy came always from their own hinterland" (207). Yet Laura, an Italian opera singer who does not respect German taboos, is oblivious to potential dangers and dismisses Eduard's fears of being apprehended for violating the GDR border. She initiates spontaneous copulation despite Eduard's protestations as to the childishness and political inappropriateness of the undertaking (207). The Wall, located on GDR territory, proves durable enough to sustain Eduard's lovemaking efforts. Love or lovemaking, then, does not cause the Wall to crumble—even if Eduard's first impression of the Wall does not correspond to his preconceived notions: "The infamous structure . . . appeared rather like the cheap version of an architectural leitmotif" (33).

The perceived shabbiness of the Wall's physical construct does not affect the pervasiveness of the ideological Wall that is evident, for example, on the level of official and officious communications. Divided Berlin is said to be a city in which there are two completely irreconcilable news versions of each "world event" (99), a statement that recalls *Der Mauerspringer*. In the latter text, the "disease of comparison" prevails, a disease that with its attendant urge "to compare distorts [the] view of [one's] own society as well as the foreign one" (69). Hence the two opposing political systems "find no justification except as negations of each other" (Anderson 1993, 366). Theo, a figure that combines traits of the narrator's friends Robert as well as Pommerer in *Der Mauerspringer*, has elevated the contentious discourse between East and West to new heights; he plays the devil's advocate and provokes his respective audience by regaling his listeners with the news version favored by the opposite camp. Similar to several figures in *Der Mauerspringer*, Theo is in search of his identity. His identity is called into question by his precarious yet privileged position as a dissident poet who walks a tightrope between East and West; for he and his wife Pauline form one of East Berlin's "partisan cells that are engaged in a war on two fronts: against the domestic miscarriage of socialism and against the Darwinian alternative in the West"(113).

Theo's war on two fronts makes it impossible for him to fully identify with either one of the two German states. As a writer he is faced with the problem of living in a country "in which veiled rhetoric is considered art, and the banning of a book is considered proof of its quality" (107). This formulation is reminiscent both of *Amanda herzlos* (182) and Becker's contention that censorship was the most important defining element of GDR literature: it enabled texts to achieve a degree of circulation in the West that was roughly comparable to the intensity of their repression in the GDR ("Wiedervereinigung" 1990, 361). Although Theo, just as his counterpart Hetmann in *Amanda herzlos*, remains ultimately in East Berlin, his distancing from the GDR becomes more pronounced as a result of an intricate ploy by the Stasi. This "apparatus of tenured torturers" (135) appears far more sinister in Schneider's text than in *Amanda herzlos*.

The cover design of *Paarungen* shows an undefined space in two different colors that is conspicuously divided by a wall. In the novel, the inhabitants of West Berlin seem oblivious of their "Wall tick" (34) that forces them to ceaselessly continue to separate and divide by erecting new walls according to the principle of cell formation. This activity, it appears to Eduard when he is visiting the Wall, resembles organic growth—although it extends from the fringes of the city to the center that is split by the Wall. The principle of division and separation, of building walls, is also noticeable in male-female relationships, particularly in Eduard's lacking "talent for exclusivity" (299) as revealed by his more or less simultaneous involvement with three women. Such lack of focus and of a center does not cause great upheavals or domestic turmoil. There is no longer any "social consensus" that would subject the "criminal in matters of love," the archetypal seducer Don Giovanni in André's and Theo's modern adaptation, to "an avenging authority" (331). Yet poetic justice prevails: in the course of amorously pursuing a young Polish woman in Warsaw, the three would-be seducers are tricked and end up without their wallets and passports—the cheaters have been cheated. Presumably, they will not draw any lesson from this incident, and we may assume that the virus of separation and (temporary) togetherness as embodied by the Wall will continue to spread unchecked.

THE LITERARY LEGACY OF THE WALL

One critic opined that after the events of November 9, 1989, the Berlin Wall has become "irrelevant" as a topical subject for the literature of united Germany (Frech 1992, 130). Leaving aside the thorny and speculative question of how and when a new national literature will develop, it seems obvious that such a farewell is premature in view of the retrospective visits of the Wall in the four post-Wall texts discussed above. These revisitations are not surprising on account of the Wall's past significance and its so-ciopolitical, psychological, and architectural legacy that presents an enormous challenge for the future. Schneider remarks in a recent essay that the removal of the Wall had caused Berlin to lose its "heart of stone," a heart that both separated and united the two halves of the city ("Chancen I" 1993, 54). The formidable task ahead is the filling of the empty space, a veritable void, left by the dismantling of the Wall—a laborious process that likely will extend beyond the year 2000 and will make demands that go beyond the spheres of city planning and architectural design. Schneider also observes that the reconstruction of the urban space in the center of the city inevitably poses the question of German identity: the old and new capital should convey to the world, as well as to its own citizens, the cosmopolitan, tolerant, democratic spirit that is a desideratum for the new Germany.

Needless to say, neither the construction of the architectural manifestations of the desirable new spirit nor the generating of such a new spirit will be an easy matter—last but not least because of the ideological and mental survival of the Wall. However, whereas texts such as those by Wolf and Maron tend to entrap their protagonists in the prison of the pre-unification past, the novels by Becker and Schneider posit the possibility of transcending the Wall by drawing attention to the physical and psychological costs of living forever in its shadow—whether in the East or in the West.

After all, as Schneider formulated in a pre-Wall essay, Berlin embodied the "myth of change" or the promise of change on the part of the two respective political systems to surpass each other in the pursuit of a better world ("Berliner Geschichten" 1988, 10). The fall of the Wall offers the chance for genuine change and the realization of this promise.

REFERENCES

Anderson, Susan C. "Walls and Other Obstacles: Peter Schneider's Critique of Unity in *Der Mauerspringer.*" *German Quarterly* 66 (1993): 362–72.
"Die ängstliche Margarete." *Der Spiegel*, January 25, 1993, 158–65.

Anz, Thomas, ed. *"Es geht nicht um Christa Wolf": Der Literaturstreit im vereinten Deutschland.* Munich: Spangenberg, 1991.

Becker, Jurek. *Amanda herzlos: Roman.* Frankfurt am Main: Suhrkamp, 1992.

————. "Gedächtnis verloren—Verstand verloren." *Die Zeit,* November 18, 1988, 61.

————. *Schlaflose Tage: Roman* [1978]. Frankfurt am Main: Suhrkamp Taschenbuch, 1980. (*Sleepless Days.* Translated by Leila Vennewitz. New York: Harcourt, 1979.)

————. "Die Wiedervereinigung der deutschen Literatur." *German Quarterly* 63 (1990): 359–66.

Biermann, Wolf. *Ein deutsch-deutscher Liedermacher/A Political Songwriter between East and West.* Translated by A. Leslie Willson. N.p.: Goethe-Institut/German Cultural Center, 1992.

————. "Der preußische Ikarus." *Die Zeit* (North American edition), December 3, 1976, 1.

————. *Preußischer Ikarus: Lieder/Balladen/Prosa/Gedichte.* Cologne: Kiepenheuer, 1978.

Bruyn, Günter de. "Intimes aus der DDR." Review of *Amanda herzlos* by Jurek Becker. *Der Spiegel,* August 3, 1992, 155–59.

Emmerich, Wolfgang. *Kleine Literaturgeschichte der DDR.* Darmstadt: Luchterhand, 1981.

Frech, Birgit. *Die Berliner Mauer in der Literatur: Eine Untersuchung ausgewählter Prosatexte seit 1961.* Pfungstadt: Ergon, 1992.

Greiner, Ulrich. "Mangel an Feingefühl." *Die Zeit,* June 1, 1990, 66–70.

Hage, Volker. " 'Wir müssen uns dem Schicksal stellen.' Über den Fall Christa Wolf." *Der Spiegel,* February 8, 1993, 197–99.

Heym, Stephan. "Aschermittwoch in der DDR." *Der Spiegel,* December 4, 1989, 55–58. Translated by Stephen Brockmann as "Ash Wednesday in the GDR." *New German Critique: Special Issue on German Unification* 52 (1991): 31–35.

Hielscher, Martin. Review of *Stille Zeile Sechs* by Monika Maron. *Deutsches Allgemeines Sonntagsblatt,* November 15, 1991. Excerpts report in *Fachdienst Germanistik* 10.1 (1992): 17.

Howe, Irving. "The Cost of Obedience." Review of *Sleepless Days* by Jurek Becker. *New York Times Book Review,* September 16, 1979, 7, 46.

James, Peter. "A Privileged Grave." Review of *Stille Zeile Sechs* by Monika Maron. *Times Literary Supplement,* November 20, 1992, 24.

Lehnert, Herbert. "Fiktionalität und autobiographische Motive. Zu Christa Wolff's Erzählung 'Was bleibt.' " *Weimarer Beiträge* 37 (1991): 423–44.

Lermen, Birgit, and Matthias Loewen. "Wolf Biermann. 'Ballade vom preußischen Ikarus.' " In *Lyrik aus der DDR: Exemplarische Analysen,* 364–70. Paderborn: Schöningh, 1987.

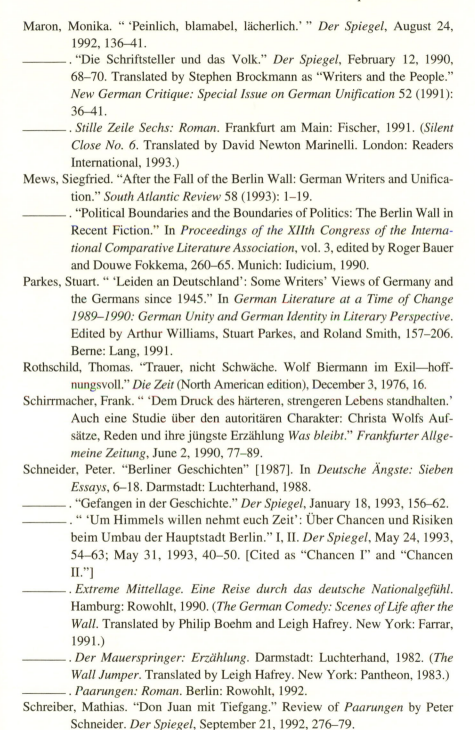

Maron, Monika. " 'Peinlich, blamabel, lächerlich.' " *Der Spiegel*, August 24, 1992, 136–41.

———. "Die Schriftsteller und das Volk." *Der Spiegel*, February 12, 1990, 68–70. Translated by Stephen Brockmann as "Writers and the People." *New German Critique: Special Issue on German Unification* 52 (1991): 36–41.

———. *Stille Zeile Sechs: Roman*. Frankfurt am Main: Fischer, 1991. (*Silent Close No. 6*. Translated by David Newton Marinelli. London: Readers International, 1993.)

Mews, Siegfried. "After the Fall of the Berlin Wall: German Writers and Unification." *South Atlantic Review* 58 (1993): 1–19.

———. "Political Boundaries and the Boundaries of Politics: The Berlin Wall in Recent Fiction." In *Proceedings of the XIIth Congress of the International Comparative Literature Association*, vol. 3, edited by Roger Bauer and Douwe Fokkema, 260–65. Munich: Iudicium, 1990.

Parkes, Stuart. " 'Leiden an Deutschland': Some Writers' Views of Germany and the Germans since 1945." In *German Literature at a Time of Change 1989–1990: German Unity and German Identity in Literary Perspective*. Edited by Arthur Williams, Stuart Parkes, and Roland Smith, 157–206. Berne: Lang, 1991.

Rothschild, Thomas. "Trauer, nicht Schwäche. Wolf Biermann im Exil—hoffnungsvoll." *Die Zeit* (North American edition), December 3, 1976, 16.

Schirrmacher, Frank. " 'Dem Druck des härteren, strengeren Lebens standhalten.' Auch eine Studie über den autoritären Charakter: Christa Wolfs Aufsätze, Reden und ihre jüngste Erzählung *Was bleibt*." *Frankfurter Allgemeine Zeitung*, June 2, 1990, 77–89.

Schneider, Peter. "Berliner Geschichten" [1987]. In *Deutsche Ängste: Sieben Essays*, 6–18. Darmstadt: Luchterhand, 1988.

———. "Gefangen in der Geschichte." *Der Spiegel*, January 18, 1993, 156–62.

———. " 'Um Himmels willen nehmt euch Zeit': Über Chancen und Risiken beim Umbau der Hauptstadt Berlin." I, II. *Der Spiegel*, May 24, 1993, 54–63; May 31, 1993, 40–50. [Cited as "Chancen I" and "Chancen II."]

———. *Extreme Mittellage. Eine Reise durch das deutsche Nationalgefühl*. Hamburg: Rowohlt, 1990. (*The German Comedy: Scenes of Life after the Wall*. Translated by Philip Boehm and Leigh Hafrey. New York: Farrar, 1991.)

———. *Der Mauerspringer: Erzählung*. Darmstadt: Luchterhand, 1982. (*The Wall Jumper*. Translated by Leigh Hafrey. New York: Pantheon, 1983.)

———. *Paarungen: Roman*. Berlin: Rowohlt, 1992.

Schreiber, Mathias. "Don Juan mit Tiefgang." Review of *Paarungen* by Peter Schneider. *Der Spiegel*, September 21, 1992, 276–79.

Walser, Martin. "Über Deutschland reden." *Die Zeit*, November 3, 1988. Reprinted as *Über Deutschland reden*. Frankfurt am Main: Suhrkamp, 1988.

Williams, Arthur, Stuart Parkes, and Roland Smith, eds. *German Literature at a Time of Change 1989–1990: German Unity and German Identity in Literary Perspective*. Berne: Lang, 1991.

Wolf, Christa. *The Author's Dimension: Selected Essays*. Introduction by Grace Paley, edited by Alexander Stephan, translated by Jan van Heurck. New York: Farrar, Straus & Giroux, 1993.

―――. *Im Dialog: Aktuelle Texte*. Berlin: Luchterhand, 1990. Partially translated in *The Author's Dimension*.

―――. *Der geteilte Himmel: Erzählung*. Halle: Mitteldeutscher Verlag, 1963. (*Divided Heaven*. Translated by Joan Becker. Berlin: Seven Seas, 1965.)

―――. *Kein Ort. Nirgends*. Darmstadt: Luchterhand, 1979. (*No Place on Earth*. Translated by Jan van Heurck. New York: Farrar, 1982.)

―――. "Der Schatten eines Traumes: Karoline von Günderrode—ein Entwurf" [1979]. In *Die Dimension des Autors: Essays und Aufsätze. Reden und Gespräche 1959–1985*, 511–71. Darmstadt: Luchterhand, 1987. ("The Shadow of a Dream: A Sketch of Karoline von Günderrode." Translated by Jan van Heurck. *The Author's Dimension*, 131–75.)

―――. *Was bleibt: Erzählung*. Frankfurt am Main: Luchterhand, 1990. (*What Remains and Other Stories*. Translated by Heike Schwarzbauer and Rick Takvorian. New York: Farrar, 1993.)

9

Berlin as Locus of Terror: *Gegenwartsbewältigung* in Berlin Texts since the *Wende*

Anna K. Kuhn

The collapse of the GDR and the ensuing and ongoing revelations about the repression and corruption of the SED (Socialist Unitary Party) regime have triggered a radical shift in discourse in the West with regard to the two Germanies. Willy Brandt's *Ostpolitik*, a watershed in postwar East-West German relations, marked the first such discursive shift. Accentuating commonalities between the two German states, *Ostpolitik* engendered a rhetoric of reciprocity and (re)conciliation: thus notions of rapprochement informed the Federal Republic's politics of detente, while the concept of *Konvergenz* (convergence) became a leitmotif of its cultural politics in the late 1970s and 1980s. The *Wende* ("Turning Point" [of 1989]), however, has resuscitated the Cold War discourse of totalitarianism,[1] with the West claiming freedom, justice, and democracy for itself and stylizing the GDR as the proper heir of Hitler's Germany. In this reading of history, *les êxtremes se touchent*, the dictatorship of the right was simply superseded by the dictatorship of the left.

Ironically, the newly resurrected discourse of totalitarianism has resulted in West Germany's (inverted) appropriation of the official GDR stance on *Vergangenheitsbewältigung*. The GDR had "come to terms with the Nazi past" by disavowing it, by facilely dissociating itself from Hitler's Germany. The whole purpose of East Germany's tedious, self-legitimating *Erbediskussion* (legacy debate)[2] was to construct a liberal democratic heritage for itself, one that culminated in the myth of wide-scale antifascistic resistance. By claiming to embody a qualitatively different political entity, the new state sought to exact liberator status for itself. Thus the GDR, created by the Soviet occupation powers as a satellite of the Soviet Union, propagated the official (communist) story of the Red Army's liberation of the German people from the yoke of fascism; invoking the Marxist-Leninist teleological capitalism-imperialism-fascism argument, it relegated fascism to the "other"—capitalist—Germany. The consequences of this (mis)reading of history are all too apparent today as we observe the return of the repressed in the form of virulent racism, (neo)Nazi rhetoric and violence, and xenophobia. These phenomena are certainly not limited to the "new Federal states," but the high incidence of (neo)Nazi-incited crimes in the East have led (Western) observers to conclude that East Germans have been even less successful than their Western counterparts in dealing with the Nazi past.

By the same token, the rhetoric of totalitarianism, by eliding Nazism and communism, allows the West to distance itself from *its* Nazi past by associating Nazism with the other "undemocratic" German state. While I am in no way trying to minimize the crimes of the East German communist state or downplay the need to scrutinize the institutional power structures of Nazism and GDR Stalinism for areas of contiguity and continuity,[3] the facile equation between the two systems all too often circulating today is shortsighted and counterproductive. Not only does this rewriting of history by the victors serve to further stigmatize the East, it smacks of self-serving, complacent *Vergangenheitsverdrängung* (repression of the [Nazi] past) on the part of the West. Such an attitude is particularly pernicious given Germany's current volatile internal political situation, and the ongoing and escalating violence toward foreigners *throughout* the Federal Republic today.

It is a commonplace that the fall of the Wall and the (re)unification of Germany have done little to abrogate differences between East and West Germans, to bridge what Peter Schneider prophetically called the "*Mauer im Kopf*," the Wall in people's heads, in his 1982 Berlin novel *Der Mauerspringer* (*The Wall Jumper*). Indeed, the current situation in Germany seems to once again substantiate the adage that psychic reality tends to limp behind material reality.

Yet, given the sheer physical materiality of the Wall—it was after all, as Schneider wittingly noted, "the only structure on earth, apart from the Great Wall of China, that . . . [could] be seen from the moon with the naked eye" (Schneider 1983, 7)—the inability of Germans to "think away" this structure, which for almost thirty years served as a constant reminder of the political, economic, and psychological division of Germany, should hardly come as a surprise. As a manifestation and instrument of power and surveillance, it was inevitable that the Wall assume its place in the political imaginary of both East and West, pointing Germans to the seemingly insurmountable task of coming to terms with their common past and ostensibly rendering a common present impossible. It is perhaps therefore not surprising—although none the less distressing—that, when suddenly and unexpectedly confronted with the reality of a common nation and the need to work for a common future, Germans in East and West should react anachronistically, projecting their fears and aggressions onto what was— but is no longer—the political Other. Indeed, the continued hostilities between Ossis and Wessis lend new meaning to the motto: "We have met the enemy and they are us."

The only way out of the current German aporia, it seems to me, is through a long and painful process of *Gegenwartsbewältigung*, a coming to terms with the GDR past within the context of the "new" German present.[4] Clearly, much of the burden of this work of memory will fall to the populace of the former GDR; it is, after all, the experiences of GDR citizens that constitute the forty-year lived reality of the SED state. But *Gegen-wartsbewältigung* cannot simply be relegated to East Germans. It is a project that must be shared by Westerners as well, for we in the West are certainly culpable of having helped legitimate and sustain what we (now) consider to have been a criminal regime.[5]

The first two literary examples of *Gegenwartsbewältigung* to emerge in the "new" (re)unified Germany,[6] Helga Schubert's *Judasfrauen* and Christa Wolf's notorious *Was bleibt* (*What Remains*), were both conceived and developed well before the *Wende*. Striking about both these narratives, as well as the other text I will be considering in detail, Monika Maron's *Stille Zeile Sechs* (*Quiet Close No. 6*), is the central role accorded Berlin in these early efforts to (re)assess the GDR's Stalinist past. Apart from positing Berlin as metonym for the SED state—from 1949 to 1989 Berlin was, after all, always invoked as the capital of the GDR—all three texts, to varying degrees, present readers with a precise topography of the city as the locus of state and *Stasi* power, and hence a potential source of intimidation and fear. Among the sites that predominate in this psychic (re)mapping of Berlin are the Alexanderplatz, the Friedrichstraße, the point of exchange between East and West, and the Pankow district of East Berlin, the early seat of the GDR government.

In the introduction to the first Western edition of *Judasfrauen*, which bears the subtitle "*Zehn Fallgeschichten weiblicher Denunziation im Drit-ten Reich*" ("Ten Case Studies of Female Denunciation in the Third Reich"), Helga Schubert is careful to note the exact date on which she is writing, namely November 24, 1989.[7] Referring to the mass demonstrations that had taken place twenty days earlier at the historic Alexanderplatz, metonym of Berlin-East,[8] Schubert explicitly invokes the events that would prove to be the GDR's nemesis. Recalling the rallies in Berlin, in which she and thousands of other GDR citizens had protested the repressive conditions in their country, Schubert voices confidence that these demonstrations had unleashed an avalanche-like movement toward democracy that could not be contained. Convinced that "the truth about the conditions of the past four decades . . . will reach the light of day" (JF1 7),[9] Schubert envisages the day on which she, as a writer, will no longer feel compelled to encode her messages in parables. "In the case of the book at hand," she goes on, "it is a matter of such an encoded message, of parables of betrayal" (7).

Schubert's introduction establishes her audience's horizon of reading: the historical specificity of her authorial comments imbues Schubert's stories about the "Third Reich" with a historical valence that transcends the narratives' diegesis. By explicitly claiming a parabolic structure for her "Fallgeschichten weiblicher Denunziation," Schubert from the outset posits a direct correlation between the "Third Reich" and the GDR, a correlation predicated on the problematic concept of totalitarianism. By appending to the East German edition of *Judasfrauen*,[10] the words "and lead us not into temptation" from the Lord's prayer (JF2 10), a clear indication that the lessons to be learned from studying the Nazi past are directly applicable to the GDR present, Schubert also implies a correlation between *Vergangenheitsbewältigung* and *Gegenwartsbewältigung*. According to Schubert, she began work on *Judasfrauen*, a project situated at the intersection of fascism, gender, and everyday history, in 1985 in an attempt to understand "the effects of a totalitarian state on the everyday behavior of its citizens as exemplified by political denunciations by women" (JF1 7). While *Judasfrauen*'s "Case Studies" are based on actual historical figures and authentic documents, Schubert embellishes her text by psychologizing and fictionalizing the historical accounts.[11] She chose to focus on National Socialist Germany, she explains, because this period had historical closure: Germany's "Thousand Year Reich" had, after all, collapsed after only twelve years and been replaced by a very different political system.[12]

Schubert's introduction explicitly states (presumably for a Western audience) what her GDR readers always knew, namely that literary texts produced under Germany's communist regime that dealt with historical subject matter often contained a subtext that referred to their current political situation.[13] By underscoring the parabolic nature of the *Judasfrauen* narratives, the introduction calls on readers to draw parallels between the "Third Reich" and the GDR—cast here as the most recent form of German totalitarianism[14]—as we read these stories of betrayal and denunciation in Nazi Germany.[15] At the same time, by situating her narratives at the juncture between very different political systems, Nazism and GDR communism/Western parliamentary democracy, *Judasfrauen* is clearly meant to instill hope in the citizens of the GDR that this regime, too, will pass.

To facilitate the reader's task, Schubert includes the autobiographical narrative "Judasfrauen," which, together with the introduction and the expository piece "Spitzel und Verräter" ("Spies and Traitors"), serves as a frame for the ten case study narratives. "Judasfrauen" outlines the difficulties the author confronted while researching the topic of women's active complicity in the Nazi state. Prime among these were the bureaucratic hurdles obstructing access to the extant archival material in the GDR and the psychological resistance offered by officials for whom her topic was ideologically suspect. Readers learn that Schubert had to obtain a special dispensation to access original Nazi *Volksgerichtshof* (People's Court) documents. Having obtained that permission, however, only marginally facilitated her task: she still had to penetrate the fortress-like edifice that housed the documents, the SED's Central Committee central party archive in the Institute for Marxism-Leninism, located in the center of Berlin. Schubert's precision in identifying the topographical coordinates of the archive in the heart of Berlin (*Berlin-Mitte*) is surpassed only by her detailed description of the complicated bureaucratic ritual visitors must observe once having gained entry to the Institute building (JF1 19–23).

Upon entering the inner sanctum of the archive, the author/narrator is confronted by the archive historian, who tries to dissuade her from pursuing her proposed line of inquiry, encouraging her instead to (re)frame her project to conform more closely to official GDR political and cultural policy. In accordance with the GDR's penchant for positive hero(ine)s, the historian urges the author/researcher to abandon her "negative" project. If she wants to study women and fascism, why, she queries, not focus on the *Trümmerfrauen* (rubble women)? Or better yet, on the role women played in *resisting* fascism? In addition to documenting the state's resistance to her project, "Judasfrauen" depicts the state's surveillance, be it through the panoptic observation of the librarian ensconced behind the glass wall overlooking the archive's reading room, through the elaborate bureaucratic apparatus that restricts access to archival materials, or through more insidious attempts at mind control.[16]

What is at stake in the ideological tug-of-war between the author and the official GDR historian is nothing less than the legitimacy of party line historiography. By seeking to recuperate a repressed aspect of German history, by uncovering and making public documents from the Nazi *Volksgerichtshof*, and juxtaposing them with postwar trial documents, the author exposes the lie within the notion of a radical historical caesura between Nazism and GDR communism. The GDR's discontinuity theory is also undermined in those passages that show how officials sought to limit the parameters of Schubert's inquiry.

But the author's research is not limited to East German documents. She receives permission to travel to West Berlin to consult records in the *Staatsbibliothek* (state library) pertaining to postwar trials of Nazi denouncers in the West. The detailed description of the stations of her thrice-weekly trips to West Berlin—early morning completion of custom forms; trip via the *S-Bahn* (city rail) to the *Bahnhof Friedrichstraße* station; crossing of border at the official East-West "glass palace" at *Friedrichstraße*; subway trip to the *Hallesches Tor* station; transfer to the bus that takes her to the *Kurfürstenstraße*; finally transfer to the bus that takes her to the *Staatsbibliothek*—provides readers (especially those familiar with Berlin) with the necessary topographical coordinates to track her itinerary through the divided city. At the same time, the description of her weekly routine—with its Monday-Wednesday-Friday trips to the SED archives and its Tuesday-Thursday-Saturday trips to the *Staatsbibliothek* in the West—underscores the schizophrenia of life in Berlin.

In the "Judasfrauen" piece, Schubert also addresses the gender-specificity of her *Judasfrauen* project. Explaining why she chose to restrict her case studies to women denouncers, Schubert maintains that she is troubled by the idealization of women: "We are not that sensitive, that tender, that cooperative, that maternal, that compassionate, that creative, that authentic. We are also evil and also dangerous, in our own way. As soon as anyone is placed on a pedestal, I would like to destroy that pedestal" (JF1 17). Much as one can applaud Schubert's desire to dismantle idealized images of the eternal (maternal) feminine, a widely held construct in Nazi Germany,[17] *Judasfrauen* ultimately merely replaces a positive cliché with a negative one, that of the treacherous woman. As the all-inclusive phrase "we are also evil and also dangerous in our way" reveals, Schubert fails to differentiate among women, thereby reaffirming the socially constructed category of "woman." By employing the generic category *"unsere Art,"* she moreover implicitly posits the generic male norm against which this feminine category is defined, thereby unwittingly reinscribing the asymmetrical categories man/woman.

In Schubert's "case studies of denunciation," men are consistently betrayed or denounced[18] by women for personal reasons, be it thwarted or unrequited love, feelings of inferiority or insecurity, etc. With the exception of the last narrative, in which we encounter a Nazi zealot, none of the women depicted in *Judasfrauen* act out of political motives. Schubert's reductive representation of women perpetrators is in keeping with her view that in totalitarian societies, women are able to manipulate the power of the state for their personal ends. Yet, as Sigrid Weigel has argued, Schubert, by invoking "a rigid gender dramaturgy, in which a female traitor, i.e., a 'Judasfrau,' confronts one or more male victims" (Weigel 1994, 208), adheres to a retrograde notion of sexual politics based on a gender-coded division of labor, in which women exploit male-dominated state apparatuses, such as the police and the court, into carrying out their private acts of revenge *for* them. By rendering their agency totally reactive, she does little to deconstruct the gender polarities she ostensibly eschews. Moreover, Schubert relied on juridical sources which were themselves already gender-coded, in which the characters of the perpetrators were strongly psychologized and their motives sensationalized. Her failure to question the reliability of her sources, together with her privatization of fascism, prevents Schubert from coming to grips with issues of institutional culpability (Weigel 1994, 208). Ultimately, Schubert's facile inversion of women's traditional victim role to that of (pseudo)perpetrator fails to problematize these binary categories; by not addressing issues of complicity (*Mittäter-schaft*), the *Judasfrauen*'s "case studies" fail to question the (false) victim/perpetrator dichotomy that informs these narratives and hardly qualify as examples of *Vergangenheitsbewältigung*.

Judasfrauen falls even shorter of the mark as an example of *Gegen-wartsbewältigung*. With only the introduction and the "Judasfrauen" narrative as tales of entry into conditions in the GDR, the reader is at a loss to make anything more than superficial connections between Nazi Germany and the SED state. East German readers will doubtless fare better than their Western counterparts and may well be able to provide concrete analogies between some *Judasfrauen* case study narratives and GDR Stasi stories; but even Schubert's ideal reader will be hard-pressed to produce the specificity of detail necessary to make the elected comparisons between the "Third Reich" and the GDR meaningful.[19]

Any attempt to compare Nazi Germany and the GDR (qua Stalinism) must include a detailed discussion of the points of similarity and difference between the two systems. That is clearly not the case in *Judasfrauen*. Instead, Schubert restricts her portrayal of the GDR to the introduction and the "Judasfrauen" frame narrative, in which she self-servingly portrays herself as a victim of the SED state, thereby begging the question as to the degree to which her "parables of betrayal" can be read as an opportunistic attempt to capitalize on the collapse of the communist East. Opportunism is, of course, the criticism that has most often been levied against Christa Wolf since the ill-timed publication of her so-called *Stasi*-narrative *Was bleibt* (*What Remains*) in 1990. As recent revelations about leading GDR writers such as Heiner Müller, Christa Wolf, Günter de Bruyn, and Monika Maron make clear, the *Stasi* is the GDR past that will not die. Wolf's disclosure in late January 1993 about her activities as an *IM* or *Inoffizielle Mitarbeiterin* (inofficial collaborator) of the *Stasi* from 1959 to 1962 unleashed a second wave of anti-Wolf writings in the German press.[20]

A prominent *Spiegel* article entitled "Die ängstliche Margarete" ("Timid Margarete"), for example, sees Christa Wolf's "*Stasi* past" as the key to illuminating opaque passages in her *oeuvre*, including the opening lines of *Was bleibt*: "Don't panic. One day I will even talk about it in that other language which, as of yet, is in my ear but not on my tongue. Today I knew would still be too soon."[21] *Spiegel* argues that Wolf had recognized the right time to speak just in the nick of time, but had failed to find the proper language. Obviously alluding to Wolf's "amnesia" about her cover name and the reports she penned as an *IM*, *Spiegel* implicitly faults her with failing to admit her complicity with the SED regime and her links to the secret police. What this article, and others like it, overlooks, however, is that the text of *Was bleibt* itself already constitutes a halting beginning at *Gegenwartsbewältigung*. At least that is the reading that I will advance here.

Written in 1979, reworked in November 1989, and published in 1990, *Was bleibt* has consistently been read as a *Stasi*-narrative. However, when viewed within the context of Wolf's entire *oeuvre* and in particular against the backdrop of her work on the Romantics in the late 1970s—*Kein Ort. Nirgends* (*No Place on Earth*) and the essays on Karoline von Günderrode and Bettine von Arnim—and in tandem with the narrative *Sommerstück*, portions of which were written around the same time as *Was bleibt* and also not published until much later (1989),[22] *Was bleibt* takes on a different valence.[23] Like *Sommerstück*, Wolf's "idyllic elegy" (Raddatz: "Ein Rückzug auf sich selbst"), *Was bleibt* can be read as a quotidian complement to *Kein Ort. Nirgends*. The text employs many of the same themes, tropes, and structures as its high cultural counterpart: both focus on the situation of the writer and problematize the function of writing in repressive times; both are informed by an overarching motif and are structured around common themes of alienation and community; and both play with notions of dystopia and utopia.[24]

In *Was bleibt* Christa Wolf again plays on the etymological root of "utopia," *u-topos*, that is, "no place," as she had earlier in *Kein Ort. Nirgends*. In the later text, however, she links the narrator's dystopic experiences to the specific (no) place of East Berlin. From the outset, Wolf carefully positions the narrator within precise topographical coordinates of the eastern half of the divided city. Thus, even more than Schubert's "Judasfrauen" frame, *Was bleibt* is a (self)consciously *East* Berlin narrative.

The opening pages of the text inform us that the narrator's apartment is located on the Friedrichstraße (*WR* 232), a name familiar to readers in East and West as the chief point of transfer between the Federal Republic and the GDR. Later we accompany the narrator as she walks down the Friedrichstraße, past the Berliner Ensemble (*WR* 245), crosses the Weidendammer Bridge (*WR* 246) and stops to contemplate the glass pavilioned transit hall, dubbed the "tear bunker" by the people (*WR* 247), that divides the two cities. Reflecting on this site, "in which the assistants of the master who controlled this city, dressed as policemen or customs officers, exercised the right to bind or to release" (*WR* 247–48), the narrator recognizes the monstrosity of this building.

Like Schubert's "glass palace," the transit hall in Wolf's text is an omnipresent reminder of Berlin's division. Unlike *Judasfrauen*, however, in *Was bleibt* it becomes the emblem of the state's (mis)use of power, triggering the narrator's reflections on her fall from innocence. She had also had to learn her mistrust of such well-established objects and had understood that they all belonged to the master who ruled the city, the advantage of the moment. Speaking from a decidedly dystopian perspective, the narrator goes on to articulate the sense of loss she experiences as she looks back at "[t]he city [that] had turned from a place into a non-place, without history, without vision, without magic, spoiled by greed, power and violence" (*WR* 248).

Leaving the "tear bunker" behind her, the narrator proceeds to a tiny liquor store beneath the Friedrichstraße rail station, window shops in the train station bookstore, and then decides to visit the new department store in the Japan Center. After completing her final errand in the post office, she retraces her steps over the Weidendammer Bridge and retreats back into her house.[25] But despite, or indeed perhaps precisely *because* of, the text's elaborate attempts to physically locate the narrator within precise topographic coordinates of East Berlin,[26] her complete psychic disorientation soon becomes manifest. Following the demoralizing visit of the young woman poet, the narrator, in articulating her ultimate sense of alienation, notes "that a tie had broken between me and the city—provided that 'city' can still stand for everything that people do to one another, both good and bad" (*WR* 277). The narrator's sense of disorientation, despair, and alienation is intensified by Wolf's use of the trope of the split self, which had played such an important role in *Kein Ort. Nirgends*. While the metaphor Wolf uses to describe the narrator's self-alienation in *What Remains*—that she is observing herself from a certain height (*WR* 276–77)—is not nearly as striking or drastic as the confrontation between Günderrode's two egos at her coffin in *Kein Ort*'s motto, [27] the gravity of the narrator's situation in *Was Bleibt* is effectively brought home to the reader through her rhetorical repetition of this phrase—it is repeated almost verbatim three times within the space of a single page.

The theme of self-alienation informs the narrative form of *Was bleibt* as well. Thus the text frequently abandons its primary mode of narration, interior monologue, in favor of an internal dialogue, that is, an imagined conversation between two of the three egos that the narrator identifies within herself. In a pivotal passage the narrator of *What Remains* speculates: "I myself. Who was that? Which of the multiple beings from which 'myself' was composed? The one that wanted to know itself? The one that wanted to protect itself? Or that third one that was still tempted to dance to the same tune as the young gentleman there outside my window?" (*WR* 262). We are confronted here by a fragmented ego acutely aware of its shortcomings and full of self-reproach. By distinguishing between the self she aspires to be (the I that wanted to know itself), what can perhaps be called an ideal or authentic self; a self-protecting self (the I that wanted to protect itself); and a conformist self (the I that was still tempted to dance to the same tune), the narrator of *Was bleibt* describes a state of profound psychic disorientation, bordering on schizophrenia. The description of her conformist self, on the other hand, vividly captures the condition of *Mittäterschaft* (complicity).

A majority of *Was bleibt*'s interior dialogue occurs between the narrator's internal voice, that is, the voice of authenticity striving for honesty of expression, and her self-protecting self, which seems to be her main persona in the text. The narrator's dilemma as a writer in a repressive society is underscored by the presence of two figures in the text who function as the objective correlatives of two of her egos, or rather, as these egos taken to their logical extremes: Jürgen M., the corrupted intellectual who has sold out to the system and who corresponds to the narrator's conformist self; and his opposite, the young dissident writer whose spirit is unbroken by prison, who writes in the new language to which the narrator aspires, and whose mere existence is a reminder of the narrator's weakness.

Given Christa Wolf's failure to provide us with specifics about the genesis and metamorphosis of the text of *Was bleibt*, it is fruitless to speculate about which passages she (re)wrote in 1989. Instead, in assessing *Was bleibt* as a post-*Wende* text, we should be attuned to Wolf's first halting attempts to come to terms with the GDR past and her role in perpetuating the SED state. For one thing, the text thematizes the writer's privileged position, both materialistically (cf. the breakfast scene in which the narrator reproaches herself for the material luxuries she enjoys like coffee and marmalade) and politically.

It is precisely her awareness of the political security that comes with the high visibility she enjoys as a popular writer that prompts her concern for those who are less visible—hence more vulnerable—like the young unpublished poet who leaves his poetry in her mailbox. Similarly, in the discussion following a public reading of her work, she tries to protect the young teacher who had brought up the word "future," only to reproach herself for being overly protective. Most importantly, however, the narrator is aware of the enormous differences between herself and the young woman writer whom she cannot deter from writing authentically—now. In a passage that registers both admiration for the young woman and self-reproach, the narrator observes that the girl cannot be held back, cannot be saved, and cannot be spoiled (*WR* 275). The only way she can justify her privileged position is by invoking her task as a writer. The only thing that remains for the narrator is to console herself with the hope of being able to write about her experiences authentically in the future in her own new language. While it may still be too soon now, it won't always be too soon: "Why not simply sit down at this desk . . . , take my pen, and begin?" (*WR* 295). It is in this spirit, in the spirit of task-setting, I submit, that we can and should read both the concluding passages of *Was bleibt* and the text as a whole.

In words that hark back verbatim to the beginning of the narrative, the narrator contemplates writing about "what remains? What is at the root of my city and what is rotting it from within?" (*WR* 295). Yet the shift in wording from "this city" in the earlier passage to "my city" in the later one is significant: it connotes a sense of responsibility for the fate of the doomed city absent in the first description. Of course, the narrator's circumlocution also underscores the fact that "Berlin" is an ambiguous signifier, one with two referents. By using the possessive "my city," rather than naming Berlin directly, she indicates that it is *East* Berlin that will be the locus of her *Gegenwartsbewältigung*.

As Christa Wolf readers know, *Vergangenheitsbewältigung* is a recurrent theme in her writings. Like many of Wolf's texts, *Was bleibt* also invokes

Nazi Germany.[28] In contrast to Wolf's earlier texts, however, in which allusions to the "Third Reich" either stand in contrast to GDR society or serve as a reminder of the work of memory and mourning that still remains to be done, in *Was bleibt* they point to parallels between the "Third Reich" and the SED-GDR state. While not entirely felicitous, Wolf's linkage of Nazism and GDR Stalinism in *Was bleibt* is more convincing than Helga Schubert's in *Judasfrauen*, both because Wolf's attempt is far more circumscribed and because her narrative about *Stasi* surveillance can tolerate comparisons with the Gestapo better than the *Judasfrauen* "case study" narratives can absorb the broad, generalizing connections Schubert insinuates between the two political systems.

In Monika Maron's *Stille Zeile Sechs*, the most powerful literary example of *Gegenwartsbewältigung* to emerge to date, the juxtaposition of Nazi and SED regimes succeeds in large degree because the question of their relationship to each other is explicitly addressed in the text. In Maron's novel the first-person narrator, Rosalind Polkowski, familiar to Maron readers from her earlier novel *Die Überläuferin* (*The Defector*), exorcises her demons by confronting and "murdering" a surrogate father-figure, Herbert Beerenbaum. By pitting the forty-two-year-old narrator—a true child of the GDR—against the *Altkommunist* Beerenbaum, a representative of the hardliner founding-father generation of the GDR, Maron has created what is arguably the first East German *Tochterroman* (daughter book), a subgenre of the *Väterromane* (father books)[29] so popular in West Germany in the 1970s.

Like *Judasfrauen* and *Was bleibt*, the action of *Stille Zeile Sechs* is set in Berlin. Unlike Schubert's and Wolf's texts, however, the narrative is not restricted to Berlin as capital of the GDR. Instead, it juxtaposes the "official" East Berlin with its countercultural antipode, the pub scene. *Stille Zeile Sechs* is driven by intergenerational conflict, by discrepancies between the values held by the founding fathers of the GDR and their children, unwilling heirs of the socialist legacy. Not consulted when the socialist blueprint was drawn up, they are now being forced to live out their fathers' "utopia." Between Rosalind Polkowski, for whom Beerenbaum incarnates all that is repressive and repulsive about both her fathers' generation and the anachronistic SED state, and Herbert Beerenbaum, for whom Rosalind's rejection of the work ethos, one of the foundational principles of the GDR, must surely be anathema, there can be no meeting of minds. By pitting representatives of two such divergent *Weltanschauungen* against each other, Maron effectively negates the possibility of dialogue, allowing only for a clash of ideas, a talking past or at each other. And that is precisely what gives *Stille Zeile Sechs*, Monika Maron's reckoning with her (step)father's generation, its power and passion: it finally gives the second generation an equal voice.

In contrast to Helga Schubert and Christa Wolf, Monika Maron's overtly critical texts (*Flugasche* [*Flight of Ashes*] and *Die Überläuferin* [*The Defector*]) were never published in the GDR, doubtless contributing to her decision to go to the West. Although, or perhaps precisely *because*, she did not leave the GDR until 1988, the once committed socialist clearly still harbors great rancor toward what she perceives as a repressive and failed regime.[30] Maron's essay "Ich war ein antifaschistisches Kind" ("I was an antifascist child" [1988/89]) reveals the autobiographical impetus of *Stille Zeile Sechs*, making clear that the stepdaughter of the leading Party functionary Karl Maron[31] was weaned on precisely the communist rhetoric that propels Beerenbaum.

From the outset Maron takes great care to establish a correlation between Beerenbaum and Rosalind's father. Again and again her first-person narrator, Rosalind, draws parallels between these two committed communists: both were advanced to academic posts in the newly founded GDR state on the basis of their politics rather than their professional training; both blur the boundary between the public and the private, subordinating the private to the point of effacement; the language of both is so cliché-riddled, so informed by the jargon of communist orthodoxy, that Rosalind can readily predict Beerenbaum's comments. The more Rosalind is struck by the similarities between these two men, the more she displaces her unresolved hostilities toward her father onto Beerenbaum.

Having, as a child, suffered from the callous indifference of her ideologically correct father, having been weaned on the antifascist resistance myth and indoctrinated by official communist ideology throughout her adult life, Rosalind—like many members of her generation—rejects both that ideology and the state that propagates it. Thus the self-declared "empiricist" Rosalind, drawing on a traumatic childhood experience, dismantles Beerenbaum's carefully constructed master narrative of communism as heroic and a morally impeccable movement by presenting her poignant definition of a communist as "someone who doesn't thank a child who gives him a big bowl of lemon cream because he happens to be too busy with world revolution" (159–60). Precisely because Beerenbaum is *not* her biological father, she is able to confront him openly, as she was never able to her own father.

Hired by Beerenbaum to record his memoirs, Rosalind is initially determined to separate head and hand, to function merely as a scribe, without

reflecting on the content of his writings. However, Beerenbaum's complacent, self-congratulatory rhetoric soon provokes her to challenge his reading
of history. Calling his hagiographic assessment of socialism's adversarial
role to Nazism into question, she insinuates structural parallels between
National Socialism and communism when she presses him about his
experiences at the Moscow Hotel Lux, from which many German communists seeking political asylum during the "Third Reich" were deported to
Siberian labor camps or killed outright.[32] As she unloads her pent up hatred
and aggression, Rosalind becomes convinced that her survival is contingent
on Herbert Beerenbaum's death and enters into a life-and-death struggle
with him. She repeatedly antagonizes Beerenbaum, whose feebleness—
symbolized by his withered, shaking right hand—invites readers to identify
him with the geriatric SED leadership.[33] By pressing Beerenbaum, who was
in Soviet exile during Hitler's regime, about taboo topics such as the Hotel
Lux and the Archipel Gulag, she calls his life, which is indistinguishable
from official communist ideology, into question.

Rosalind's strategy of discrediting Beerenbaum by pointing out the
discrepancy between communist theory and praxis had already been adum-
brated by Maron's choice of narrative setting. *Stille Zeile Sechs* derives its
title from Herbert Beerenbaum's (fictional) address, an imaginary street in
the historically authentic Pankow district of East Berlin. In Maron's novel,
this exclusive residential neighborhood, which housed the GDR government until the end of the 1950s, is referred to by the local populace as
"*Städtchen*" ("little city"), a term evocative of the notion of the "state within
the state," as the *Stasi* came to be known. In contrast to *Judasfrauen* and
Was bleibt, Maron's Berlin no longer emanates fear and dread; instead the
Pankow she invokes is characterized by a lack, an absence of power—since
power withdrew when the seat of government was moved behind the city
borders of Berlin, to *Berlin-Mitte*. Some houses, now used as official
governmental guest houses, remain, serving as reminders of past glory;
others, such as that of the GDR's first general secretary, were torn down,
because it is rumored that so many bugs had been installed in the walls over
the years that no one was able to remove them all, "making the house
unacceptable to other tenants" (6). Once a high-security area, guarded and
cordoned off, the *Städtchen*, this former citadel of power, still a sanctuary
of Party functionaries, has now taken on the quality of a ghost town: "It
was as bleak as a mining town after a gold rush. . . . Order was maintained,
as if by ghosts, as if those who had left were still there" (7).

Although the topography of Berlin in *Stille Zeile Sechs* is not nearly as
precisely drawn[34] as it was in *Judasfrauen* or *Was bleibt*, the narrator takes

great care to deliberately and repeatedly associate Beerenbaum with Pankow. In so doing, she underscores the discrepancy between Beerenbaum's self-understanding as a man of the people and his privileged life experience, while simultaneously bearing out the lie of the GDR's self-definition as a classless society, as the *Arbeiter- und Bauernstaat* (workers' and peasants' state). What is ultimately at stake in the generational conflict between Rosalind and Beerenbaum is not simply a struggle for the validation of the narrator's or Beerenbaum's identity, it is the legitimacy of the GDR and the way the GDR will be remembered and recorded in the annals of history. In other words, *Stille Zeile Sechs* is about historiography, about who gets to interpret what has happened in the past, a not insignificant contest, given that whoever controls the past also controls the future.

The choice of historiographers will, of course, determine the perceptions of Berlin that are disseminated as well. Clearly Beerenbaum's impressions of the city diverge from those of Rosalind. For the committed communist, Berlin would signify the yardstick by which to measure the success of the valorous class struggle. Subordinating personal relationships, including his and his wife's, to visions of their shared commitment to this higher cause, for Beerenbaum Berlin doubtless signifies both the site of the failed Spartacist uprising of 1919 and of the Red Army's triumphal victory over fascism in 1945. In lieu of Beerenbaum's liberation narrative, a tribute to the "Red Army who freed the German people from the yoke of fascism,"[35] Rosalind would likely present GDR history as a narrative of repression. As someone who gives personal history precedence over monumental history, she would likely inscribe Berlin as the site of the injustices the individual had to bear at the hands of a ruthless and tyrannical state. She might well also invoke the workers' uprising in 1953 which was brutally suppressed by Soviet forces. Unlike Beerenbaum's perception of Berlin as a site of dynamic change and moral justification, in Rosalind's view, Berlin under the SED would likely come to signify petrification, stasis, fear, and dread.

Like Helga Schubert's *Judasfrauen*, Monika Maron's *Stille Zeile Sechs* consciously plays with the *Opfer/Täter* dialectic—with considerably more success. Indeed, the underlying question that informs the text is one taken from revolutionary dramatist Ernst Toller's diaries, namely, whether action always entails guilt,[36] a question that *Stille Zeile Sechs* seems to answer in the affirmative. Both Rosalind and Beerenbaum perceive themselves as victims. Rosalind, as the unwilling beneficiary of the society created by Beerenbaum and his ilk, holds Beerenbaum personally responsible for the repressive state under which she suffers; Beerenbaum, on the other hand, has stylized himself as liberator-hero of succeeding generations of Germans, a role that is dependent on his status as victim of Nazi oppression.

Yet, to confound the issue, Beerenbaum's claim to victim status is not simply empty rhetoric: his personal narrative is the very stuff of which the GDR antifascist resistance myth is made. In retaliation for Rosalind's aggressive, insistent questions about Soviet Stalinism,[37] Beerenbaum invokes the greater evil against which Stalinism was ostensibly pitted: Nazism. In the following session he dictates: "My wife [Grete] was arrested during autumn of 1939. . . . She was taken to Ravensbrück concentration camp. . . . That's not in Siberia" (116–17). Frustrated by Beerenbaum's all-too-familiar ploy of stifling criticism of communism by invoking Nazi persecution, Rosalind continues their psychological tug-of-war by recording: "Grete was arrested in the autumn of 1939. They put her in Ravensbrück concentration camp. Siberia is located near Ravensbrück (117). Rosalind's deliberate (mis)writing of Beerenbaum's history establishes the proximity between Nazism and Stalinism that Beerenbaum is so intent upon disavowing and reveals the broader political ramifications of their ostensibly personal conflict.

In the final showdown that culminates in Beerenbaum's heart attack, Rosalind, using knowledge gleaned from the countercultural *Kneipe* (pub) scene, charges the former university administrator with having denounced a colleague to the *Stasi*. Beerenbaum's attempt at self-justification illustrates how fine the line between *Opfer* and *Täter* is drawn. Again falling back on his victim status, he goes on to claim the state's intellectual proprietorship of its citizens: "We weren't permitted to go to university. We paid so that others could go to university, always. First, as proletarians with our sweat, then with the money of our state. The Worker's Penny. This education was our property; anyone who ran away with it was a robber" (172). In one of *Stille Zeile Sechs*'s most forceful passages, Rosalind lashes back with an Orwellian vision of the futuristic communist utopia: "Confiscating brains. You confiscated grey matter because you had too little of it yourselves. In the century to come you would have amputated them and hung them on wires to save prison costs. Servitude of the brain instead of serfdom of the body" (173). In Rosalind's view, Beerenbaum and his cohorts are guilty not only of intellectual vampirism, but also of mortgaging the lives of her generation. As she reproaches him: "We know nothing . . . because we weren't allowed to live. Your own life was not enough for you, it was too mean, so you used up our life too. You are cannibals, slave owners with an army of torturers" (174). Through Beerenbaum's story Maron accomplishes what Schubert's *Judasfrauen* case study narratives purport to do, namely, to show how someone can be an *Opfer* in one set of historical circumstances and a *Täter* in another. Maron's far more imaginative text teases out the *Opfer/Täter* problematic still further through her portrayal of Rosalind as victim and perpetrator simultaneously. Thus the text furnishes ample evidence to mount a case that Rosalind, guinea pig of the German communist experiment, is a victim of Beerenbaum's politics, while at the same time presenting her as the aggressor. It is, after all, Rosalind who throws down the gauntlet, initiating open conflict with Beerenbaum; it is she who rejects his attempts at rapprochement; it is she who deliberately stalks her physically weakened opponent in their final confrontation, taking sadistic pleasure in imagining physically abusing him.

In a scene reminiscent of *Was bleibt*, Maron's narrator steps outside herself and observes/imagines in horror as her bloodthirsty alter ego, avenging herself for past indignities, thrashes the defenseless Beerenbaum and then waits for him to die. By blurring the line between fantasy and reality, by splitting Rosalind's consciousness, Maron allows her protagonist to imagine her full potential for violence without actually physically laying a hand on Beerenbaum. Maron complicates the *Opfer/Täter* problematic still further by playing on the double meaning of *Opfer* in German, namely "victim" and "sacrifice." Thus Beerenbaum, a victim of Nazi oppression, blithely sacrifices succeeding generations to the socialist cause, only to have his victim, Rosalind, become his "murderer" and in turn sacrifice him for the sake of her future. Only after Beerenbaum has been buried can Rosalind begin to empathize with her biological father; only after her rage has been spent are other emotions possible and the emotional rigor mortis that characterized her dealings with her father's generation somewhat abated.

Stille Zeile Sechs's conclusion precludes the possibility of closure and adds a final twist to the novel, relativizing the psychological resolution that Beerenbaum's death seems to bring. For although Beerenbaum is dead, he lives on through his memoirs—which he bequeaths to her. The open-ended conclusion distinctly holds out the possibility that Rosalind will indeed one day return to (re)evaluate Beerenbaum's story and her relationship to that story. Staring at the packet that Beerenbaum's son has handed her, Rosalind proclaims emphatically that she will not open it: "I shall throw it in the next rubbish bin. I shall bury it between the mountains of papers on the lowest shelf of my bookcase" (184), leaving the reader to speculate about just how long it will take her to open the packet.

At the end of *Stille Zeile Sechs* both Rosalind's story and the history of the GDR are open. As the beneficiary of Beerenbaum's memoirs, Rosalind has the option of (re)viewing his writings, augmenting or revising them (in line with her newly gained insights about her own capacity for *Täterschaft*) and publishing them—thereby adding to the official historical record—or suppressing them. The end of *Stille Zeile Sechs* finds its protagonist psychologically poised to embark on the process of *Gegenwartsbewältigung*. To be productive, this process requires overcoming the simple assigning of guilt and the facile dochotomization of *Opfer* and *Täter*, which still characterized Rosalind's conflicts with Beerenbaum, in favor of empathy and relentless self-scrutiny, a task which Rosalind now seems equipped to do.

As we have seen in the three narratives under discussion that have begun the laborious task of *Gegenwartsbewältigung*, the city of Berlin, quite logically, has, and will doubtless continue to have, a unique role to play in this process. More than any other German city, Berlin embodies the point of intersection of numerous strands of German history. On the one hand, its divided status symbolizes retribution for Germany's murderous National Socialist past; at the same time, East Berlin, as capital of the GDR, is emblematic both of the SED state and of forty years of GDR history. The decision to move the capital of the newly (re)unified Germany to Berlin moreover marks it as the site of Germany's future. Beyond that, Berlin's divided status underscores the consequences of the simplistic *Opfer-Täter* dichotomy operable in Cold War politics, even as it serves as the embodied reminder of the complicated enmeshment of these two categories. Its topography, marked by such scars of Nazi and GDR history as Bendlerstraße (Gestapo headquarters) und Plötzensee, the Wall, and Normannenstraße (*Stasi* headquarters), is therefore the obvious terrain on which to determine both what will remain of GDR history and culture and to forge a viable collective future, one based on having come to terms with both Germany's Nazi and Stalinist past.

NOTES

Research for this chapter was funded in part by a fellowship from the Center for German and European Studies, located at U.C. Berkeley. I would like to thank the Center for supporting my project.

1. As Ian Kershaw has pointed out, theories of totalitarianism that conflated fascism and communism did not arise in the post–World War II period. Such theories were already extant in the early 1930s but gained unprecedented popularity during the Cold War era (Kershaw 1993, 7). In the postwar period it was above all Hannah Arendt's *The Origins of Totalitarianism* (1951) that was the most influential in recuperating this term.

2. True, the battle for the construction of a specifically East German heritage (*Erbe*) was fought primarily on the cultural front; its agenda was, however, clearly political.

3. As Marie-Luise Gättens has noted, continuity entails disruptions and differences and is not the same as identity (Gättens 1995, 217).

4. I have chosen to retain this rather vexed term for heuristic reasons. The term *Gegenwartsbewältigung*, an obvious homology to *Vergangenheitsbewältigung*, has by now achieved a common currency and can serve as a shorthand to invoke the work of memory and mourning that informs both this project of coming to terms with the GDR's Stalinist past and *Vergangenheitsbewältigung*, coming to terms with the Nazi past. Nonetheless, I am concerned by false distinctions between past and present that surface when these two terms are played off against each other. I therefore want to underscore that, in my understanding, both *Vergangenheitsbewältigung* and *Gegenwartsbewältigung* in no way entail a "mastering" of the past, but rather a working through of the past in the present for the sake of individual and collective psychic health in the future. Moreover, while I am aware that both the term *"Vergangenheitsbewältigung"* and *"Gegenwartsbewältigung"* rely heavily on psychological processes, I am convinced that individual psychological responses to historical events such as Nazism and Stalinism are necessary first steps that can lead to a broader societal response.

5. Precisely the desire both to probe the West's complicity in upholding the GDR and its failure to help shape post-*Wende* debates in more productive ways informs the 1992 collection of essays edited by Cora Stephan entitled *Wir Kollaborateure*. Addressing such issues as the Western Left's investment in maintaining a *sozialistischer Staat auf deutschem Boden* (a socialist state on German territory), this slim volume confronts issues of Western complicity in GDR history in a more judicious fashion than does Brigitte Seebacher-Brandt's polemic against the 1968 student generation, *Die Linke und die Einheit*. In doing so, *Wir Kollaborateure* gets beyond the finger-pointing and obsession with *Stasi-Geschichten* all too pervasive today. Together with Lothar Baier's important text *Volk ohne Zeit: Essay über das eilige Vaterland*, in which he takes the Federal Republic to task for what he perceives to be its colonization of the GDR, *Wir Kollaborateure* constitutes an important first step in establishing an East-West dialogue about Germany's most recent German past.

6. In the East, attempts at *Gegenwartsbewältigung* on the part of well-known writers date back to the hectic, historic days in autumn 1989. Understandably, these first ventures were not cast in traditional literary forms. Instead, writers like Christa Wolf and Helga Königsdorf turned to shorter, more immediate genres, such as the essay, letter, and interview as they tried to process the impressions, thoughts, and emotions aroused by the events that were occurring with such breakneck speed and that would ultimately topple the SED regime. Thus volumes such as Christa Wolf's *Im Dialog: Aktuelle Texte* and *Angepaßt oder mündig: Briefe an Christa Wolf im Herbst 1989* and Helga Königsdorf's *1989 oder ein Moment der Schönheit, Aus dem Dilemma eine Chance machen* and *Adieu DDR: Protokolle eines Abschieds* document the euphoria, confusion, frustration, and

disillusionment of two loyal socialists convinced of the viability of a socialist "third way."

7. This information is missing from the introduction to the paperback version, published by Deutscher Taschenbuch Verlag in 1992. All further references to the first (hardcover) edition of *Judasfrauen* of 1990 will be cited as JF1 in parentheses in the text; references to the paperback edition of 1992 will be cited as JF2 in parentheses in the text.

8. The remarks of a young East German after the *Wende* make explicit this metonymic relationship: "It is so ugly, our Alex . . . , but it is our Berlin. . . . It would be so beautiful, an East Germany independent and democratic." Quoted by Karl Heinz Bohrer in his essay "Why We Are Not a Nation and Why We Should Become One" (1991, 75).

9. All translations from *Judasfrauen* are my own.

10. Although the manuscript of *Judasfrauen* was submitted to the Ostberliner publishing house in 1988, it was not published in the GDR until after the first free elections and the dissolution of the *Stasi* (JF2 10).

11. Schubert incorporated some documents in montage form; she also psychologized the figures by inventing fictional monologues for several historical perpetrators and for one actual victim (JF2 9–10).

12. Schubert stresses that the reader of her book knows from the outset that the "Thousand Year Reich" did last for only twelve years despite terror, internal mind police, and ethnic murder. The reader is also aware of the fact, according to Schubert, that a different political system followed this one.

13. This textual strategy was widespread in the GDR. Christa Wolf's *Kein Ort. Nirgends* (*No Place on Earth*) is perhaps the best known example of such an encoding of contemporary material in historical subject matter. Written after dissident poet and songwriter Wolf Biermann's expatriation from the GDR in 1976, the text explores the dilemma of the German Romantics Heinrich von Kleist and Karoline von Günderrode who, like Wolf and many of her compatriots, felt that they were superfluous in their society. Wolf chose to make her strategy readily decipherable for her non-GDR audience by explicitly mapping out the similarities between her situation and that of her Romantic protagonists in an interview with Fraucke Mayer-Gosau, "Projektionsraum Romantik," and in essays about the women Romantics such as "Nun Ja! Das nächste Leben geht aber heute an" [about Bettine von Arnim] and "Der Schatten eines Traumes" [about Karoline von Günderrode].

14. In the revised introduction, written for the paperback edition of *Judasfrauen*, Schubert explicitly calls the GDR a totalitarian state. Describing the reaction of GDR readers to a reading of the unpublished manuscript, Schubert maintained that they were astounded about the parallels that were discernible to their own totalitarian state (*eigenen totalitären Staat*) (JF2 8).

15. At the same time, the double focus presented here creates a utopian space for its GDR readership, keeping alive hope for the possibility of a complete

political upheaval. In "Spitzel und Verräter," the second part of *Judasfrauen*'s tripartite frame, the narrator/writer, harkening back to the "Introduction," differentiates between the time of betrayal and the time "afterward," that is, after the fall of the regime. For, she argues, "there is always an afterward; every era has an end" (JF1 13).

16. I am indebted to Marie-Luise Gättens for her discussion of Michel Foucault's theories of the disciplines in the context of *Judasfrauen* in her chapter "Law, Gender, and Complicity: Helga Schubert's Judasfrauen," in *Women Writers and Fascism: Reconstructing History*.

17. As Katharina von Ankum has persuasively shown, the image of woman as mother also informed the pronatal policies of the GDR for many years. It distinguished itself from Nazi policy in that in the GDR woman was also conceived as worker.

18. In "Spitzel und Verräter" ("Spies and Traitors"), the short expository piece that, together with the introduction and the expository piece "Judasfrauen" constitutes the narrative's frame, Schubert distinguishes between these two types of perpetrators: "A spy is to a traitor as a murderer is to a manslaughterer. Like the murderer, the spy acts with intention: s/he wants to report about those closest to her/him. . . . A traitor, on the other hand, tells an interested official something s/he may have known for a long time. S/he has kept it to himself until now. Now s/he wants to avenge himself, or s/he is forced to make a statement" (JF1 11). According to Schubert, what distinguishes the traitor from the spy is not just premeditation, but also duplicity. "The spy . . . dissembles. No one would trust him with any information otherwise. The spy must dissemble, must pretend to embrace a different opinion, laugh about a forbidden joke, must tell one himself. S/he must lay the bait" (JF1 11). Yet, despite Schubert's rather dubious differentiation within the category of perpetrator, she does not problematize the category itself—or, for that matter, its opposite.

19. The failure of Schubert's *Judasfrauen* project as *Gegenwartsbewältigung* can in part be attributed to the author's reliance on the discourse of totalitarianism, a discourse repudiated in the 1970s for its inability to differentiate between Nazism and Stalinism with sufficient precision. See Ian Kershaw for a discussion of the limitations of the notion of totalitarianism.

20. The situation took on a bizarre twist when Frank Schirrmacher and Ulrich Greiner, who had spearheaded the *Was bleibt* polemic in 1990, reversed themselves. Schirrmacher in "Fälle: Wolf und Müller" ("Cases: Wolf and Müller") defended Wolf and Müller by arguing against precisely the kind of *ad hominem/ad feminam* attack that he had advanced in the case of Wolf in 1990, and Greiner, who had been instrumental in initiating the *Stasi* debate, issued a "Plädoyer für Schluß der *Stasi*-Debatte" ("Plea for an End to the *Stasi* Debate"). Greiner's appeal for an end to the debate was based on the belief that this debate had failed to achieve the desired goal of coming to terms with the GDR past. While somewhat suspicious of Greiner's motives in faulting the coverage of the *Stasi* stories in the German

feuilletons—I wonder to what degree his dismay about news coverage of the latest revelations hinges on the fact that his paper was "scooped" by other news media— I concur with his conclusions. The "*Stasi* debate" has in fact been counterproductive; it has amounted to little more than meaningless searches for *Opfer* and *Täter*. A lot of finger-pointing has gone on; but the debate, by focusing on the intelligentsia, by framing its discussion on the abstracted level of *Geist und Macht*, has failed to deal with the specific crimes of the SED state or to discuss in any meaningful way the price paid by those oppressed, which included loss of lives, etc. Thus I would argue that it was not *Was bleibt* that was an affront to the "real victims" of the Honecker regime, as Greiner argued in his infamous review of *Was bleibt* in the June 1, 1990 edition of *Die Zeit*, but rather the media hype surrounding Wolf's text and around ensuing *Stasi* revelations concerning leading members of the GDR literary establishment. See, for example, "Die ängstliche Margarete" and Raddatz, "Von der Beschädigung der Literatur durch ihre Urheber." In June 1993, Luchterhand, with Christa Wolf's blessings, published *Zerrbild und Dialog*, a facsimile of Wolf's *Stasi* files together with the West German press's reaction to the revelation of Wolf's "*Stasi* past." The volume speaks for itself: the discrepancy between the minimalist, scarcely incriminating files and the media hype again makes clear the degree to which the press scapegoated Wolf.

21. Wolf, *What Remains* 1993, 232. Further references to the English translation will be cited as *WR* in parentheses. The German original reads: "Nur keine Angst. In jener anderen Sprache, die ich im Ohr, noch nicht auf der Zunge habe, werde ich eines Tages auch darüber reden. Heute, das wußte ich, wäre es noch zu früh. Aber würde ich spüren, wenn es an der Zeit ist" (7). Further references to the German original will be cited as *WB*.

22. Wolf worked on *Sommerstück* for many years; early versions date back to 1982–83; Wolf reworked the text again four years later before publishing it in 1989.

23. For a more detailed analysis of *Was bleibt* within the context of Wolf's *oeuvre* as a whole, see my " 'Zweige vom selben Stamm'? . . ." Portions of the analysis of *Was bleibt* presented in this chapter overlap with those of the earlier piece.

24. To be sure, aesthetically, *Was bleibt* is no match for *Kein Ort. Nirgends*; it cannot begin to approximate the formal and stylistic brilliance and poetic subtlety of Wolf's "wished for legend." More than any other text, *Kein Ort. Nirgends* demonstrates how successful Christa Wolf was in making an artistic virtue out of the evil of censorship; her "mastery of analogy," as Jürgen Engler put it, allowed GDR readers to read the story of the fictive meeting between Kleist and Günderrode as an eminently GDR-specific book and to understand the figure of Kleist as a direct analogue to Wolf Biermann. Critics in the West tended toward a more general reading of *Kein Ort. Nirgends* as a *Künstler* narrative. Pointing to Wolf's strategy of melding the figural narrative perspectives of her two main characters with that of the authorial perspective of the narrator, they discussed *Kein Ort.*

Nirgends first as a generic *Künstlererzählung* then as the displaced articulation of Wolf's own crisis as a writer.

Yet precisely the strategy that makes the historical narrative *Kein Ort. Nirgends* so effective—indirect metaphorical expression—fails when it is transposed to *Was bleibt*'s contemporary setting. I am thinking in particular of the passage in *Was bleibt* in which the narrator describes the "master who rules her city" as "der rücksichtslose Augenblicksvorteil" (*WB* 35). Given what we now know about the *Stasi* and Erich Honecker, this description, as Ulrich Greiner was quick to point out, is inadequate at best. Indeed, even without the benefit of extrinsic information, based solely on the pervasive atmosphere of fear that permeates the narrative, this circumlocution seems feeble.

25. As Marilyn Fries (1991, 12) has noted, the narrator's trajectory in *Was bleibt* is the reverse of that of the narrator of *Unter den Linden*.

26. The narrator later drives to the hospital to visit her husband; from there she goes to the cultural center to give a reading and then finally returns home. While not nearly as detailed as before, readers are again provided with specific names of places, such as the Leninallee (*WR* 279), the Oranienburgerstraße (*WR* 293), and the Alexanderplatz (*WR* 280), enabling them again to determine the narrator's (general) location in Berlin.

27. In Wolf's narrative about the Romantics, two quotations, one from Kleist, the other from Günderrode, precede the narrative, sounding the theme of (self-)alienation that resonates throughout the text. Günderrode's motto, taken from her letters, reads: "Deswegen kömmt es mir aber vor, als sähe ich mich im Sarg liegen und meine beiden Ichs starren sich ganz verwundert an."

28. These include the shopkeeper's story of her Jewish friend who, together with her entire family, was killed by the Nazis, and the narrator's leitmotific use of "men in leather coats" to describe the young men who are observing her, a motif that recalls the "men in trenchcoats" in *Kindheitsmuster* who are sent to intimidate Charlotte Jordan.

29. Prototypical *Väterromane* are fictionalized auto/biographical texts in which members of the first post–World War II generation sought to clarify their fathers' role in the "Third Reich" in an effort to understand their own histories better. Intermeshing filial and paternal narratives, these confessional texts recorded the fathers' stories while simultaneously registering the childhood traumas of the children, traumas incurred largely at the hands of the father. In doing so, *Väterromane* often explored the residual effects of Nazism on everyday postwar familial life. Part of the wave of "New Subjectivity," father books seem to have been driven more by a desire to understand than to condemn. Thus, while the sheer existence of these texts calls the fathers' past into question, the children rarely challenge their fathers directly within the narrative. Instead, writing serves a therapeutic function, allowing the children both to confront their own past and to gain a clearer understanding of how their fathers' biography shaped their behavior.

30. Maron was one of the few women who were vocal during the (re)unification process, often called upon by the Western press to present her views on the GDR and on the prospects for unification. See also her correspondence with Joseph von Westphalen from 1987 to 1988, *Trotzdem herzliche Grüße: Ein deutsch-deutscher Briefwechsel* (Frankfurt: Fischer, 1989).

31. Karl Maron was head of the *Volkspolizei* (People's Police) and then from 1955–63 served as the GDR's Minister of the Interior.

32. Like the Archipel Gulag, the Hotel Lux was among the Soviet atrocities considered a taboo subject in the GDR. Christa Wolf was one of the first GDR writers to break that taboo. In *Kindheitsmuster* (*Patterns of Childhood*, 1976) she alludes both to the Hotel Lux and Grete Mühsam, the wife of the poet Erich Mühsam, who was among those sent to Siberia from the Hotel Lux. In *Stille Zeile Sechs* Monika Maron also invokes Grete Mühsam's name, adding to it that of Alice Abramowitz (139–40).

33. Thomas Brasch's 1977 novel, *Vor den Vätern sterben die Söhne* (The Sons Die Before the Fathers), one of the first East German *Väterromane*, distinguished itself from its West German counterparts through its angry attack on the older generation. *Stille Zeile Sechs* follows Brasch's lead; it also differs from typical *Töchterromane* in that Rosalind is far less benevolent toward the "father" than most children-protagonists of this genre. In fact, *Stille Zeile Sechs* is propelled by a series of increasingly hostile confrontations between the dropped-out historian Rosalind, who has concluded that it is immoral to "think for money" and has quit her job to pursue individual interests and pleasures, and Beerenbaum, a (former) high-level Party functionary.

34. Maron's innovation is her detailed description of the countercultural *Kneipenszene* (pub scene). Ironically, the *Kneipe*, which in Maron's text constitutes one of niches of the so-called *Nischengesellschaft-DDR*, was ostensibly conceived as a haven for dispossessed intellectuals. It emerges here however as a dominating, hierarchically structured, competitive, and intolerant sphere. In short, it replicates precisely those characteristics it seeks to escape.

35. So reads the inscription on the monument erected in East Berlin dedicated to the Red Army.

36. The communist writer Toller participated in the aborted communist revolution of 1918, emigrated to the United States in 1933, and committed suicide in New York in 1939. The passage from his diary that Rosalind contemplates in *Stille Zeile Sechs* is: "Must the activist perforce become guilty? Or, if he doesn't want to become guilty, perish?" My translation; the published English translation is misleading. ("Muß der Handelnde schuldig werden, immer und immer? Oder, wenn er nicht schuldig werden will, untergehen?" [41].)

37. In one of their sessions, Rosalind literally draws blood from Beerenbaum (nosebleed) by tormenting him about the nefarious Hotel Lux and the fate suffered by Alice Abramowitz at the hands of Soviet communists. Sent to Siberia from the Hotel Lux, a crippled Abramowitz returned to Germany after the war to

find that her son had rejected her because he had been told that his mother was a Nazi spy.

REFERENCES

"Die ängstliche Margarete." *Der Spiegel*, January 25, 1991, 158–65.

Arendt, Hannah. *The Origins of Totalitarianism*. New York: Harcourt, Brace, 1951.

Baier, Lothar. *Volk ohne Zeit: Essay über das eilige Vaterland*. Berlin: Verlag Klaus Wagenbach, 1990.

Bohrer, Karl Heinz. "Why We Are Not a Nation and Why We Should Become One." *New German Critique* 52 (1991): 72–83.

Brasch, Thomas. *Vor den Vätern sterben die Söhne*. Berlin: Rotbuch-Verlag, 1977.

Ebbinghaus, Angelika, ed. *Opfer und Täterinnen: Frauenbiographien des Nationalsozialismus*. Nördlingen: Franz Greno, 1987.

Engler, Jürgen. "Herrschaft der Analogie." *Neue Deutsche Literatur* 7 (1979): 128–32.

Foucault, Michel. *Discipline and Punish: The Birth of the Prison*. New York: Vintage, 1979.

Fries, Marilyn. "When the Mirror is Broken. What Remains?: Christa Wolf's *Was bleibt*." *GDR Bulletin* 17/1 (Spring 1991): 11–18.

Gättens, Marie-Luise. "Law, Gender and Complicity: Helga Schubert's Judasfrauen." In *Women Writers and Fascism: Reconstructing History*, 216–81. Gainesville: University of Florida Press, 1995.

Greiner, Ulrich. "Plädoyer für Schluß der *Stasi*-Debatte." *Die Zeit*, February 12, 1993, 12.

Kershaw, Ian. *The Nazi Dictatorship: Problems and Perspectives of Interpretation*. London/New York/Melbourne/Auckland: Edward Arnold, 1993.

Königsdorf, Helga. *1989 oder ein Moment der Schönheit*. Berlin: Aufbau, 1990.

———. *Adieu DDR: Protokolle eines Abschieds*. Reinbek bei Hamburg: Rowohlt, 1990.

———. *Aus dem Dilemma eine Chance machen*. Darmstadt/Neuwied: Luchterhand, 1990.

Kuhn, Anna K. " 'Zweige vom selben Stamm?': Christa Wolf's *Was bleibt, Kein Ort. Nirgends* and *Sommerstück*." *German Monitor* 30 (1993): 187–205.

Kukutz, Irena, and Katja Havemann. *Geschützte Quelle: Gespräche mit Monika H., alias Karin Lenz, mit Faksimiles, Dokumenten und Fotos*. Berlin: Basis Druck, 1990.

Loest, Erich. *Die Stasi war mein Eckermann: oder Mein Leben mit der Wanze*. Leipzig: Steidl, 1991.

Maaz, Joachim. *Der Gefühlsstau: Ein Psychogramm der DDR*. Berlin: Argon, 1990.

———. *Das gestürzte Volk: Die unglückliche Einheit*. Berlin: Argon, 1991.

Maron, Monika. *Die Überläuferin*. Frankfurt am Main: Fischer, 1986. (*The Defector*. Translated by David Newton Marinelli. London: Readers International, 1988.)

———. "Ich war ein antifaschistisches Kind." In *Nach Maßgabe meiner Begreifungskraft: Artikel und Essays*. Frankfurt: Fischer, 1993.

———. *Stille Zeile Sechs*. Frankfurt: Fischer, 1991. (*Silent Close No. 6*. Translated by David Newton Marinelli. London: Readers International, 1993.)

Raddatz, Fritz. "Ein Rückzug auf sich selbst: Christa Wolfs 'Sommerstück.'" *Die Zeit*, March 24, 1989.

———. "Von der Beschädigung der Literatur durch ihre Urheber." *Die Zeit*, January 21, 1993, 15.

Schirrmacher, Frank. "Fälle: Wolf und Müller." *Frankfurter Allgemeine Zeitung*, January 22, 1993, 29.

Schneider, Peter. *Der Mauerspringer*. Darmstadt/Neuwied: Luchterhand, 1982. (*The Wall Jumper*. Translated by Leigh Hafrey. New York: Pantheon Books, 1983.)

Schubert, Helga. *Judasfrauen: Zehn Fallgeschichten weiblicher Denunziation im Dritten Reich*. Darmstadt/Neuwied: Luchterhand, 1990. (JF1)

———. *Judasfrauen: Zehn Fallgeschichten weiblicher Denunziation im Dritten Reich*. Munich: Deutscher Taschenbuch Verlag, 1992. (JF2)

Seebacher-Brandt, Brigitte. *Die Linke und die Einheit*. Berlin: Siedler, 1991.

Stephan, Cora, ed. *Wir Kollaborateure: Der Westen und die deutschen Vergangenheiten*. Reinbek bei Hamburg: Rowohlt, 1992.

Vinke, Hermann, ed. *Akteneinsicht Christa Wolf: Zerrspiegel und Dialog*. Darmstadt/Neuwied: Luchterhand, 1993.

Weigel, Sigrid. "Erinnerung vor Gericht: Zum Opfer-Täter Diskurs über den Nationalsozialismus in Helga Schuberts 'Judasfrauen' und ihren Gerichts-Quellen." In *Bilder des kulturellen Gedächtnisses: Beiträge zur Gegenwartsliteratur*, 198–231. Dülmen/Hiddingsel: tende, 1994.

Wolf, Christa. *Angepaßt oder mündig: Briefe an Christa Wolf im Herbst 1989*. Darmstadt/Neuwied: Luchterhand, 1990.

———. *Im Dialog: Aktuelle Texte*. Darmstadt/Neuwied: Luchterhand, 1990.

———. "Kultur ist, was erlebt wird. Ein Interview mit Fraucke Mayer-Gosau." *Alternative* 144/45 (April/June 1982): 117–27. Reprinted as "Projektionsraum Romantik" in Christa Wolf, *Die Dimension des Autors*. Darmstadt/Neuwied: Luchterhand, 1987, pp. 878–95. ("Culture Is What You Experience—An Interview with Christa Wolf." Translated by Jeannette Clausen, *New German Critique* 27 [Fall 1982]: 89–100.)

———. *Was bleibt*. Darmstadt/Neuwied: Luchterhand, 1990. (*What Remains and Other Stories*. Translated by Heike Schwarzbauer and Rick Takvorian. New York: Farrar, Straus and Giroux, 1993.)

———. "Nun Ja! Das nächste Leben geht aber heute an." In *Die Dimension des Autors*, 572–610. Darmstadt/Neuwied: Luchterhand, 1987. ("Your Next

Life Begins Today: A Letter about Bettine." Translated by Jan van Heurek. Christa Wolf, *The Author's Dimension*, edited by Alexander Stephan, 187–216. New York: Farrar, Straus & Giroux, 1993.)

————— . "Der Schatten eines Traumes: Karoline von Günderrode—ein Entwurf." In *Die Dimension des Autors*, 511–71. Darmstadt/Neuwied: Luchterhand, 1987. ("The Shadow of a Dream: A Sketch of Karoline von Günderrode." In *The Author's Dimension*, edited by Alexander Stephan, 131–75. New York: Farrar, Straus & Giroux, 1993.)

Selected Bibliography

BIBLIOGRAPHIES

Glass, Derek. "Literary Images of Berlin: A Select Bibliography." In *Berlin. Literary Images of a City. Eine Großstadt im Spiegel der Literatur.* Edited by Derek Glass, et al., 188–210. Berlin: Schmidt, 1989.

Kreusel, Gert, et al. *Berlin in der Belletristik. Empfehlende thematische Bibliographie.* Berlin: Staatsbibliothek, 1987.

Literaturverzeichnis Berlin mit Umgebung. Eine Bibliographie lieferbarer Bücher, Karten und neuer Medien. Berlin: Buchhandlung Kiepert, 1995.

Schäfer, Ute and Rainald Stromeyer, et al. *Berlin-Bibliographie (1978 bis 1984) in der Senatsbibliothek.* Berlin/New York: de Gruyter, 1987.

Speier, Hans-Michael. "Eine Auswahlbibliographie Berliner Lyrik von der Gründerzeit bis zur Gegenwart." In *Poesie der Metropole. Die Berlin-Lyrik von der Gründerzeit bis zur Gegenwart im Spiegel ihrer Anthologien.* Berlin: Colloquium Verlag, 1990, pp. 57–164.

Wallace, Ian. *Berlin.* Oxford/Santa Barbara/Denver: Clio Press, 1992.

Wittneben, Jürgen, ed. *Berlin-Literatur in der Amerika-Gedenkbibliothek/Berliner Zentralbibliothek.* Berlin: Amerika-Gedenkbibliothek, 1985.

HISTORY AND POLITICS

Beyme, Klaus von. *Hauptstadtsuche: Hauptstadtfunktionen im Interessenkonflikt zwischen Bonn und Berlin.* Frankfurt am Main: Suhrkamp, 1991.

Hillenbrand, Martin J. *The Future of Berlin.* Montclair, N.J.: Allanheld, Osmun Publishers, 1980.

Keiderling, Gerhard. *Berlin 1945–1986. Geschichte der Hauptstadt der DDR*. 2nd ed. Berlin: Dietz Verlag, 1987.

Lange, Annemarie. *Berlin in der Weimarer Republik*. Berlin: Dietz Verlag, 1987.

———. *Berlin zur Zeit Bebels und Bismarcks. Zwischen Reichsgründung und Jahrhundertwende*. Berlin: Dietz, 1972.

———. *Das wilhelminische Berlin. Zwischen Jahrhundertwende und November-revolution*. Berlin: Dietz, 1967.

Langguth, Gerd, ed. *Berlin vom Brennpunkt der Teilung zur Brücke der Einheit*. Köln: Verlag Wissenschaft und Politik, 1990.

Leonhard, Wolfgang. *Spurensuche. 40 Jahre nach Die Revolution entläßt ihre Kinder*. Cologne: Kiepenheuer & Witsch, 1992.

Mahncke, Dieter. *Berlin im geteilten Deutschland*. Munich/Vienna: Oldenbourg, 1973.

Read, Anthony, and David Fischer. *Berlin Rising: A Biography of a City*. New York/London: Norton, 1994.

Ribbe, Wolfgang, ed. *Geschichte Berlins*. 2 vols. Munich: Beck, 1987–1988.

Schäfer, Hans-Dieter. *Berlin im Zweiten Weltkrieg. Der Untergang der Reichshauptstadt in Augenzeugenberichten*. Munich: Piper, 1986.

Schmid, Thomas. *Berlin, der kapitale Irrtum. Argumente für ein föderalistisches Deutschland*. Frankfurt am Main: Eichborn, 1991.

Simmons, Michael. *Berlin, the Dispossessed City*. London: H. Hamilton, 1988.

Sutterlin, James S., and David Klein. *Berlin: From Symbol of Confrontation to Keystone of Stability*. New York/Westport/London: Praeger, 1989.

Wetzlaugk, Udo. *Berlin und die deutsche Frage*. Cologne: Verlag Wissenschaft und Politik, 1985.

———. *Die Aliierten in Berlin*. Berlin: Arno Spitz, 1988.

Wolff, Michael W. *Die Währungsreform in Berlin 1948/49*. Berlin: de Gruyter, 1991.

THE WALL

Armstrong, Anne. *Berliners: Both Sides of the Wall*. New Brunswick, N.J.: Rutgers University Press, 1973.

Gelb, Norman. *The Berlin Wall*. London: Joseph, 1986.

Haupt, Michael. *Die Berliner Mauer. Vorgeschichte—Bau—Folgen*. Munich: Bernard & Graefe Verlag, 1981.

Mehls, Hartmut, ed. *Im Schatten der Mauer*. Berlin: Deutscher Verlag der Wissenschaften, 1990.

Scholze, Thomas, and Falk Blask. *Leben im Schatten Der Maurer*. Berlin: Basis Druck, 1992.

THE *WENDE* AND UNIFICATION

Darnton, Robert. *Berlin Journal 1989–1990*. New York: Norton, 1991. (*Der letzte Tanz auf der Mauer: Berliner Journal 1989–1990*. Munich: Hanser, 1991.)

Glaessner, Gert-Joachim. *The Unification Process in Germany: From Dictatorship to Democracy*. Translated by Colin B. Grant. New York: St. Martin's Press, 1992.

Grosser, Dieter, ed. *German Unification. The Unexpected Challenge*. Oxford: Berg, 1992.

McAdams, James A. *Germany Divided: From the Wall to Reunification*. Princeton, N.J.: Princeton University Press, 1993.

Momper, Walter. *Grenzfall: Berlin im Brennpunkt der Geschichte*. Munich: Bertelsmann, 1991.

Nooteboom, Cees. *Berliner Notizen. Berichte aus der Wendezeit*. Frankfurt: Suhrkamp, 1991.

Pond, Elizabeth. *Beyond the Wall: Germany's Road to Unification*. Washington, D.C.: Brookings Institution, 1993.

BIOGRAPHIES, MEMOIRS, FICTION

Adlon, Hedda. *Hotel Adlon, Berlin: The Life and Death of a Great Hotel*. Translated by Norman Denny. London: Barrie Books, 1958.

Baker, Leonard. *Days of Sorrow and Pain: Leo Baeck and the Berlin Jews*. New York: Macmillan, 1978.

Benjamin, Walter. "A Berlin Chronicle." In *Reflections: Essays, Aphorisms, Autobiographical Writings*. Translated by Edmund Jephcott. New York: Harcourt, Brace, Jovanovich, 1978.

Brandt, Willy. *Erinnerungen*. Berlin/Frankfurt am Main: Propyläen, 1990. (*My Life in Politics*. Translated by Anthea Bell. London: Hamish Hamilton, 1992.)

de Bruyn, Günter. *Zwischenbilanz. Eine Jugend in Berlin*. Frankfurt am Main: Fischer, 1992.

Deutschkron, Inge. *Ich trug den gelben Stern*. Cologne: Verlag Wissenschaft und Politik, 1978. (*Outcast: A Jewish Girl in Wartime Berlin*. Translated by Jean Steinberg. New York: Fromm International Publication Corporation, 1989.)

Dietrich, Marlene. *Ich bin, Gott sei dank, Berlinerin*. (*My Life*. Translated by Salvator Attanasio. New York: Grove Press, 1989.)

Döblin, Alfred. *Berlin Alexanderplatz. Die Geschichte vom Franz Biberkopf* [1929]. (*Berlin Alexanderplatz: The Story of Franz Biberkopf*. Translated by Eugene Jolas. Harmondsworth: Penguin, 1978.)

Drewitz, Ingeborg. *Gestern war Heute. Hundert Jahre Gegenwart.* Düsseldorf: Claassen, 1978.

Isherwood, Christopher. *Mr. Norris Changes Trains* [1935]. *Goodbye Berlin* [1939]. London: Chatto & Windus, 1985.

Krüger, Ingrid, and Eike Schmitz. *Berlin, du deutsche Frau. Eine literarische Chronik der geteilten Stadt mit Texten und Bildern von Autoren aus Ost und West.* 2nd ed. Darmstadt/Neuwied: Luchterhand, 1987.

Plivier, Theodor. *Berlin. Roman* [1954]. (*Berlin, a Novel.* Translated by Louis Hagen and Vivian Milroy. Garden City: Doubleday, 1957.)

Richter, Hans Werner, ed. *Berlin, ach Berlin.* Munich: dtv, 1984.

Schneider, Peter. *Der Mauerspringer.* Darmstadt/Neuwied: Luchterhand, 1982. (*The Wall Jumper.* Translated by Leigh Hafrey. New York: Random House, 1983.)

Speier, Hans-Michael. *Poesie der Metropole. Die Berlin-Lyrik von der Gründerzeit bis zur Gegenwart im Spiegel ihrer Anthologien.* Berlin: Colloquium Verlag, 1990.

————, ed. *Berlin! Berlin! Eine Großstadt im Gedicht.* Stuttgart: Reclam, 1987.

Wittstock, Uwe, ed. *Berlin erzählt. 19 Erzählungen.* Frankfurt: Fischer, 1991.

CULTURAL INSTITUTIONS AND CITY DISTRICTS

Bergler, Andrea, and Heike Sporkhorst, eds. *Kreuzberg schwarz auf weiß: Ein Literaturverzeichnis.* Berlin: Kunstamt Kreuzberg, Kreuzberger Museum, Stadtbibliothek Kreuzberg, 1992.

Dahn, Daniela. *Prenzlauer Berg-Tour.* Leipzig: Mitteldeutscher-Verlag, 1987. (Published in West Germany as *Kunst und Kohle.* Darmstadt/Neuwied: Luchterhand, 1987.)

Elkins, T. H., and B. Hofmeister. *Berlin: The Spatial Structure of a Divided City.* London/New York: Methuen, 1988.

Escher, Felix. *Neukölln.* Berlin: Colloquium, 1988.

Hofmeister, Burkhardt. *Berlin. Eine geographische Strukturanalyse der zwölf westlichen Bezirke.* Darmstadt: Wissenschaftliche Buchgesellschaft, 1990.

Jaeckel, Garhard. *Die Charité. Die Geschichte eines Weltzentrums der Medizin.* Bayreuth: Hestia, 1987.

Knaak, Heinrich. *Kreuzberg.* Berlin: Colloquium Verlag, 1988.

Liebmann, Irene. *Berliner Mietshaus.* Halle: Mitteldeutscher-Verlag, 1982; Frankfurt: Frankfurter Verlagsanstalt, 1990.

Ribbe, Wolfgang, and Wolfgang Schache. *Die Siemensstadt. Geschichte und Architektur eines Industriestandortes.* Berlin: Ernst & Sohn, 1985.

Roskamp, Heiko, ed. *Verfolgung und Widerstand: Tiergarten, ein Bezirk im Spannungsfeld der Geschichte 1933–1945.* Berlin: Edition Hentrich, Frölich & Kaufmann, 1984.

Stein, Rosemarie. *Die Charité 1945–1992: Ein Mythos von innen.* Berlin: Argon Verlag, 1992.

Tebbe, Krista, ed. *Kreuzberg—Prenzlauer Berg: Annähernd alles über Kultur.* Berlin: Kunstamt Kreuzberg, 1990.

Zimm, Alfred, ed. *Berlin und sein Umland.* 3rd ed. Darmstadt: Wissenschaftliche Buchgesellschaft, 1990.

METROPOLIS AND CULTURE

Boberg, Jochen, Tilman Fichter, and Eckart Gillen. *Die Metropole. Industriekultur in Berlin im 20. Jahrhundert.* Munich: Beck, 1986.

Brunn, Gerhard, and Jürgen Reulecke, eds. *Metropolis Berlin. Berlin als deutsche Hauptstadt im Vergleich europäischer Hauptstädte 1871–1939.* Bonn/Berlin: Bouvier, 1992.

————. *Berlin: Blicke auf die deutsche Metropole.* Essen: Reimar Hobbing Verlag, 1989.

Grzywatz, Berthold, et al., eds. Stadtgeschichte als Kulturarbeit: Beiträge zur Geschichtspraxis in Berlin-Ost und -West. Berlin: Stapp Verlag, 1991.

Haxthausen, Charles W., and Heidrun Suhr, eds. *Berlin: Culture and Metropolis.* Minneapolis/Oxford: University of Minnesota Press, 1990.

Joachimides, Christos M., and Norman Rosenthal, eds. *Metropolis: International Art Exhibition 1991.* New York: Rizzoli, 1991.

Kirchhoff, Gerd, ed. *Views of Berlin.* Boston/Basel/Berlin: Birkhäuser, 1989.

Petras, Renate. *Die Bauten der Berliner Museumsinsel.* Berlin: Stapp, 1987.

Schade, Günter. *Die Berliner Museumsinsel: Zerstörung, Rettung, Wiederaufbau.* Berlin: Henschel, 1986.

Steinfeld, Thomas, and Heidrun Suhr. *In der großen Stadt. Die Metropole als kulturtheoretische Kategorie.* Frankfurt: Anton Hain, 1990.

Tomerius, Lorenz. *Berlin—Kulturhauptstadt Europas 1988: Cultural City of Europe 1988: Ville Européenne de la Culture 1988.* Frankfurt am Main/Berlin: Ullstein, 1988.

Walker, Ian. *Zoo Station: Adventures in East and West Berlin.* London: Martin, Secker & Warburg, 1987.

Westermann, Karin. *Mitte und Grenze: Motive konservativer Kulturpolitik am Beispiel Berlins 1945 bis 1985.* Frankfurt am Main: Peter Lang, 1989.

Die Zukunft der Metropolen: Utopischer Ort Berlin—Historische Topographie. Katalog der Ausstellung in der TU Berlin, vol. 3. Berlin: Technische Universität, 1984.

LITERARY CULTURE AND IMAGES

Allen, Roy F. *Literary Life in German Expressionism and the Berlin Circles.* 2nd ed. Ann Arbor, Mich.: University of Michigan Press, 1983.

Bentele, Günter, and Otfried Jaren. *Medienstadt Berlin.* Berlin: Vistas, 1988.

Bienert, Michael. *Die eingebildete Metropole: Berlin im Feuilleton der Weimarer Republik*. Stuttgart: Metzler, 1992.

Böthig, Peter, and Klaus Michael, eds. *MachtSpiele. Literatur und Staatssicherheit im Fokus Prenzlauer Berg*. Leipzig: Reclam, 1993.

Cohen, Mitch, ed. *Berlin: Contemporary Writing from East and West Berlin*. Santa Barbara: Bandanna Books, 1983.

Eckhardt, Wolf von, and Sander Gilman. *Bertolt Brecht's Berlin: A Scrapbook of the Twenties*. Lincoln, Neb./London: University of Nebraska Press, 1993.

Fries, Marilyn Sibley. *The Changing Consciousness of Reality: The Image of Berlin in Selected German Novels from Raabe to Döblin*. Bonn: Bouvier, 1980.

Glass, Derek, Dieter Roesler, and John J. White, eds. *Berlin: Literary Images of a City: Eine Großstadt im Spiegel der Literatur*. Berlin: Erich Schmidt Verlag, 1989.

Helbig, Jörg, ed. *Welcome to Berlin: Das Image Berlins in der englischsprachigen Welt von 1700 bis heute*. Berlin: Stapp, 1987.

Hermsdorf, Klaus. *Literarisches Leben in Berlin: Aufklärer und Romantiker*. Berlin: Akademie Verlag, 1987.

Kramer, Jane. *Eine Amerikanerin in Berlin*. Berlin: Edition Tiamat, 1993.

POPULATION, IMMIGRATION, VIOLENCE

Barkowski, Hans, and Gerd Hoff, eds. *Berlin interkulturell: Ergebnisse einer Konferenz zu Migration und Pädagogik*. Berlin: Colloquium Verlag, 1991.

Borneman, John. *Belonging in the Two Berlins: Kin, State, Nation*. Cambridge: Cambridge University Press, 1992.

Conradt, Sylvia, and Kirsten Heckmann-Janz. *Reichstrümmerhauptstadt: Leben in Berlin 1945–1961*. Darmstadt/Neuwied: Luchterhand, 1987.

Emre, Gültekin. *300 Jahre Türken an der Spree*. Berlin: n.p., 1983.

Farin, Klaus, and Eberhard Seidel-Pielen. *"Ohne Gewalt läuft nichts." Jugend und Gewalt in Deutschland*. Cologne: Bund-Verlag, 1993.

Frick, Dieter. *The Quality of Urban Life: Social, Psychological, and Physical Conditions*. Berlin: de Gruyter, 1986.

Gross, Leonard. *Versteckt. Wie Juden in Berlin die Nazi-Zeit überlebten*. Hamburg: Rowohlt, 1983.

Hewartz-Emden, Leonie. *Türkische Familien und Berliner Schule—Einstellungen, Erwartungen und Erfahrungen türkischer Eltern: Eine empirische Untersuchung*. Berlin: Express Edition, 1986.

Höcker, Karla. *Beschreibung eines Jahres. Berliner Notizen 1945*. Berlin: Arani Verlag, 1984.

Kardoff, Ursula von. *Berliner Aufzeichnungen 1942–1945*. Edited by Peter Hartl. Munich: Beck, 1992.

Merten, Roland, ed. *Rechtsradikale Gewalt im vereinigten Deutschland. Jugend im gesellschaftlichen Umbruch.* Opladen: Leske und Budrich, 1993.

Runge, Irene. *Vom Kommen und Bleiben. Osteuropäische jüdische Einwanderer in Berlin.* Berlin: Ausländerbeauftragte des Senats, 1992.

Schilling, Heinz-Dieter. *Ich bin wer: Stadtreportagen.* Berlin: Express Edition, 1983.

Schoeps, Julius H., ed. *Juden in Berlin.* Berlin: n.p., 1986.

WOMEN

Anselm, Sigrun, and Barbara Beck, eds. *Triumph und Scheitern in der Metropole: Zur Rolle der Weiblichkeit in der Geschichte Berlins.* Berlin: Dietrich Reimer Verlag, 1987.

Arndt, Marlies, et al. *Ausgegrenzt und mittendrin—Frauen in der Wissenschaft: Dokumente einer Tagung an der Humboldt-Universität am 22./23. Okt. 1993.* Berlin: Edition Sigma Bohn, 1993.

Berlinerinnen. Bekannte und unbekannte Frauen in Berlin aus drei Jahrhunderten. Ausstellungskatalog. Berlin: Berlin Museum, 1975.

Diemer, Susanne. *Patriarchalismus in der DDR: Strukturelle, kulturelle und subjektive Dimensionen der Geschlechterpolarisierung.* Opladen: Leske & Budrich, 1994.

Eifert, Christiane, and Susanne Rouette, eds. *Unter allen Umständen: Frauengeschichte(n) in Berlin.* Berlin: Rotation Verlag, 1986.

Hermann, Kai, and Horst Rieck, eds. *Die Kinder vom Bahnhof Zoo* [1978]. (*Christiane F.: Autobiography of a Girl of the Streets and Heroin Addict.* Translated by Susanne Flatauer. Toronto/New York: Bantam Books, 1982.)

Hübner, Sabine. *Rückenwind für Technikfrauen. Erfahrungen einer Servicestelle mit Vernetzung und institutioneller Kooperation in Berlin.* Pfaffenweiler: Centaurus, 1992.

Nickel, Hildegard Marie. "Women in the German Democratic Republic and in the New Federal States: Looking Backwards and Forwards." *German Politics and Society* 24–25 (Winter 1991–92): 34–52.

Scholz, Hannelore. "East-West Women's Culture in Transition: Are East German Women the Losers of Unification?" *Journal of Women's History* 5, 3 (Winter 1994): 109–16.

Toksöz, Gülay. *Ja sie kämpfen—und sogar mehr als die Männer: Immigrantinnen, Fabrikarbeit und gewerkschaftliche Interessenvertretung.* Berlin: Verlag für Wissenschaft und Bildung, 1991.

Index

About the Contributors

BARBARA BECKER-CANTARINO is Research Professor at Ohio State University. Her teaching and research interests center on early modern and contemporary German culture and literature. She has repeatedly held a Visiting Professorship at the Free University of Berlin. Her most recent publications include *Diskurse der Freundschaft* (1991) and *The Enlightenment and Its Legacy* (1992). Her study on German Romantic women authors will be published in Germany next year. She is currently at work on a book entitled *Women in Post-War Berlin*.

CAROL AISHA BLACKSHIRE-BELAY is Associate Professor at Temple University in Philadelphia. Her field of expertise is German language and cultural/ethnic studies, German–African relations, and minorities in contemporary German society. She also serves as the Director of the International African-German Network. Among her most recent books are *The Image of Africa in German Society, Language Contact: Verb Morphology in German of Foreign Workers* and *The German Mosaic: Cultural and Linguistic Diversity in Society*.

FRIEDERIKE EIGLER is Associate Professor of German at Georgetown University. Her research interests include twentieth-century literature, feminist criticism, and the history and theory of autobiography. Among her publications are articles on recent developments in the former GDR, a monograph on Elias Canetti, and an edited volume (with Peter C. Pfeiffer) entitled *Cultural Transformations in the New Germany* (1993).

ANKE GLEBER teaches German film and literature at Princeton University. She has published on images of women in Nazi cinema, the figure of the flaneur in twentieth-century German literature, travel literature of the Weimar Republic, the Weimar *Kino-Debatte*, and articles on Arno Schmidt, Thomas Bernhard, and Heiner Müller.

ANNA K. KUHN is Professor of German at the University of California, Davis. Her research interests center on contemporary German literature and culture, feminist theory, and film studies. Among her numerous publications is the study *Christa Wolf's Utopian Vision: From Marxism to Feminism* (1988). Her current research project includes a study of the cinematic representation of foreigners in contemporary German film and a volume called "Rereading Christa Wolf."

HANNA LABRENZ-WEISS studied at the University of Warsaw and received a fellowship for the Free University of Berlin where she earned a doctorate at the Otto-Suhr-Institut of Political Science. She published *Das Bild Preußens in der polnischen Geschichtsschreibung* in 1986. She holds a research position at the Division on Education and Research at the Gauck Commission headquarters in Berlin.

SIEGFRIED MEWS is Professor of German at the University of North Carolina at Chapel Hill. His many publications on modern German literature and culture include volumes on Carl Zuckmayer, Bertolt Brecht, Günter Grass, and Ulrich Plenzdorf.

BRIGITTE PEUCKER is Professor of German at Yale University where she teaches film and literature and chairs the Film Studies Program. Besides her work on poetry, her publications include articles on Werner Herzog, Wim Wenders, Rainer Werner Fassbinder, and studies on cinema, most recently *Incorporating Images: Film and the Rival Arts* (1995).

HANNELORE SCHOLZ teaches history of German literature and German women's literature at Humboldt University, Berlin, where she headed the Center for Interdisciplinary Research on Women, 1991–1993. Her publications include *Widersprüche im bürgerlichen Frauenbild* (1992) and articles on Sophie Tieck, women authors of the GDR and Eastern Europe, and on women and the *Wende*.